CASE WORKER

ARCO

CASE WORKER

HY HAMMER
PHYLLIS COHEN

MACMILLAN
U.S.A.

Macmillan General Reference
A Simon & Schuster Macmillan Company
1633 Broadway
New York, NY 10019-6785

An Arco Book

MACMILLAN is a registered trademark of Macmillan, Inc.
ARCO is a registered trademark of Prentice-Hall, Inc.

Library of Congress Cataloging-in-Publication Data

Case Worker: social investigator, eligibility specialist / edited by
    Hy Hammer, Phyllis Cohen.—10th ed.
        p.   cm.
    ISBN 0-671-84713-9
        1. Social service—United States—Examinations, questions, etc.
2. Public welfare—United States—Examinations, questions, etc.
3. Civil service—United States—Examinations. I. Hammer, Hy
II. Cohen, Phyllis.
HV11.5.C37 1992   92-30786
361.7'076—dc20   CIP

Manufactured in the United States of America

10 9 8 7 6 5 4

CONTENTS

Part Three—Background Material and Examination Questions Classified by Subject Matter

WHAT THIS BOOK WILL DO FOR YOU

ARCO Publishing has followed testing trends and methods ever since the firm was founded in 1937. We specialize in books that prepare people for tests. Based on this experience, we have prepared the best possible book to help *you* score high.

To write this book we carefully analyzed every detail surrounding the forthcoming examination:

• the job itself

• official and unofficial announcements concerning the examination

• all the previous examinations, many not available to the public

• related examinations

• technical literature that explains and forecasts the examination

Can You Prepare Yourself For Your Test?

You want to pass this test. That's why you bought this book. Used correctly, your "self-tutor" will show you what to expect and will give you a speedy brush-up on the subjects tested in your exam. Some of these are subjects not taught in schools at all. Even if your study time is very limited, you should:

• Become familiar with the type of examination you will have.

• Improve your general examination-taking skill.

• Improve your skill in analyzing and answering questions involving reasoning, judgment, comparison, and evaluation.

• Improve your speed and skill in reading and understanding what you read—an important part of your ability to learn and an important part of most tests.

This book will tell you exactly what to study by presenting in full every type of question you will get on the actual test.

This book will help you find your weaknesses. Once you know what subjects you're weak in, you can get right to work and concentrate on those areas. This kind of selective study yields maximum test results.

This book will give you the *feel* of the exam. Almost all of our sample and practice questions are taken from actual previous exams. On the day of the exam, you'll see how closely this book follows the format of the real test.

This book will give you confidence *now*, while you are preparing for the test. It will build your self-confidence as you proceed and will prevent the kind of test anxiety that causes low test scores.

This book stresses the multiple-choice type of question because that's the kind you'll have on your test. You must not be satisfied with merely knowing the correct answer for each question. You must find out why the other choices are incorrect. This will help you remember a lot you thought you had forgotten.

After testing yourself, you may find that you are weak in a particular area. You should concentrate on improving your skills by using the specific practice sections in this book that apply to you.

Part One

Applying and Studying
for the Examination

PREPARING YOURSELF FOR THE CIVIL SERVICE EXAMINATION

About seven million people are employed by our state and local departments and agencies—approximately 1,700,000 by the fifty states and over 5,200,000 by the thousands of local government units and school districts. The employment opportunities cover practically every skill and profession in our complex modern social order. Every year thousands of new jobs are created and tens of thousands of replacements are needed on existing jobs.

Most federal, state, and municipal units have recruitment procedures for filling civil service positions. They have developed a number of methods to make job opportunities known. Places where such information may be obtained include:

1. The offices of the State Employment Services. There are almost two thousand throughout the country. These offices are administered by the state in which they are located, with the financial assistance of the federal government. You will find the address of the one nearest you in your telephone book.

2. Your state Civil Service Commission. Address your inquiry to the capital city of your state.

3. Your city Civil Service Commission—if you live in a large city. It is sometimes called by another name, such as the Department of Personnel, but you will be able to identify it in your telephone directory under the listing of city departments.

4. Your municipal building and your local library.

5. Complete listings are carried by such newspapers as *The Chief-Leader* (published in New York City), as well as by other city and state-wide publications devoted to civil service employees. Many local newspapers run a section on regional civil service news.

6. State and local agencies looking for competent employees will contact schools, professional societies, veterans organizations, unions, and trade associations.

7. School Boards and Boards of Education, which employ the greatest proportion of all state and local personnel, should be asked directly for information about job openings.

The Format of the Job Announcement

When a position is open and a civil service examination is to be given for it, a job announcement is drawn up. This generally contains everything an applicant has to know about the job.

The announcement begins with the job title and salary. A typical announcement then describes the work, the location of the position, the education and experience requirements, the kind of examination to be given, the system of rating. It may also have something to say about veteran preference and the age limit. It tells which application form is to be filled out, where to get the form, and where and when to file it.

Study the job announcement carefully. It will answer many of your questions and help you decide whether you like the position and are qualified for it.

There is no point in applying for a position and taking the examination if you do not want to work where the job is. The job may be in your community or hundreds of miles away at the other end of the state. If you are not willing to work where the job is, study other announcements that will give you an opportunity to work in a place of your choice. A civil service job close to your home has an additional advantage since local residents usually receive preference in appointments.

The words **Optional Fields**—sometimes just the word **Options**—may appear on the front page of the announcement. You then have a choice to apply for that particular position in which you are especially interested. This is because the duties of various positions are quite different even though they bear the same broad title. A public relations *clerk*, for example, does different work from a payroll *clerk*, although they are considered broadly in the same general area.

Not every announcement has options. But whether or not it has them, the precise duties are described in detail, usually under the heading **Description of Work**. Make sure that these duties come within the range of your experience and ability.

Most job requirements give a **deadline for filing** an application. Others bear the words, *No Closing Date* at the top of the first page; this means that applications will be accepted until the needs of the agency are met. In some cases a public notice is issued when a certain number of applications has been received. No application mailed past the deadline date will be considered.

Every announcement has a detailed section on **education and experience requirements** for the particular job and for the optional fields. Make sure that in both education and experience you meet the minimum qualifications. If you do not meet the given standards for one job, there may be others open where you stand a better chance of making the grade.

If the job announcement does not mention **veteran preference**, it would be wise to inquire if there is such a provision in your state of municipality. There may be none or it may be limited to disabled veterans. In some jurisdictions surviving spouses of disabled veterans are given preference. All such information can be obtained through the agency that issues the job announcement.

Applicants may be denied examinations and eligible candidates may be denied appointments for any of the following reasons:

> intentional false statements
> deception or fraud in examination or appointment
> use of intoxicating beverages to the extent that ability to perform the duties of the position
>   is impaired
> criminal, infamous, dishonest, immoral, or notoriously disgraceful conduct

The announcement describes **the kind of test** given for the particular position. Please pay special attention to this section. It tells what areas are to be covered in the written test and lists the specific subjects on which questions will be asked. Sometimes sample questions are given.

Usually the announcement states whether the examination is to be **assembled** or **unassembled**. In an assembled examination applicants assemble in the same place at the same time to take a written or performance test. The unassembled examination is one where an applicant does not take a test; instead, he or she is rated on his or her education and experience and whatever records of past achievement the applicant is asked to provide.

In the competitive examination all applicants for a position compete with each other; the better the mark, the better the chance of being appointed. Also, competitive examinations are given to determine desirability for promotion among employees.

Civil service written tests are rated on a scale of 100, with 70 usually as the passing mark.

Filling Out the Application Form

Having studied the job announcement and having decided that you want the position and are qualified for it, your next step is to get an application form. The job announcement tells you where to send for it.

On the whole, civil service application forms differ little from state to state and locality to locality. The questions, which have been worked out after years of experimentation, are simple and direct, designed to elicit a maximum of information about you.

Many prospective civil service employees have failed to get a job because of slipshod, erroneous, incomplete, misleading, or untruthful answers. Give the application serious attention, for it is the first important step toward getting the job you want.

Here, along with some helpful comments, are the questions usually asked on the average application form, although not necessarily in this order.

Name of examination or kind of position applied for. This information appears in large type on the first page of the job announcement.

Optional job (if mentioned in the announcement). If you wish to apply for an option, simply copy the title from the announcement. If you are not interested in an option, write *None*.

Primary place of employment applied for. The location of the position was probably contained in the announcement. You must consider whether you want to work there. The announcement may list more than one location where the job is open. If you would accept employment in any of the places, list them all; otherwise list the specific place or places where you would be willing to work.

Name and address. Give in full, including your middle name if you have one, and your maiden name as well if you are a married woman.

Home and office phones. If none, write *None*.

Legal or voting residence. The state in which you vote is the one you list here.

Height without shoes, weight, sex. Answer accurately.

Date of birth. Give the exact day, month, and year.

Lowest grade or pay you will accept. Although the salary is clearly stated in the job announcement, there may be a quicker opening in the same occupation but carrying less responsibility and thus a lower basic entrance salary. You will not be considered for a job paying less than the amount you give in answer to this question.

Will you accept temporary employment if offered you for (a) one month or less, (b) one to four months, (c) four to twelve months? Temporary positions come up frequently and it is important to know whether you are available.

Will you accept less than full-time employment? Part-time work comes up now and then. Consider whether you want to accept such a position while waiting for a full-time appointment.

Were you in active military service in the Armed Forces of the United States? Veterans' preference, if given, is usually limited to active service during the following periods: 12/7/41 - 12/31/46; 6/27/50 - 1/31/55; 6/1/63 - 5/7/75; 6/1/83 - 12/1/87; 10/23/83 - 11/21/83; 12/20/89 - 1/3/90; 8/2/90 to end of Persian Gulf hostilities.

Do you claim disabled veterans credit? If you do, you have to show proof of a war-incurred disability compensable by at least 10%. This is done through certification by the Veterans Administration.

Special qualifications and skills. Even though not directly related to the position for which you are applying, information about licenses and certificates obtained for teacher, pilot, registered nurse, and so on is requested. List your experience in the use of machines and equipment and whatever other skills you have acquired. Also list published writings, public speaking experience, membership in professional societies, honors and fellowships received.

Education. List your entire educational history, including all diplomas, degrees, special courses taken in any accredited or Armed Forces school. Also give your credits toward a college or a graduate degree.

References. The names of people who can give information about you, with their occupations and business and home address, are often requested.

Your health. Questions are asked concerning your medical record. You are expected to have the physical and psychological capacity to perform the job for which you are applying. Standards vary, of course, depending on the requirements of the position. A physical handicap usually will not bar an applicant from a job he can perform adequately unless the safety of the public is involved.

Work history. Considerable space is allotted on the form for the applicant to tell about all his past employment. Examiners check all such answers closely. Do not embroider or falsify your record. If you were ever fired, say so. It is better for you to state this openly than for the examiners to find out the truth from your former employer.

Case Worker
Notice of Examination

The City of New York is an Equal Opportunity Employer.

TEST DATE Candidates will be notified by mail when to report for the written test.

LIST ESTABLISHMENT Eligible lists will be established in groups periodically as needed. Each list will be terminated one year from the date it is established unless extended by the City Personnel Director.

SALARY AND VACANCIES The appointment rate is $20,275 per annum. Vacancies exist in the Human Resources Administration/Department of Social Services and the Department of Juvenile Justice.

REQUIREMENTS

MINIMUM REQUIREMENTS A baccalaureate degree from an accredited college by January 1988. The minimum requirements must be met by the date of appointment.

Candidates who were educated in countries other than the United States must file DP-404 for evaluation of foreign education with their experience paper. Foreign education will be evaluated by the Department of Personnel to determine its comparability to education received in domestic accredited institutions.

Section 424-a of the New York Social Services Law requires an authorized agency to inquire whether a candidate for employment with child-caring responsibilities is or has been the subject of a child abuse and maltreatment report. The Agency has the discretion to assign a candidate who has been the subject of a child abuse and maltreatment report to a position with no childcaring responsibilities.

At the time of interview for appointment, all candidates for positions in Special Services for Children and Crisis Intervention Services will be required to complete a satisfactory writing sample in English.

JOB DESCRIPTION

DUTIES AND RESPONSIBILITIES Under supervision, with considerable latitude for independent action, individually or as a team member, identifies, develops and implements social service plans for disadvantaged clients, including recipients of public and medical assistance and child welfare services, adults/children receiving or needing institutional care, and homeless adults/families; may also determine eligibility for these services; may perform counseling and investigative activities; performs related work.

SPECIAL WORKING CONDITIONS Eligibles appointed to this position may be required to work shifts including nights, Saturdays, Sundays, and holidays.

TEST INFORMATION

TESTS   Written, weight 100, 70% required. The written test will be of the multiple-choice type and may include questions on techniques of gathering, organizing, and assessing information; interpretation of agency rules, regulations, and procedures, Federal, State, and City social service laws and guidelines; preparation of narrative reports, letters, and case records; forms completion, record keeping, basic arithmetic, and other related areas.

Accomodations are available for certified disabled applicants. Applications for accommodations must be submitted as early as possible and in no event later than 15 work days before the test or part of a test for which accommodation is requested. Consult General Examination Regulations for further requirements.

The Department of Personnel makes provisions for candidates claiming inability to participate in an examination when originally scheduled because of the candidates' religious beliefs. Such candidates should consult the City Personnel Director's Rule 4.4.6 for applicable procedures in requesting a special examination.

APPOINTMENTS

SELECTIVE CERTIFICATION   The eligible list resulting from this examination may be selectively certified to fill vacancies in the title of Caseworker which require six months of casework experience in child welfare, shelter care for the homeless, or protective services for adults. This requirement must be met by the last date for filing.

Candidates who wish to be selectively certified in any or all of the above fields must complete Experience Paper Form A, including all of the required information in the boxes provided and describing their duties clearly.

Candidates who do not wish to be considered for selective certification should complete the education section of Experience Paper Form A *only*.

QUALIFYING LANGUAGE ORAL TEST FOR SELECTIVE CERTIFICATION   The eligible list resulting from this examination may be selectively certified to fill vacancies for Caseworker which require a working knowledge of both English and another language. Those who pass the written test and are placed on the eligible list may be permitted to take a qualifying language oral test to determine ability to speak and understand other languages as needed. Candidates wishing to take such a qualifying test must so indicate at the time of the written test the language for which they wish to be tested. Only those who pass the qualifying oral test will be eligible for such selective certification.

Eligibility Specialist
Notice of Examination

The City of New York is an Equal Opportunity Employer.

In conjunction with the holding of this examination, a promotion examination will be held. The names appearing on the promotion list will receive prior consideration in filling vacancies. However, it is expected that there will be sufficient vacancies so that the open competitive list will be used as well.

The Department of Personnel makes provisions for candidates claiming inability to participate in an examination when originally scheduled because of the candidates' religious beliefs.

SELECTIVE CERTIFICATION The eligible list resulting from this examination may be selectively certified to fill vacancies in the title of Eligibility Specialist which require a working knowledge of both English and another language.

SALARY AND VACANCIES The appointment rate for this position is $18,030 per annum. There are 3 (three) assignment levels for this position: for Level I, the appointment rate is $18,030; for Level II, $18, 701; for Level III, $19,850. After original appointment, appointees may be assigned to any of these levels as the needs of the service require. Vacancies exist in the Human Resources Administration/Department of Social Services.

PROMOTION OPPORTUNITIES Employees in the title of Eligibility Specialist are accorded promotion opportunities, when eligible, to the title of Principal Administrative Associate.

REQUIREMENTS

MINIMUM REQUIREMENTS

1. An associate degree from an accredited college or completion of two years of study (60 credits) at an accredited college; or

2. A four-year high school diploma or its equivalent, and two years of full-time experience in the following areas: interviewing for the determination of eligibility for public assistance or unemployment, health, or other insurance benefits; bookkeeping; preparation of statistical reports; validation of vouchers, warrants, invoices; or

3. Education and/or experience equivalent to "1" or "2" above. However, all candidates must have a high school diploma or its equivalent.

Candidates who were educated in countries other than the United States must file form DP-404. Foreign education will be evaluated by the Department of Personnel to determine comparability to education received in domestic accredited educational institutions.

Experience Paper must be filled out completely and in detail and filed with your application.

At the time of appointment and at the time of investigation, candidates must present all the official documents and proof required to qualify, as stated in the Notice of Examination. Failure to present required documents, including proof of education and experience requirements, will result in disqualification for appointment.

The minimum requirements must be met by the last date for the receipt of applications.

Applicants may be summoned for the written test prior to the determination of whether they meet the minimum requirements.

RESIDENCY REQUIREMENTS A person who enters City service on or after September 1, 1986 shall be a resident of the City on the date that he or she enters City service or shall establish City residence within ninety days after such date, and shall thereafter maintain City residence as a condition of employment. Failure to establish or maintain City residence as required shall constitute a forfeiture of employment. This requirement does not apply to some City agencies.

JOB DESCRIPTION

DUTIES AND RESPONSIBILITIES This position encompasses the performance of tasks, under supervision, with some latitude for independent action or decision. This work is performed under well-defined procedures of the Human Resources Administration/Department of Social Services in Income Maintenance, Food Stamps, Medical Assistance, and Crisis Intervention Services; determining and verifying initial and continuing eligibility for Public Assistance, Medicaid, and Food Stamps through the use of agency procedures, automated systems, and/or based on face to face client interviews. There are three assignment levels within this class of positions. All personnel perform related work.

TEST INFORMATION

TESTS Written weight 100, 70% required. The written test will be of the multiple-choice type and may include questions on reading comprehension, including the interpretation and application of appropriate rules and regulations and the ability to obtain pertinent data from documents, printouts, files, and coding; ability to communicate effectively both orally and in writing, with clients and others; knowledge and application of interviewing techniques in face-to-face client contact or by telephone; ability to follow instructions and to complete forms accurately; knowledge of clerical functions, general office procedures, and filing systems; ability to perform basic mathematical computations; ability to prepare statistical and activity reports, as required.

There is a two- to four-week training program prior to assignment. Candidates who do not successfully complete this training may be terminated from employment with Human Resources Administration/Department of Social Services.

QUALIFYING LANGUAGE ORAL TEST FOR SELECTIVE CERTIFICATION The competitive written test will be in English. Those who pass the written test and who meet the minimum requirements and are placed on the eligible list may be permitted to take a qualifying language oral test to determine ability to speak and understand another language. Candidates wishing to take this qualifying test must so indicate at the time the written test is given. Candidates who do not so indicate at the time the written test is given will not be permitted to take the qualifying language oral test. Only those who pass this qualifying test will be eliglble for selective certification to fill vacancies which require a working knowledge of both English and another language. Eligibles will be called for the qualifying language oral test in groups as the needs of the service require.

Promotion to Eligibility Specialist
Notice of Examination

The City of New York is an Equal Opportunity Employer.

Accommodations are available for certified disabled applicants. Applications for accommodations must be submitted as early as possible and in no event later than 15 work days before the test or part of a test for which accommodation is requested. Consult General Examination Regulations for further requirements.

The Department of Personnel makes provisions for candidates claiming inability to participate in an examination when originally scheduled because of the candidates' religious beliefs.

SELECTIVE CERTIFICATION The eligible list resulting from this examination may be selectively certified to fill vacancies in the title of Eligibility Specialist which require a working knowledge of both English and another language.

PROMOTION OPPORTUNITIES Employees in the title of Eligibility Specialist are accorded promotion opportunities, when eligible, to the title of Principal Administrative Associate.

REQUIREMENTS

ELIGIBILITY Open to each employee of Human Resources Administration/ Department of Social Services who on the date of the written test: (1) is permanently employed in the title of Office Aide and meets the minimum requirements below; and (2) is not otherwise ineligible.

The admission of permanent Office Aides to this test is on a collateral basis and applies to this examination only; it is not to be considered a precedent for future examinations.

MINIMUM REQUIREMENTS

1. An associate degree from an accredited college or completion of two years of study (60 credits) at an accredited college; or

2. A four-year high school diploma or its equivalent, and two years of full-time experience in the following areas: interviewing for the determination of eligibility for public assistance or unemployment, health, or other insurance benefits; bookkeeping; preparation of statistical reports; validation of vouchers, warrants, invoices; or

3. Education and/or experience equivalent to "1" or "2" above. However, all candidates must have a high school diploma or its equivalent.

   Experience Paper Form A must be filled out completely and in detail and filed with your application.

   At the time of appointment and at the time of investigation, candidates must present all the official documents and proof required to qualify, as stated in the Notice of Examination. Failure to present required documents, including proof of education and experience requirements, will result in disqualification for appointment.

Candidates who were educated in countries other than the United States must file form DP-404. Foreign education will be evaluated by the Department of Personnel to determine comparability to education received in domestic accredited educational institutions.

The minimum requirements must be met by the last date for the receipt of applications.

Applicants may be summoned for the written test prior to the determination of whether they meet the minimum requirements.

Persons who are on an eligible list for Office Aide and who are appointed to such eligible title by the date of the test may file for this examination. However, filing fees will *not* be refunded for persons who are not appointed by the date of the test. Late applications from those appointed after filing closes will be accepted prior to the date of the test if they are submitted by HRA's personnel office with a covering letter confirming late eligibility. The filing fee must be paid by check or money order; cash will *not* be accepted.

JOB DESCRIPTION

DUTIES AND RESPONSIBILITIES   This position encompasses the performance of tasks, under supervision, with some latitude for independent action or decision. This work is performed under well-defined procedures of the Human Resources Administration/Department of Social Services in Income Maintenance, Food Stamps, Medical Assistance, and Crisis Intervention Services; determining and verifying initial and continuing eligibility for Public Assistance, Medicaid, and Food Stamps through the use of agency procedures, automated systems, and/or based on face-to-face client interviews. There are three assignment levels within this class of positions. All personnel perform related work.

TEST INFORMATION

TESTS   Seniority, weight 15; written, weight 85, 70% required. The written test will be of the multiple-choice type and may include questions on reading comprehension, including the interpretation and application of appropriate rules and regulations and the ability to obtain pertinent data from documents, printouts, files, and coding; ability to communicate effectively both orally and in writing, with clients and others; knowledge and application of interviewing techniques in face-to-face client contact or by telephone; ability to follow instructions and to complete forms accurately; knowledge of clerical functions, general office procedures, and filing systems; ability to perform basic mathematical computations; ability to prepare statistical and activity reports, as required; standards of employee conduct, including provisions of the Mayor's Executive Order No. 16 (1978).

There is a two- to four-week training program prior to assignment. Candidates who do not successfully complete this training may be reassigned to their former Civil Service title.

QUALIFYING LANGUAGE ORAL TEST FOR SELECTIVE CERTIFICA- TION   The competitive written test will be in English. Those who pass the written test and who meet the minimum requirements and are placed on the eligible list may be permitted to take a qualifying language oral test to determine ability to speak and understand another language. Candidates wishing to take this qualifying test must so indicate at the time the written test is given. Candidates who do not so indicate at the time the written test is given will not be permitted to take the qualifying language oral test. Only those who pass this qualifying test will be eligible for selective certification to fill vacancies which require a working knowledge of both English and another language. Eligibles will be called for the qualifying language oral test in groups as the needs of the service require.

SAMPLE STATE ANNOUNCEMENT

SOCIAL WORKER I	PSYCHIATRIC SOCIAL WORKER I
SOCIAL WORKER II	PSYCHIATRIC SOCIAL WORKER II

As a Social Worker I you would perform a wide variety of social services depending upon the facility which you join and the specific unit and/or department in which you work. For example, you may be working in an inpatient or outpatient setting, or in a Social Services or Community Services Department.

In whichever setting you work, your tasks would be likely to include a case work load, therapy work (individual and/or group), and work with community resources and services. Also you would most likely be working as a member of an intra- or inter-disciplinary team—helping to make referrals and helping to organize and participate in various interdisciplinary activities as a part of a team.

As a Social Worker II your tasks, in principle, would be similar to those of the Social Worker I. The difference lies in the degree of development displayed. As a Social Worker II, you would be expected to handle complex work assignments with less supervision and with an expertise honed by two years of experience. At times, a part of the job may be creating, organizing, and/or supervising special projects and programs.

As a Psychiatric Social Worker I you would perform a wide variety of social services depending upon the facility which you join and the specific unit and/or department in which you work. For example, you may be working in an inpatient or outpatient setting, or in a Social Services or Community Services Department.

In whichever setting you work, your tasks would be likely to include a case-work load, therapy work (individual and/or group), and work with community resources and services. You would most likely be working as a member of an intra- or inter-disciplinary team—helping to make referrals and helping to organize and participate in various inter-disciplinary activities as a part of a team.

As a Psychiatric Social Worker II your tasks, in principle, would be similar to those of the Psychiatric Social Worker I. The difference lies in the degree of development displayed. As a Psychiatric Social Worker II, you would be expected to handle complex work assignments with less supervision and with an expertise honed by two years of experience. At times, a part of the job may be creating, organizing, and/or supervising special projects and programs.

Minimum Qualifications: On or before the date of filing your application, you must have a master's degree in social work from a regionally accredited college or university, or one recognized by the State Education Department as following acceptable educational practices.

Applicants for Social Worker II must have had, in addition, two years of social work experience, one year of which must be professionally supervised post-master's degree experience.

If eligible, you may compete in both Social Worker I and Social Worker II examinations by filing one application, listing both examination numbers and titles.

If you are an applicant for Psychiatric Social Worker II, you must have had, in addition, two years of social work experience. One year of this experience must be professionally supervised post-master's degree experience, and one year must be in the field of mental health.

If eligible, you may be compete in both Psychiatric Social Worker I and Psychiatric Social Worker II examinations by filing one application, listing both examination numbers and titles.

Selection: There will be neither written nor oral tests for these positions. The examinations will consist of an evaluation of your training and experience in relation to the duties and requirements of the position(s). Final scores will be based on the ratings given in this evaluation.

You are urged to give complete and accurate information on your application. Vagueness and omissions will not be decided in your favor. For example: Include a full description of duties and the percentages of time spent working on each aspect of the job; indicate the specific setting(s) in which you've worked, whether you've engaged in team work, whether you've worked with behavior modification and/or token economy programs, and experience with community resources and agencies. Describe your continuing education: graduate courses taken beyond the master's degree; attendance at seminars, conferences, and workshops; professional papers written; etc.

Some of these positions require the ability to understand and speak a second language fluently. Positions are so designated because of the nature of the client group served. Fluency must be demonstrated prior to appointment.

Although promotion examinations are also being announced for Social Worker II and Psychiatric Social Worker II, it is expected that appointments will also be made as a result of these open-competitive examinations. Candidates eligible for the promotion examinations will NOT be admitted to the open-competitive examinations.

SAMPLE FEDERAL GOVERNMENT ANNOUNCEMENT

This announcement is used to fill all professional Social Worker positions nationwide at grades GS-9 through GS-12.

Government social workers work in a kaleidescopic range of settings—from remote Indian reservations to crowded inner city facilities, from one-person offices to involvement with a team of medical specialists.

Of more than 2400 social workers and social work program specialists who work in the federal government, only 10% work in Washington, D.C. Of those who work outside the capital area, 85% work in Veterans Administration hospitals, outpatient clinics and special settings, such as mental hygiene clinics, day treatment centers, restoration centers, domiciliaries and with veterans in community care and outreach programs. The other major employers are the Department of Health and Human Services; Department of Justice (Bureau of Prisons); Department of the Interior (Bureau of Indian Affairs); and the Army. In Washington, D.C. the Government of the District of Columbia is the major employer.

QUALIFICATIONS REQUIRED
SOCIAL WORKER—VETERANS ADMINISTRATION
Note: Most VA social workers are originally hired at GS-9 and GS-11.

Education

Completion of all requirements for a master's degree in social work which includes field practice assignments from a school of social work accredited by the Council of Social Work Education.

Training and Experience

Experience gained prior to the completion of all requirements for the master's degree is not qualifying.

GS-9: No additional experience or training is required.

GS-11: In addition to the basic education requirements, you must have a minimum of 1 year of professional social work experience, under qualified social work supervision, which demonstrates the potential to perform advanced assignments independently. To be qualifying, the experience must have been obtained in the social work program of a hospital, clinic, or other voluntary or public social or health agency.

GS-12: In addition to the GS-11 requirements, you must have a minimum of one additional year of professional social work experience which demonstrates broad knowledge of social work and superior skill and judgment in professional practice. For research and education positions, this additional year must be in social work education (class or field instruction) or social work research as appropriate.

For all positions except social work research, one year of the total qualifying experience must have been in professional social work in a clinical setting. A clinical setting is a medical or psychiatric hospital or clinic, a residential treatment center, or any other type of facility where social work is involved in collaborative treatment and is identified with the medical profession.

For social work research positions, applicants must have knowledge of research methods and have demonstrated potential or observed skill in planning, developing, and carrying through studies of social work practice or processes.

For positions with social work educational responsibilities, the required experience must have included planning or conducting a staff development program for graduate social workers or extensive field instruction of social work students or teaching in an accredited school of social work.

Substitution of Additional Education

For specialized staff or research positions at GS-12, you may substitute successful completion of the advanced curriculum beyond a master's degree in an accredited school of social work on a year-for-year basis in your specialization for a maximum credit of 2 years.

SOCIAL WORKER AND
SOCIAL WORK PROGRAM SPECIALIST

For agencies other than the Veterans Administration.

Education

Successful completion of all requirements for a master's degree in social work from a school of social work accredited by the Council on Social Work Education.

Training and Experience

Experience gained before completion of all requirements for the master's degree is not qualifying.

GS-9: No additional experience is required if your education has included field practice assignments in professional social work. Otherwise, 1 year of professional social work experience under professional supervision is required.

GS-11: In addition to meeting the requirements for GS-9, you must have a minimum of 1 year of professional social work experience, under professional supervision, which demonstrates the ability to perform advanced assignments independently.

GS-12: In addition to meeting the requirements for GS-11, you must have a minimum of 1 additional year of professional social work experience which demonstrates a broad knowledge of social work and superior skills and professional judgment.

For Social Work Program Specialist positions, your experience must have included one, or in some cases a combination of two or more, functions, such as program planning, program development, program evaluation, consultation, and cooperative community relationships in an agency providing social work service to families, children, or adults; or supervisory, administrative, or consultative work in a public or voluntary welfare or health agency with an organized social work program. This experience must have demonstrated the ability to analyze, evaluate, and advise on overall aspects of social work program, plans, and operations and to work effectively with representatives of other agencies and groups in developing program standards and requirements.

For positions with staff development responsibilities, the required experience must have included experience in planning or conducting social work education or staff development program in a health or welfare agency, or teaching in an accredited school of social work.

How You Are Rated

There is no written test. You will be rated on your professional experience, education, and training as described in your application, along with any additional information which may be obtained. If you meet the qualifications, your name will go on a list with names of other qualified applicants and may be referred to federal agencies as vacancies occur. For specialized jobs, only names of applicants whose qualifications meet the special needs of the job will be referred.

Describe Your Experience Fully

Be sure to provide sufficient information on your background and accomplishments so that you can be evaluated fairly. Formal job titles, official position descriptions, elaborate terminology describing positions held will not be accepted as establishing the quality of value of your experience. Describe your duties and responsibilities in your own words.

For field practice assignments during your graduate study, please give the dates and a brief statement of your duties and responsibilities. If the assignments involved working with drug addicts and/or alcoholics, indicate this as well.

Part-Time or Unpaid Experience

Pertinent part-time or unpaid experience will be evaluated on the same basis as paid experience. If you have such experience, which is relevant to the kind of job you are applying for, you should describe it on your application in detail, showing the actual number of hours per week in the activity.

Graduate Students

Applications will be accepted from candidates for graduate social worker degrees who expect to complete all requirements for the degree, including acceptance of the thesis, within nine months of the date of filing. Applications should be accompanied by a list of courses, including a full description of field practice assignments and semester hours, which will be completed within the nine-month period.

If you qualify on the basis of an anticipated degree, you may not start work until all educational requirements have been successfully completed.

Eligibility

If you are qualified, you will be eligible for job consideration for 12 months from the date on your notice of rating. If you want to extend your eligibility, you must submit an up-to-date Personal Qualifications Statement (SF 171) after 10, but no more than 12 months from that date.

How To Apply

Send 1. A Personal Qualifications Statement, SF 171, clearly indicating the locations where you are available to work.
2. Supplemental Qualifications Statement for Social Worker CSC Form 1170/14.
3. A transcript of your grades to date: or CSC Form 1170/17 or CSC Form 226 which transmit the same information.
4. Standard Form 15, with the required proof, if you are claiming 10-point veteran preference.
to: Washington D.C. Area Office, EWM
U.S. Civil Service Commission 20415.

If you are interested in a Correctional Treatment Specialist job, you should contact a Federal Job Information Center in the area where you want to work in order to find out whether applications are being accepted.

Application forms, current salaries, and additional information on government employment can be obtained from federal job information centers. Federal job information centers are listed in the white pages of major metropolitan area phone directories under "U.S. Government."

TECHNIQUES OF STUDY AND TEST-TAKING

Although a thorough knowledge of the subject matter is the most important factor in succeeding on your exam, the following suggestions could raise your score substantially. These few pointers will give you the strategy employed on tests by those who are most successful in this not-so-mysterious art. It's really quite simple. Do things right from the beginning. Make these successful methods a habit. Then you'll get the greatest dividends from the time you invest in this book.

PREPARING FOR THE EXAM

- **Budget your time.** Set aside definite hours each day for concentrated study. Keep to your schedule.

- **Study alone.** You will concentrate better when you work by yourself. Keep a list of questions you cannot answer and points you are unsure of to talk over with a friend who is preparing the same exam. Plan to exchange ideas at a joint review session just before the test.

- **Eliminate distractions.** Disturbances caused by family and neighbor activities (telephone calls, chit-chat, TV programs, etc.) work to your disadvantage. Study in a quiet, private room.

- **Use the library.** Most colleges and universities have excellent library facilities. Some institutions have special libraries for the various subject areas: physics library, education library, psychology library, etc. Take full advantage of such valuable facilities. The library is free from those distractions that may inhibit your home study. Moreover, research in your subject area is more convenient in a library since it can provide more study material than you have at home.

- **Answer all the questions in this book.** Don't be satisfied merely with the correct answer to each question. Do additional research on the other choices which are given. You will broaden your background and be more adequately prepared for the "real" exam. It's quite possible that a question of the exam which you are going to take may require you to be familiar with the other choices.

- **Get the "feel" of the exam.** The sample questions which this book contains will give you that "feel" since they are virtually the same as those you will find on the test.

- **Take the sample tests as "real" tests.** With this attitude, you will derive greater benefit. Put yourself under strict examination condition. Tolerate no interruptions while you are taking the sample tests. Work steadily. Do not spend too much time on any one question.

If a question seems too difficult, go to the next one. If time permits, go back to the omitted question.

- **Tailor your study to the subject matter. Skim or scan.** Don't study everything in the same manner. Obviously, certain areas are more important than others.

- **Organize yourself.** Make sure that your notes are in good order—valuable time is unnecessarily consumed when you can't find what you are looking for quickly.

- **Keep physically fit.** You cannot retain information well when you are uncomfortable, headachy, or tense. Physical health promotes mental effency.

How To Take An Exam

- **Get to the Examination Room about Ten Minutes Ahead of Time.** You'll get a better start when you are accustomed to the room. If the room is too cold, too warm, or not well ventilated, call these conditions to the attention of the person in charge.

- **Make Sure that You Read the Instructions Carefully.** In many cases, test-takers lose credits because they misread some important point in the given directions—example: the **incorrect** choice instead of the **correct** choice.

- **Be Confident.** Statistics conclusively show that you are more likely to receive high scores when you are prepared. It is important to know that you are not expected to answer every question correctly. The questions usually have a range of difficulty and differentiate between several levels of skill.

- **Skip Hard Questions and Go Back Later.** It is a good idea to make a mark on the question sheet next to all the questions you cannot answer easily and go back to those questions later. First answer the questions you are sure about. Do not panic if you cannot answer a question. Go on and answer the questions you know. Usually the easier questions are presented at the beginning of the exam and the questions become gradually more difficult.

   If you do skip ahead on the exam, be sure to skip ahead also on your answer sheet. A good technique is to check periodically the number of the question on the answer sheet with the number of the question on the test. You should do this every time you decide to skip a question. If you fail to skip the corresponding answer blank for that question, all of the following answers will be wrong.

   Each student is stronger in some areas than in others. No one is expected to know all the answers. Do not waste time agonizing over a difficult question because it may keep you from getting to other questions that you can answer correctly.

- **Guess If You Are Not Sure.** No penalty is given for guessing when these exams are scored. Therefore, it is better to guess than to omit an answer.

- **Mark the Answer Sheet Clearly.** When you take the examination, you will mark your answers to the multiple-choice questions on a separate answer sheet that will be given to you at the test center. If you have not worked with an answer sheet before, it is in your best interest to become familiar with the procedures involved. Remember, knowing the correct answer is not enough! If you do not mark the sheet correctly, so that it can be machine-scored, you will not get credit for your answers!

   In addition to marking answers on the separate answer sheet, you will be asked to give your name and other information, including your Social Security number. As a precaution bring along your Social Security number for identification purposes.

Read the directions carefully and follow them exactly. If they ask you to print your name in boxes provided, write only one letter in each box. If your name is longer than the number of boxes provided, omit the letters that do not fit. Remember, you are writing for a machine; it does not have judgment. It can only record the pencil marks you make on the answer sheet.

Use the answer sheet to record all answers to questions. Each question, or item, has four or five answer choices labeled (A),(B),(C),(D),(E). You will be asked to choose the letter that stands for the best answer. Then you will be asked to mark your answer by blackening the appropriate space on your answer sheet. Be sure that each space you choose and blacken with your pencil is **completely** blackened. The machine will "read" your answers in terms of spaces blackened. Make sure that only one answer is clearly blackened. If you erase an answer, erase it completely and mark your new answer clearly. The machine will give credit only for clearly marked answers. It does not pause to decide whether you really meant (B) or (C).

- **Read Each Question Carefully**. The exam questions are not designed to trick you through misleading or ambiguous alternative choices. On the other hand, they are not all direct questions of factual information. Some are designed to elicit responses that reveal your ability to reason, or to interpret a fact or idea. It's up to you to read each question carefully, so know what is being asked. The exam authors have tried to make the questions clear. Do not go astray looking for hidden meanings.

- **Don't Answer Too Fast**. The multiple-choice questions on your exam are not superficial exercises. They are designed to test not only your memory but also your understanding and insight. Do not place too much emphasis on speed. The time element is a factor, but it is not all-important. Accuracy should not be sacrificed for speed.

- **Materials and Conduct at the Test Center.** You need to bring with you to the test center your admission form, your Social Security number, and several No. 2 pencils. Arrive on time as you may not be admitted after testing has begun. Instructions for taking the test will be read to you by the test supervisor and time will be called when the test is over. If you have questions, you may ask them of the supervisor. Do not give or receive assistance while taking the exams. If you do, you will be asked to turn in all test materials and told to leave the room. You will not be permitted to return and your test will not be scored.

Part Two

Five Practice Examinations

Answer Sheet for Sample Practice Examination I

1. Ⓐ Ⓑ Ⓒ Ⓓ
2. Ⓐ Ⓑ Ⓒ Ⓓ
3. Ⓐ Ⓑ Ⓒ Ⓓ
4. Ⓐ Ⓑ Ⓒ Ⓓ
5. Ⓐ Ⓑ Ⓒ Ⓓ
6. Ⓐ Ⓑ Ⓒ Ⓓ
7. Ⓐ Ⓑ Ⓒ Ⓓ
8. Ⓐ Ⓑ Ⓒ Ⓓ
9. Ⓐ Ⓑ Ⓒ Ⓓ
10. Ⓐ Ⓑ Ⓒ Ⓓ
11. Ⓐ Ⓑ Ⓒ Ⓓ
12. Ⓐ Ⓑ Ⓒ Ⓓ
13. Ⓐ Ⓑ Ⓒ Ⓓ
14. Ⓐ Ⓑ Ⓒ Ⓓ
15. Ⓐ Ⓑ Ⓒ Ⓓ
16. Ⓐ Ⓑ Ⓒ Ⓓ

17. Ⓐ Ⓑ Ⓒ Ⓓ
18. Ⓐ Ⓑ Ⓒ Ⓓ
19. Ⓐ Ⓑ Ⓒ Ⓓ
20. Ⓐ Ⓑ Ⓒ Ⓓ
21. Ⓐ Ⓑ Ⓒ Ⓓ
22. Ⓐ Ⓑ Ⓒ Ⓓ
23. Ⓐ Ⓑ Ⓒ Ⓓ
24. Ⓐ Ⓑ Ⓒ Ⓓ
25. Ⓐ Ⓑ Ⓒ Ⓓ
26. Ⓐ Ⓑ Ⓒ Ⓓ
27. Ⓐ Ⓑ Ⓒ Ⓓ
28. Ⓐ Ⓑ Ⓒ Ⓓ
29. Ⓐ Ⓑ Ⓒ Ⓓ
30. Ⓐ Ⓑ Ⓒ Ⓓ
31. Ⓐ Ⓑ Ⓒ Ⓓ
32. Ⓐ Ⓑ Ⓒ Ⓓ

33. Ⓐ Ⓑ Ⓒ Ⓓ
34. Ⓐ Ⓑ Ⓒ Ⓓ
35. Ⓐ Ⓑ Ⓒ Ⓓ
36. Ⓐ Ⓑ Ⓒ Ⓓ
37. Ⓐ Ⓑ Ⓒ Ⓓ
38. Ⓐ Ⓑ Ⓒ Ⓓ
39. Ⓐ Ⓑ Ⓒ Ⓓ
40. Ⓐ Ⓑ Ⓒ Ⓓ
41. Ⓐ Ⓑ Ⓒ Ⓓ
42. Ⓐ Ⓑ Ⓒ Ⓓ
43. Ⓐ Ⓑ Ⓒ Ⓓ
44. Ⓐ Ⓑ Ⓒ Ⓓ
45. Ⓐ Ⓑ Ⓒ Ⓓ
46. Ⓐ Ⓑ Ⓒ Ⓓ
47. Ⓐ Ⓑ Ⓒ Ⓓ
48. Ⓐ Ⓑ Ⓒ Ⓓ

49. Ⓐ Ⓑ Ⓒ Ⓓ
50. Ⓐ Ⓑ Ⓒ Ⓓ
51. Ⓐ Ⓑ Ⓒ Ⓓ
52. Ⓐ Ⓑ Ⓒ Ⓓ
53. Ⓐ Ⓑ Ⓒ Ⓓ
54. Ⓐ Ⓑ Ⓒ Ⓓ
55. Ⓐ Ⓑ Ⓒ Ⓓ
56. Ⓐ Ⓑ Ⓒ Ⓓ
57. Ⓐ Ⓑ Ⓒ Ⓓ
58. Ⓐ Ⓑ Ⓒ Ⓓ
59. Ⓐ Ⓑ Ⓒ Ⓓ
60. Ⓐ Ⓑ Ⓒ Ⓓ
61. Ⓐ Ⓑ Ⓒ Ⓓ
62. Ⓐ Ⓑ Ⓒ Ⓓ
63. Ⓐ Ⓑ Ⓒ Ⓓ
64. Ⓐ Ⓑ Ⓒ Ⓓ

65. Ⓐ Ⓑ Ⓒ Ⓓ
66. Ⓐ Ⓑ Ⓒ Ⓓ
67. Ⓐ Ⓑ Ⓒ Ⓓ
68. Ⓐ Ⓑ Ⓒ Ⓓ
69. Ⓐ Ⓑ Ⓒ Ⓓ
70. Ⓐ Ⓑ Ⓒ Ⓓ
71. Ⓐ Ⓑ Ⓒ Ⓓ
72. Ⓐ Ⓑ Ⓒ Ⓓ
73. Ⓐ Ⓑ Ⓒ Ⓓ
74. Ⓐ Ⓑ Ⓒ Ⓓ
75. Ⓐ Ⓑ Ⓒ Ⓓ
76. Ⓐ Ⓑ Ⓒ Ⓓ
77. Ⓐ Ⓑ Ⓒ Ⓓ
78. Ⓐ Ⓑ Ⓒ Ⓓ
79. Ⓐ Ⓑ Ⓒ Ⓓ
80. Ⓐ Ⓑ Ⓒ Ⓓ

PRACTICE EXAMINATION I

Case Worker—Hospital Environment

Direction For Answering Questions: Each question has four suggested answers, lettered A, B, C, and D. Decide which one is the best answer and on the sample answer sheet locate the question number and with a soft pencil darken the area which corresponds to the answer that you have selected.

TIME ALLOWED FOR ENTIRE EXAMINATION: 3 HOURS

1. You have scheduled an hour's time for an interview with a patient. As the time is almost up and you must go on to your next patient, the patient suddenly starts talking about what he believes to be a new problem. It would be best for you to

   (A) conclude the interview and schedule another appointment with the patient in the near future
   (B) permit the patient to take all the time he needs and skip your next scheduled interview
   (C) request the patient's reason for bringing up the problem as the interview is about to end
   (D) tell the patient that you have no more time to spend with him.

2. You have been assigned to a case involving a deteriorating relationship between the parents of a hospitalized child who was the victim of an accident caused by the father. Your counseling of the child's parents has resulted in a marked improvement in their relationship. The child is now about to be discharged from the hospital and you are engaged in a final interview with the parents. At this interview you should

   (A) tell the parents their problem has been solved
   (B) offer to continue your counseling with the parents
   (C) once more lecture the parents on what they should and should not do
   (D) declare to the parents that you were responsible for improving their relationship.

3. One of your clients, an adult male out-patient, has been meeting with you for several months. He has failed to keep his last two appointments and has not communicated with you since his last visit. His physician calls you saying that one of his laboratory tests indicates that he must undergo additional testing. You have been unsuccessful in trying to reach him by telephone, mail, or telegram. You should then

   (A) contact a neighbor telling him to persuade the patient to come to the hospital
   (B) contact a relative of the patient and request that he persuade the patient to visit the hospital
   (C) write to the patient telling him that he is endangering his life by not visiting the hospital
   (D) make an emergency visit to the patient's home explaining that it is very important that he undergo additional testing.

4. An elderly woman patient who has been admitted to the hospital has been assigned to you as a client. The woman is unable to speak with sufficient coherence to identify herself. However a card has been found in her possession which contains her name and an address which is a short distance from the hospital. The telephone company has no phone listed at the address in the name of the woman. Although she is talkative, her remarks do not make sense and she keeps repeating that she must cook dinner for her brother. It would be most advisable under the circumstances for you to

(A) send the security guards to the address to tell her relatives that she has been hospitalized

(B) send a visiting nurse to look after the patient's brother

(C) call the public assistance agency to determine if the woman is on welfare

(D) make a visit yourself to the address to try to determine more information about the woman.

5. Assume that you are a Case Worker assigned to the Alcoholism Clinic. One of your clients appears for a scheduled interview in an intoxicated state. It would be best for you to

(A) conduct a session completely devoted to the evils of drinking

(B) cancel the interview, make another appointment for the client, and tell him that you cannot interview him while he is intoxicated

(C) tell the client in an authoritative manner that you are about to close his case

(D) recommend that he be referred for further medical assistance because your counseling is not of any help.

6. Assume that you are a Case Worker in a Family Planning Clinic. One of your clients is an unmarried pregnant girl who wants an abortion even though her boyfriend is encouraging her to have the child after marrying him. She is bewildered and does not know what to do. It would be best for you to

(A) lecture her, emphasizing that it was her carelessness that caused her present predicament

(B) encourage the patient to make up her own mind and you will support her decision

(C) encourage her to do what her boyfriend wants her to do because he is offering to marry her

(D) try to determine if the girl's uncertainty in this matter is a result of her religious upbringing.

7. You are interviewing a new client who tells you that he is on public assistance and is receiving as much money as when he was working. He further states that he cannot understand why anyone would really want to work when they can receive as much money by being on assistance and not working. In response it would be most appropriate for you to

(A) strongly state that you disagree with the client

(B) state that it all depends on an individual's values

(C) agree with the client

(D) refuse to discuss this matter with the client.

8. During a follow-up interview with a young woman client, she suddenly states, "Stop all this professional stuff, let us be friends." It would be best for you to respond by saying,

(A) "If we were friends, it would be very difficult for me to help you as I should."

(B) "We can be friends, but I will have to get you assigned to some one else."

(C) "Our rules and regulations prohibit this."

(D) "I am too busy to make any new friends."

9. On the basis of an interview with a new male client you discover that he is on probation, having been recently released from prison. You feel that it would be desirable to contact the client's Probation Officer in order to secure additional information concerning the client. It would be appropriate for you to contact the Probation Officer

(A) after the interview, only with the client's consent
(B) after the interview, without the client's consent
(C) at the completion of the interview without telling the client
(D) only if the client can be present during the discussion.

10. During your first interview, a newly hospitalized patient tells you of her son's truancy from school. She seems to be very concerned about this matter. Your initial response should be

(A) "This is your son's problem, your problems are more important at this point."
(B) "Will this matter bother you during your hospitalization?"
(C) "Has your son failed any subjects because of his truancy?"
(D) "I am too busy to discuss your son with you today."

11. A young woman, one of your clients, gave birth three days ago. She refuses to see her baby and is very abusive to the staff. At this point it would be most appropriate for you to

(A) remonstrate with the woman, pointing out that she is acting like a child
(B) speak to the woman, telling her that she will feel differently after she sees her child
(C) interview the woman in an effort to understand why she is acting like she is
(D) threaten the woman with a transfer to the psychiatric ward if she does not conform to acceptable behavior.

12. A young woman about to be admitted to the hospital refuses to be admitted because she says there will be no one to take care of her three young children while she is hospitalized. You speak to the physician who has examined her and he declares that immediate hospitalization is an absolute necessity. The action you should take first is to

(A) suggest that the patient get a neighbor to care for the children
(B) suggest that the children be admitted to the hospital also
(C) look for the children's father and urge him to care for the children
(D) tell the patient that you will be able to arrange for the care of her children while she is hospitalized.

13. You are a Case Worker in a Methadone Maintenance Clinic. As you complete a scheduled interview with one of your clients he asks to borrow ten dollars from you. In this instance you should

(A) tell your client that you are prohibited by rules and regulations from lending him the money
(B) lend the client the ten dollars
(C) suggest he borrow it from a friend or a relative
(D) tell him to request the loan from another member of the staff.

14. You have been assigned as a client a young woman who is pregnant but wants to have an abortion because she feels that she may not be able to properly care for her baby. An appropriate first response would be for you to say

(A) "What do you consider to be proper care?"
(B) "You are going to be an excellent mother."
(C) "Who is the baby's father?"
(D) "In what month of your pregnancy did you start to have these thoughts?"

15. In your capacity as a Case Worker the best reason for you to utilize the questioning technique while interviewing your clients is to

(A) reinforce your own impressions concerning the case
(B) obtain necessary information to process the case
(C) bring to light any fraudulent intent on the part of the client
(D) reveal misinformation given by the client.

16. Properly acting Case Workers should "accept" a client even though they may differ with the client in his or her feelings, attitudes, and general behavior. This means that Case Workers should

(A) agree with client as to what he or she says, feels, and does
(B) indicate their respect for the client as a person
(C) form no strong opinion concerning their client's beliefs
(D) attempt to change their sense of values so that they coincide with the client's.

17. The Case Worker should attempt to fully prepare before visiting a client. All of the following except one should be included in the Case Worker's preparation. Indicate the one that should not.

(A) obtaining all relevant information from the client's medical history
(B) trying to perceive how the client will feel
(C) owning up to his or her prejudices
(D) deciding on a solution to the client's problems.

18. Following your introduction to a new client, the most appropriate of the following questions to ask first is

(A) "Will you be having visitors today?"
(B) "Which doctor is treating you?"
(C) "How can I help you?"
(D) "Do you carry hospitalization insurance?"

19. You can best clarify a statement made by a client during an interview by

(A) asking the client to rephrase his or her statement
(B) rephrasing the statement and asking the client if that is what he or she meant
(C) telling the client that you do not understand what he or she is saying
(D) making your own assumptions where necessary.

20. At the conclusion of an interview with a client in which you have resolved a number of problems it would be most appropriate for you to

(A) caution the client to be punctual at the next appointment
(B) advise your client as to what actions you will take and what actions you expect the client to take before the next visit
(C) caution the client to medicate himself if he should get depressed
(D) advise the client to come in with some new problems at his next visit.

21. In the midst of interviewing a married patient with young children who is about to undergo surgery, she asks if you are married. It would be appropriate for you to reply

(A) with your marital status, but requesting the reason for her question
(B) that you are not, but you are engaged to be married
(C) that the question is entirely out of order
(D) that you were married but are now divorced

22. After you've introduced yourself to a new patient, she proceeds to give you a lengthy description of her illness. It would be proper for you in this instance to show your concern by

    (A) making brief comments and asking relevant questions
    (B) making no comments so that the patient is not interrupted
    (C) frequently interrupting so that you may clear up in your mind points you do not understand
    (D) requesting that the patient pause at specific intervals so that you may ask pointed questions.

23. An adult patient in your care has been receiving your counseling for about a month. He is about to be discharged from the hospital but his place of residence is still an undecided issue. The final decision concerning this matter should be made by

    (A) you in the capacity of his Case Worker
    (B) the patient's relatives
    (C) the patient, with the assistance of the Case Worker if it is required
    (D) the patient, based upon the advice of the doctors.

24. One of the patients assigned to you asks you for advice concerning his unhappy marital status. For you to decide how to respond in this instance all but one of the following should enter your consideration. Which one should you not consider?

    (A) the level of anxiety the patient may be experiencing
    (B) whether the patient will be able to follow through on your advice
    (C) the seriousness of the problem
    (D) whether you are inclined to believe the patient will accept your advice.

25. Good case work technique indicates that while interviewing a young child close attention should be paid to the child's behavior, feelings, and mood, in addition to what the child says. Close observation is necessary because it

    (A) provides pertinent information about the child
    (B) aids the relationship
    (C) warns the Case Worker about the proper time to offer consolation
    (D) offers clues about the proper time to humor the child.

26. You decide it would be proper to refer one of your patients who is about to be discharged for psychiatric help. He agrees to cooperate but requests that you withhold in your report certain information that he has given to you in confidence. For you to include this information in your report to the psychiatrist without the patient's permission would be

    (A) proper, because the psychiatrist will need this information
    (B) improper, because you would be violating a confidence
    (C) proper, because the client's welfare is of utmost importance
    (D) improper, because the patient would probably find out eventually that the confidence was breached.

27. One of your clients, a woman who had been severely beaten by her husband, is visibly upset and embarrassed about relating detailed information concerning the beating to you. It would be best in this instance for you to

    (A) insist that she tell her entire story of the beating including details
    (B) tell the patient you are leaving and will return when she is ready to tell her story
    (C) tell the woman she need not tell you the details of the beating at this time and ask her how you can help her
    (D) put off the interview until such time that the husband can be present to give his side of the story.

28. A retired 78-year-old school teacher is about to be discharged from the hospital after a brief illness. Upon to this point he has spoken clearly and seems to be well-oriented. As you enter his room to confer with him he fails to recognize you and his speech is rambling and incoherent. It would be most appropriate for you to react to this change of behavior by

(A) telling the patient in an authoritative tone to come to his senses
(B) leaving the room and telling the patient you will return when he comes to his senses
(C) advising the patient's physician of the change of behavior
(D) telling the patient that discharge plans will be cancelled and a transfer to a state hospital will be processed.

29. In your capacity as a Case Worker you are assisting a client to complete his application for Medicaid. He appears to be eligible but he is reluctant to disclose to you information necessary to complete the form. In this situation it would be best for you to

(A) inform your supervisor of your client's uncooperativeness and recommend that the case be closed
(B) advise the patient that if he does not complete the form he cannot be treated in the clinic
(C) request from the patient the reason for his reluctance to apply for the aid for which he is apparently eligible
(D) tell the client his bill will be turned over to a collection agency for payment if he does not complete the form at once.

30. One of your clients who has been admitted to the hospital on a medical emergency appears to be depressed over the fact that he has become ill during a period when his wife and children are away. In the past you have had a similar experience which you dealt with successfully. In this instance it would be most appropriate for you to

(A) tell the man of your experience and tell him to use the same approach
(B) tell the man of your experience and show your sympathy
(C) tell him to get a good night's sleep and he will feel better tomorrow
(D) tell the man you dealt with this situation and discover how he feels about taking the same approach as you did.

31. You are assigned as a Case Worker on the Pediatric Service and you receive a phone call from a woman who reports that her neighbor's infant has black and blue marks all over its body. She says that she has heard sounds from her neighbor's apartment that lead her to believe that the child has been beaten. It would be most proper for you to respond to this call by

(A) referring the matter to the proper agency responsible for the welfare of children
(B) advising the caller that you cannot act on the basis of a phone call
(C) informing the caller to mind her own business
(D) telling the woman to call the police and have the parents of the child arrested.

32. You have been assigned a long-term patient and have been advising her for a considerable period of time. However, due to an impending reorganization this patient is about to be assigned to a new Case Worker in the near future. It would be most appropriate for you to tell the patient of her imminent reassignment to a new Case Worker

(A) at once, so that the patient may prepare herself for the change
(B) at the first visit of the new Case Worker, so that the patient will not attribute the change to you
(C) at your final visit and at the same time telling the patient what you know about the new Case Worker
(D) at the conclusion of your final visit in order to avoid a sentimental farewell.

33. You are assigned to a Psychiatric Clinic as a Case Worker. While on duty you receive a phone call from a man who says his wife just ingested twenty sleeping pills following an argument. You can be of most help in this matter by

    (A) advising the man to stay calm because the dose is probably not lethal
    (B) advising the man to give his wife plenty of black coffee
    (C) offering him an appointment for marital counseling
    (D) advising the man to get immediate emergency help for his wife.

34. As you, a Case Worker assigned to a large hospital, enter your place of employment, you observe an elderly man tripping over the curb and falling to the ground. You should first

    (A) inform the administrator of the hospital of the accident
    (B) assist the man to his feet and walk him into the hospital where he can sit down
    (C) stay with the man and caution him not to move until help can be summoned
    (D) call the police from the nearest phone.

35. One of your clients is in the midst of relating to you the details of her previous surgery and the problems she had with it, including her post-operative treatment. She encountered many adverse reactions from her family during this period. She is now scheduled to undergo similar surgery and she is anxious to avoid the same problems she encountered before. The amount of notes taken during this interview should have been

    (A) a great deal; there were many details related in the interview
    (B) a small amount; the discussion demanded your entire attention and notes should have been recorded after the interview was completed
    (C) a great deal; the client will then be impressed by your apparent interest
    (D) a small amount; complete notes should be taken at the end of the interview, not during it.

36. As a Case Worker you are interviewing a patient for the second time and you find your relationship considerably strained. You can best handle this situation by first

    (A) considering this situation to be routine, and reviewing your own attitudes and reactions towards the client during your initial interview
    (B) considering this to be unusual and trying to analyze your client's reasons for his or her attitude
    (C) considering it to be routine and request that the client be assigned to another Case Worker
    (D) considering it to be unusual and requesting the client to explain his or her hostility toward you.

37. As a Case Worker you have been assigned a client who is a diabetic 50-year-old woman who is medicated with insulin injections. She has been admitted to the hospital frequently in a diabetic coma because she has great difficulty in injecting herself with insulin. Instruction in the clinic has failed to solve the problem and the case had been referred to you. You should first

    (A) refer her for psychiatric evaluation and possible therapy
    (B) speak to her husband to ascertain whether he would be willing to inject his wife
    (C) warn the woman she will have to remain hospitalized until she is able to inject herself with insulin
    (D) attempt to convince the woman it would be in her best interests to learn to inject herself as many diabetics do.

38. A young waitress has been to the emergency room twice in the last few days because of on-the-job accidents. On both occasions she has indicated to the physicians who have treated her that she is tired and tense almost continuously. She has been referred for a

complete medical workup and you have been assigned to counsel her. You can be of assistance to her by

(A) requesting copies of all medical tests as they are taken
(B) interviewing the waitress to ascertain if any non-medical problems are contributing to her condition
(C) recommending her for an immediate psychiatric evaluation
(D) not interviewing her until the results of the medical workup are made available to you.

39. A female patient frequently fails to keep clinic appointments because she is more interested in coping with non-medical problems than with her medical condition, which the doctor feels is sufficiently significant to warrant frequent and regular treatment. You are assigned to counsel her and attempt to convince her of the importance of keeping her medical appointments. You can best accomplish this by

(A) telling her no problem could be more important than her medical problem
(B) interviewing her in an attempt to evaluate her other problems and ascertain just how much help you can supply to her
(C) telling her you will be happy to help her with her other problems only after she keeps all of her medical appointments
(D) warning her she will be discharged if she misses one more medical appointment.

40. A Case Worker assigned to a hospital would have the primary responsibility of

(A) instructing the nurse concerning the patient's medication
(B) contacting relatives as to when they should visit
(C) observing a patient for signs of anxiety concerning his or her illness
(D) keeping full records of the patient's visitors.

41. You have been assigned to look after the welfare of a young child whose parents have both been hospitalized following an automobile accident. Of the following, your primary concern would be to

(A) encourage the child to react as a grownup because that is what is expected of him
(B) spend your time playing games with the child
(C) get the child to tell you his true feelings and reassure him that you will give him help when he may need it
(D) convince the child that he has no real fears.

42. One of your clients has many real medical and social problems and is in need of a great deal of case work assistance. In order to be of most help to this client it would be best for you to

(A) try to convince the client of the unimportance of his or her problems
(B) assist the client to have a realistic view of his or her problems and assure him or her you will help as much as you can
(C) enunciate to the client those areas in which you can help and those areas which you feel are beyond help
(D) discourage the client from trying to help himself or herself and encourage dependence on you.

43. In a discussion with one of your clients you find that she is eligible for public assistance and you therefore refer her to the Department of Social Services. She replies that she will be unable to discuss this matter with anyone else but you. You should then

(A) emphasize to the client that you cannot help her in this matter
(B) offer to accompany her to the public assistance office, but work on her future independence
(C) since your client's emotional outlook is more important, discourage your client from pursuing the matter
(D) direct your client to get a friend to accompany her.

44. A newspaper reporter approaches you saying he has received many complaints concerning long waits for emergency treatment. Your most appropriate response would be

(A) tell the reporter that there are more cases with less help available
(B) refer the reporter to the head of your division
(C) assure the reporter that the emergency room is most efficient
(D) direct the reporter to speak to the hospital employee responsible for public relations.

45. You are assigned a client whose problems seem to be typical of those of many of your other clients. Of the following, it would be most appropriate to

(A) attempt to learn more about the client to ascertain if there are significant differences
(B) just handle this client as you do your other clients
(C) discuss the matter with another Case Worker
(D) tell the client that there are many others with similar problems.

46. A patient informs you as his Case Worker that someone has stolen his shoes. He is about to be discharged and he tells you that he has no means for replacing them. It would be most appropriate for you to first

(A) suggest he speak to the ward nurse about that matter
(B) advise him to buy a new pair in a neighborhood store
(C) tell him you will see if there is an available pair in the hospital clothing room
(D) question him to find out if he was wearing a pair when he was admitted.

47. You receive a complaint from the parents of a hospitalized child that their child is being ignored by the attending nurses. From your extensive experience you know that this condition does not exist in the pediatric ward. You should assume that the parents are

(A) acting in this manner because it is natural outgrowth of their concern about their child's illness
(B) chronic complainers
(C) complaining because they do not care for the facilities in the hospital
(D) complaining because they feel that this will entitle their child to special treatment.

48. As a Case Worker, you have been assigned a young attractive female as a client who as a result of an automobile accident will not be able to walk again. At your first interview your client is distraught over the fact that now she will never be able to get married because young men will no longer be interested in her. Of the following it would be best for you to tell her that

(A) she might very well be mistaken about her future chances of marrying
(B) she has her entire life in front of her
(C) she is young and pretty and very intelligent
(D) she should be happy that she is alive.

49. A man enters your office without an appointment and tells you that he is a close friend of one of your clients who is a terminal cancer patient. He seats himself in a chair next to your desk. Your first remark to the man should be

(A) "You probably want to know how your friend is doing."
(B) "You know that your friend is dying of cancer."
(C) "May I help you?"
(D) "Have you a problem?"

50. While conducting an interview with a new client, your mind wanders and you feel that you might have missed some important details that your client has been telling you. At that point it would be best for you to

(A) let the patient continue and hope that he or she will repeat what you may have missed

(B) tell the client to rephrase what he or she has been saying

(C) admit that you did not get part of the client's story and ask him or her to repeat it from the part you last remember

(D) assume that part which you may have missed was not important.

51. In the midst of your client relating to you her family makeup, she suddenly says, "Three of my children go to school and my oldest, who is eighteen. . . . " At this point she stops speaking. The most appropriate action that you could take at this point is to

(A) say, "works?"

(B) say, "left school?"

(C) prompt, "What about the fourth child?"

(D) remain silent for a short time and hope your client will continue.

52. An eight-year-old has been referred to the Pediatric Clinic because he frequently falls asleep in class. The examining pediatrician can find no medical reason for this behavior. You decide to pay a visit to the boy's home where you determine that there is continual quarreling between the boy's parents. The boy has two younger brothers. The father has been unemployed for several months. Your best course of action at this point would be to

(A) refer the case to the agency that has jurisdiction over cases of child neglect

(B) take immediate steps to place the three boys in foster homes

(C) offer to obtain a job for the father and to seek a second medical opinion

(D) ask your superior to refer this case to a social worker in order to obtain a proper evaluation of the overall family situation.

53. A ten-year-old boy who requires a complete body cast to correct an orthopedic condition will be ready for discharge in about two weeks. He will be required to return weekly to the orthopedic clinic. His mother is the sole support of the child and you are asked to prepare for the discharge and the subsequent follow-up treatment. You should

(A) recommend that she use her vacation time during her son's convalescence

(B) suggest that she place her son in a rehabilitation center until he is completely well

(C) advise her to quit her job until he is completely well

(D) help her to decide what will be best for both herself and for her child.

54. A five-year-old boy is required to take oral medication five times daily to control a chronic condition. This type of therapy is almost always successful in treating this medical condition. However, the boy does not seem to respond to the medication, even though his mother insists she follows the doctor's orders religiously. In this situation it would be best for you to

(A) direct the mother to keep a complete record of just when she gives her son the medication

(B) discuss the matter with the boy's father, asking him to make sure his wife administers the medication as required

(C) interview the mother and father at the same time, evaluating if the medicine is actually being given to the child as required

(D) suggest to the doctor that the child be hospitalized until it can be definitely determined whether the medication will help the child.

55. Mrs. Rodriguez has been visiting her husband who has been hospitalized for about one week. Visiting hours are from 2 p.m. to 4 p.m. Each day she arrives about 3:30 and

stays to 4:30. The nurses cannot continue to permit this and ask you, her husband's Case Worker, to speak to her. In this instance you should ask the nurses to

(A) continue to permit her to set her own visiting hours because Mrs. Rodriguez does not understand that there are fixed visiting hours

(B) permit her to continue to visit during these hours until you can get Mrs. Rodriguez to understand the restricted visiting hours

(C) restrict Mrs. Rodriguez to the hospital visiting hours and if she refuses to conform, she should be evicted

(D) restrict Mrs. Rodriguez to the visiting hours and explain that enforcing visiting hours is their responsibility.

56. Which one of the following would be an appropriate health facility for an aged disabled individual who becomes acutely ill at home?

(A) nursing home
(B) hospital
(C) extended day facility
(D) home attendant.

57. You have been assigned to place an elderly patient who is ready for discharge from a hospital and who will be able to manage for herself but who will require some supervision. The most suitable accommodation that you could place her in would be a

(A) nursing home
(B) rehabilitation center
(C) chronic care facility
(D) health-related facility.

58. One of your clients, a married woman with three children, will be hospitalized for some time. Her children are all younger than ten and her husband works days regularly. In this instance it would be best for you to arrange for the children's care by arrangements that would provide for

(A) a foster home
(B) facilities at a day care center
(C) a homemaker
(D) a visiting nurse.

59. One of your clients, an elderly woman, is getting ready to be discharged. She will need a significant amount of attention for her personal needs because she lives alone. You should therefore recommend

(A) a housekeeper
(B) a homemaker
(C) a home attendant
(D) a companion.

60. Which type of facility would be suitable for a patient in a psychiatric facility who is scheduled to be returned to community living?

(A) a halfway house
(B) a rehabilitation center
(C) a community center
(D) a nursing home.

61. One of your clients requires services from another city agency. The proper way to make this referral is to

(A) telephone the agency and advise them he is on his way
(B) have the client contact the agency on his own
(C) write a referral letter for the client and have him bring it with him
(D) have the client execute a release of information and forward it to the agency with a summary of the client's problem and request that an appointment be set up for him.

62. A woman who speaks little English is having great difficulty in setting up an appointment for her young son who is afflicted with severe abnormal behavior. He has been referred to the psychiatric clinic by a physician who found no medical reason for the child's erratic behavior. You determine that the woman has not filled out and returned the required forms and in the interim the child's behavior has grown much worse. You should
    (A) tell the woman nothing can be done until she completes and returns the required forms
    (B) send the woman to the clinic to explain her problem
    (C) help the woman to complete the forms
    (D) tell the recommending physician about the child's worsening condition and request that he or she seek immediate help for the child.

63. A seven-year-old girl is about to be discharged from the hospital after a long stay. She formerly lived with her sick grandmother because her mother had died and her father had deserted her. The grandmother tells you that she cannot possibly continue to care for her so you have arranged to have her placed in a foster home. It would then be most appropriate for you to
    (A) convince the child she would be happier living apart from her grandmother
    (B) inform the child that she is going to a new home where she will have many new friends
    (C) inform the child in the presence of her grandmother of the plans for her new home and reasons for it, giving her the opportunity to consent to the foster home
    (D) inform the child of the plans that you have made for her future and ask her to be brave.

Answer questions 64 through 66 based on the information given in the following report.

Margaret Brown
Age: 54
Single
Parents Deceased
Closest Relative: Sister Myra Farlow, Age 56, Married
Diagnosis: Muscular Dystrophy

The patient, a high school graduate, supported herself as a typist since graduation. She lived at home with parents until their death in an automobile accident fifteen years ago. After their death she maintained her own apartment until she became ill and could no longer work. A medical workup resulted in the diagnosis of muscular dystrophy, which has proved to be progressive. The time came when she could no longer take care of her needs and when she took a serious fall she was hospitalized. Arrangements have been made to have her placed in a nursing home, where she will be ready to be discharged in a short time. Her sister will be unable to take care of her because she has to maintain a home for her family. Margaret Brown is unhappy over the prospect of going to a nursing home and she is under the impression that her sister, Myra Farlow, is putting her there to be rid of her. Ms. Farlow is requesting assistance from the Case Worker assigned to her sister.

64. Margaret Brown is probably most resentful of the decision to put her in a nursing home for which of the following reasons?
    (A) her illness has warped her thought process
    (B) she has disliked her sister all of her life
    (C) she had no say in the decision to place her in the nursing home
    (D) she always sought help from others before she became ill.

65. The Case Worker can be of most assistance to Myra Farlow in this situation by

(A) assuring Ms. Farlow everything will come out right

(B) telling Ms. Farlow you are sure you can straighten out her sister's thinking about the matter

(C) helping Ms. Farlow to understand her sister's feelings concerning her imminent transfer to a nursing home

(D) requesting that Ms. Farlow visit her sister and explain why she is being put into a nursing home.

66. A nursing home for Margaret Brown should be selected on the basis of giving primary consideration to which one of the following four factors?

(A) the number of male residents in the nursing home

(B) an accessible location to Ms. Farlow's home

(C) the availability of a private room for Margaret Brown since she has always had her own bedroom

(D) the average age of the nursing home's residents

Answer questions 67 through 69 on the basis of the following case record.

Mary Jordan
Age: 38
Single
Children: Robert, 8, and Geraldine, 4
Diagnosis: Paralysis of left side following stroke

Patient completed eighth grade before leaving school to work at variety of jobs in factories and as a lunchroom waitress. She is now supported by public assistance. In May 1986, a hysterectomy was performed as well as the removal of a benign tumor on her left kidney. In February 1987, she suffered a cerebrovascular episode; diagnosed as hemiparesis left. In June 1987, she had a cystoscopy operation. Discharged August 1988, patient was scheduled for bi-weekly visits to Rehabilitation Clinic for treatment of paralysis. She has followed therapy faithfully and has recovered to the point where she can walk with the aid of a cane. However, her left hand and arm have not responded well to treatment.

Patient displays a poor attitude during interviews with the Case Worker. She feels she is being punished for a sin she has committed. She is very concerned about the welfare of her children who appear to be doing well in school and are healthy.

67. The most important reason for the Case Worker being able to understand the medical terms in this report is that

(A) it will enable the Case Worker to participate in medical discussions with the treating physicians

(B) it will enable the Case Worker to understand the patient's symptoms

(C) it will enable the Case Worker to sound professional

(D) it will enhance the promotional opportunities of the Case Worker.

68. The Case Worker will best be able to handle Mary Jordan's fear that she is being punished for sins she has committed by

(A) discussing with her superior the possibility of referring Mary Jordan for psychiatric evaluation

(B) advocating that the fear be treated psychiatrically

(C) reassuring Mary Jordan that what she thinks is definitely not so

(D) accepting Mary Jordan's fears as an indication that she is psychotic

69. The Case Worker should understand that the reason that Mary Jordan is overly concerned about the children's welfare is that

(A) she doubts her future ability to take care of her children adequately
(B) she is convinced that she has not properly brought up her children
(C) she depends on her children to make her feel worthy
(D) she has ambitions to provide for her children better than she was provided for in her childhood.

Answer questions 70 through 73 solely on the information contained in the following passage.

At the completion of an interview the Case Worker should record the essential points in a manner so that it will serve several purposes. The record of an interview can insure continuity of service to a client by an agency even though a client is to be served by several Case Workers for one reason or another. The record also serves as a permanent record of the service extended to a client and is also an indicator of the agency's accountability to the community. The Case Worker who is about to record the record of an interview is faced with the problem of just what is to go into the record and the manner in which the essential information brought to light during the interview is to be presented. The purpose of a record is not an end in itself. However it does provide a means to an end in that it may provide the basis for required training of the staff, or it can be an indicator for improvement of methods and procedures and used for purposes of research. There is no universal opinion of the most important reason for the recording of case work interviews; therefore, in reality, recording has proved to be limited effectiveness and has not truly served any of its purposes with true efficiency.

The cost of recording is considerable and it usually takes three times as much worker time as the actual interview. Not to be overlooked is the time of the transcriber, the filing time, and the time of the record reviewer. In addition there is the expense of the filing equipment and the space that this equipment occupies. There is no question that the recording of interviews is of utmost importance but the value of interviewing in such a way is questionable.

70. The passage indicates that the recording of an interview for social work purposes

(A) takes three times as long as the actual interview
(B) is a less expensive process than the actual interview
(C) is equal to the money expanded for the actual interview
(D) is too expensive to serve any worthwhile purpose.

71. A specific purpose of the recording process mentioned in the passage is

(A) conservation of time
(B) overall economy
(C) a source of research
(D) a labor-saving device.

72. According to the passage, one of the major expenses that a social agency may incur by its recording process is

(A) supervision
(B) on-the-job training
(C) research
(D) record reviewing.

73. From this passage you may infer that the author's opinion regarding the ultimate usefulness that social work recording achieves is that it is

(A) very useful
(B) limited
(C) not readily measured
(D) of no value.

Answer questions 74 through 76 based solely on the information contained in the following passage.

The Governor, in an effort to improve the administration of the Medical program so that it can deliver services to its beneficiaries, has appointed a committee whose purpose will be to advise the State Commissioner of Social Welfare concerning medical care services. This committee is comprised of members of the medical, dental, pharmaceutical, nursing and social work professions and also includes representatives from the fields of mental health, home health agencies, nursing homes, educational facilities, public health and welfare administrations, and the public. The committee includes a number of physicians in private practice who look after the interests of all private physicians who treat Medicaid patients.

The committee makes appropriate recommendations concerning the standards, quality, and costs of medical services, personnel, and facilities and also helps to bring to light unmet needs. It also assists in long-range planning and serves to evaluate the effectiveness and utilization of services. When requested, it advises on administrative and financial matters and acts to interpret the program and its goals to professional groups. Midland City contributions to the effort are depicted in the process of representatives of the medical societies meeting periodically with administrators representing Medicaid to discuss problems and to mull over proposals. One objective is to gain the cooperation of the county medical societies so that they will eventually inform the citizenry of just where they can avail themselves of medical care under Medicaid.

74. One might infer that the group on the advisory committee least likely to be objective in their recommendations would be

(A) public health and welfare administrations
(B) representatives of the general public
(C) private physicians
(D) schools of health science.

75. You might also infer from the passage that a major problem of the Medicaid program in Midland City is that

(A) the Mayor has not appointed a committee to assist in improving Medicaid's operation
(B) a sizeable number of citizens do not know where to go to obtain medical care under Medicaid
(C) insufficient meetings are held by the committee members to deal effectively with the problems at hand
(D) citizens are lacking the initiative to seek medical care offered under the Medicaid program.

76. The passage states that the Governor's purpose in appointing the committee to act in an advisory capacity concerning Medicaid was to

(A) obtain increased cooperation from the county medical societies
(B) encourage committee members to provide medical care to Medicaid beneficiaries
(C) assist in improving the Medicaid program all around and to make for better administration and for better provision of services
(D) indicate to private physicians and other health care professionals that it would be to their benefit to accept Medicaid patients.

77. You, a Case Worker, have been assigned a very difficult case. You are to counsel and provide for an eight-year-old boy whose parents have been seriously injured in an automobile accident. Your initial approach should be to

(A) convince the child that he will be able to handle the situation without difficulty
(B) play games with him and always let him win
(C) permit the child to "open up" and tell you of his fears and reassure him that you and others will provide him with the assistance he will need
(D) tell the child he really does not have any problems.

78. The record of an interview is properly recorded when it contains

(A) sufficient details to provide the reader with an understanding of the client's problems and needs
(B) as much detail as possible so that it will not be necessary to have to resort to memory
(C) verbatim quotes from the client so as to preclude future misunderstandings
(D) as few notes as possible and a heavy reliance on the memory of the Case Worker.

79. You, as a Case Worker, are preparing to write a summary of a case giving the essential facts in a clear and concise manner. The best form to use in this instance would be a

(A) programming record
(B) request for medical services
(C) case file
(D) face sheet.

80. Of the following records the most useful to you as a Case Worker in the preparation of a treatment plan for a patient is the

(A) Medical Services Order
(B) face sheet
(C) Social Service Medical Record
(D) Psychosocial Summary.

Correct Answers for Practice Examination I

CASE WORKER (for assignment to Hospital Corporation)

1. A	17. D	33. D	49. C	65. C
2. B	18. C	34. C	50. C	66. B
3. D	19. A	35. B	51. D	67. B
4. D	20. B	36. A	52. D	68. A
5. B	21. A	37. D	53. D	69. A
6. B	22. A	38. B	54. D	70. A
7. B	23. C	39. B	55. B	71. C
8. A	24. D	40. C	56. B	72. C
9. A	25. A	41. C	57. D	73. B
10. B	26. B	42. B	58. C	74. C
11. C	27. C	43. B	59. C	75. B
12. D	28. C	44. D	60. A	76. C
13. A	29. C	45. A	61. D	77. C
14. A	30. D	46. C	62. D	78. A
15. B	31. A	47. A	63. B	79. D
16. B	32. A	48. A	64. C	80. D

Explanations of Correct Answers for Practice Examination I

1. **(A)** Good social work case practice requires that appointment schedules be kept unless emergency situations arise. There is nothing in the situation presented to indicate the client's "new" problem is actually a "new" one or requires immediate discussion. Concluding the interview and scheduling the next meeting for the near future to discuss the new problem will solve the issue.

2. **(B)** From the information given, you know the relationship has improved but that further counseling may be needed or desired. The best solution is to offer such service if desired.

3. **(D)** You are responsible for informing the patient of the need for more testing and usual methods to contact him have been unsuccessful. Since he has shown reluctance to communicate, it is essential that you *personally* follow up and convince him directly of the need for the tests. Note that this medical information *must* be given *only* to the patient himself.

4. **(D)** In the situation described, more information is needed about both the woman's medical, social, and financial situations and her brother. It is *your* responsibility as the Case Worker in charge to find out these situations. To do so, a visit to the patient's address is indicated.

5. **(B)** In the situation described, no practical purpose is served by attempting to interview the client. A lecture on the evils of drinking or a threat to close the case may not be absorbed by a drunk client. Recommending further medical assistance without counseling is an abdication of your responsibility as a counselor for an alcoholism clinic. Since there is no indication that the patient has been intoxicated persistently at interviews,

your best procedure is to cancel the interview. Schedule another and impress upon the client that he will not be counseled unless he is sober.

6. **(B)** Good case work practice requires that you be concerned with solutions, not past actions, and that you *not* make decisions for the client. It is your responsibility to discuss with the client all social, economic, religious, and moral factors involved. Help the client to see all the possible consequences of selecting the easiest alternative and, when she arrives at a decision, assure her of your full support, regardless of your personal opinions on the matter.

7. **(B)** Good case work procedure requires that a client's viewpoint be discussed and respected, but that society's values be fully understood by the client. Your personal attitude towards receiving public assistance is *not* at issue. In this instance, the Case Worker must explain society's values towards work and must explore with the client his own attitudes towards self-support.

8. **(A)** Good case work practice demands the maintenance of a professional client/worker relationship. You must make the client understand that failure to maintain such an objective relationship may impair your ability to help her reach the correct decisions about her problems.

9. **(A)** Confidentiality of information received from or about a client and complete honesty with the client are basic requisites in any client/Case Worker relationship. The client must be made aware of and agree to your need to consult with his probation officer in order for you to help the client reach any decisions.

10. **(B)** Your first and primary concern must be the welfare of the newly hospitalized client. You must therefore initially determine whether her son's truancy will adversely affect her medical condition.

11. **(C)** In the circumstances given, the first thing that must be determined is the reasons the client thinks are the causes of her actions. Only after you understand her feelings can action be taken towards protecting the future well-being of the infant and towards correcting the abusive relationship with hospital staff.

12. **(D)** In this situation, the client is faced with the very real problems of the need to enter the hospital *immediately* and the need to be assured that her children will be cared for while she is hospitalized. Good case work procedure calls for *first* assuring her that the children will be looked after *and also* effectuating *immediate* hospitalization. Wrong answers (A) and (C) may delay the hospitalization. Suggesting hospitalization for the well children is contrary to good health care procedure.

13. **(A)** Good case work procedure and public welfare regulations mandate that neither the individual Case Worker nor any employee of the facility lend or give money to clients. This must be carefully explained to the client so that a good relationship continues between you and the client and so that future requests to you or to other staff are prevented.

14. **(A)** You are asked for the correct *first* response to the client's stated desire for an abortion. You only know that she believes she may not be able to take proper care of a baby. Only when you know what she believes "proper care" to be can you fully discuss with her the many aspects connected with this request. The other proposed answers will not give you any basic information to help you begin the discussion.

15. **(B)** Correct case work procedure mandates that you seek information from the client, that you accept this information as true, and that you form no prior opinions without first obtaining needed data from the client. Only by asking pertinent questions can a

Case Worker obtain the necessary data to determine eligibility for public assistance for any specific service requested by the client.

16. **(B)** The statement given in this question is one of the most basic tenets of all good case work practice. *Acceptance* of the client does *not* mean Case Workers must either adopt clients' values for themselves or attempt to change the client in these respects. The *acceptance* of the client means that workers realize and understand that the clients are entitled to their own feelings and attitudes. A solution to any problem must conform to those individual attitudes and beliefs and be acceptable to the client.

17. **(D)** The question asks for something the Case Worker should *not* do in preparing to visit clients. A worker should not decide on a solution to a client's problems, but rather should be prepared to work with the client to arrive at solutions which will be the *client's* solutions and thus acceptable to him or to her.

18. **(C)** Good case work procedure mandates that the hospitalized client learns immediately that you, the case worker, are there to assist with problems. Only after this is fully understood and accepted by the client can you ask the questions needed to elicit information to help.

19. **(A)** Good case work interviewing technique requires that you obtain the most complete and accurate statements possible. By asking clients to rephrase a response you didn't fully understand, you enable them to rethink the statement and tell you what they really meant to say. Rephrasing the statement yourself may result in a client's apparent agreement to something not really meant. Explaining you didn't understand may cause loss of confidence in you, resentment, or agitation. Making your own assumptions can be fatal to full understanding of the statement.

20. **(B)** After a meeting at which a number of important problems have been resolved, it is *most* important that both you and the client know exactly what has been decided, and what actions you and the client will take as a result of the decisions reached. This will ensure the success of the meeting so that at the next session you can begin in a positive, progressive manner.

21. **(A)** The client is asking what to her may be an important question. She is seeking to assure herself that you are sympathetic to her very real problems. It may be that she believes your marital status will provide that assurance. It is insufficient for you to merely tell her your marital status. You must explore the reasons for the question and give her the assurance that regardless of your marital status you appreciate her problems and can help her with them.

22. **(A)** The first meeting is primarily an exploratory one where you and the client begin to understand and respect each other while the client is made confident of your desire and ability to help her. The best way to do this is to allow her to freely discuss the problem which is bothering her the most—her illness. By making brief comments and asking pertinent questions you are indicating both sympathy with her illness and awareness of related social, marital, economic problems but *not* interrupting her train of thought. This will increase her confidence in your sympathy and ability and will help you to prepare for the next meeting where problems relevant to her situation can be discussed. Answer B may lead her to think you are not really listening; answer C disturbs her thoughts and may result in her feeling the interview is too regimented.

23. **(C)** In the situation described, there is no indication that the client is unwilling or unable to arrive at his own decision regarding his residence after discharge from the hospital. Good case work procedure requires that the patient make the decision himself. Your suggestions or advice should be made available to him as well as your assistance in obtaining the residence he desires, but the final decision is his to make. Doctors'

advice is limited to physical necessities (e.g., client can't climb stairs). Relatives cannot make the decision; they can only offer or refuse to offer financial help or the availability of their own residence for his consideration.

24. **(D)** In this situation, the client has asked for your advice and you must honor that request. Whether or not he will accept it is irrelevant. In advising him, you *should* consider all the points given in the wrong answers.

25. **(A)** A child is usually unable to hide his feelings, emotions, and moods, but may often be unable to verbalize them. Good case work technique requires you to observe these nonverbal actions and learn the reasons for them in order to fully understand the child's problems. Thus, for example, the child who says school is "ok" but who is always feeling sick at breakfast probably is indicating problems at school.

26. **(B)** In most situations, the information given to you "in confidence" should *not* be released to anyone without the client's consent. The situation described in this question contains no extenuating circumstance which merits your violating the confidence.

27. **(C)** From the situation described, good case work technique requires you to wait until the client is willing to tell you the details of the situation or to respect her inability/ unwillingness to tell you anything at all. The best course for you to take is to move on to the practical question of how to help her to handle the situation which has arisen.

28. **(C)** In this situation, an elderly, well-educated, well-oriented person has suddenly exhibited a marked change in ability to speak clearly and to recognize a familiar face. The best possible response for the Case Worker is to tell the attending physician about the change as quickly as possible so that the doctor can determine if further medical assistance is needed and whether the immediate hospital discharge is still feasible.

29. **(C)** In this situation, you are concerned with an ill person who appears to be eligible for Medicaid but does not appear willing to disclose the information needed to complete the eligibility form. Your primary responsibility is to determine the reasons for his reluctance. Is he afraid to disclose information he has kept from hospital records? Does he feel that Medicaid is charity and is unwilling to be considered poor? Does he distrust what you will do with the information? Before you can intelligently deal with the problem you must understand its nature.

30. **(D)** The Case Worker's responsibility in dealing with this emergency medical problem is to try to relieve any anxieties the patient may have, and to assure the patient you will give all the aid possible in dealing with any problems. The correct answer in the situation presented in this question gives the patient a possible solution to his problem and the opportunity to accept or reject it.

31. **(A)** As a general rule, a Case Worker should refer all problems that are not the specific responsibility of his/her agency to the proper governmental agency—in this instance to the child welfare or child abuse agency. If uncertain about the proper authority, consult your supervisor.

32. **(A)** When a long-term counselor/patient relationship, as described in this question, is going to be terminated, the best approach is to inform the patient sufficiently in advance of the change in Case Worker so that the patient has time to prepare for the change. Waiting until your final visit will give the patient no time to ask questions regarding the change, or to bring up important points she has put off telling you and which she may be even more reluctant to discuss with a new counselor. NOTE: This principle applies to *all* types of long-term counselor/client relationships. The client should feel neither deserted nor at fault and must understand that the change in counselor will not be injurious.

33. **(D)** In the situation described, the woman has ingested a dangerous number of sleeping pills and immediate medical help is needed. Your best advice is to have the man call for immediate emergency help. To make the call yourself may delay the medical personnel from giving the man vital instructions he should follow *immediately,* i.e., before the medical personnel arrive at the house.

34. **(C)** A basic principle in the situation described in this section requires that the injured person *not* move or *not* be moved by an unskilled person. Since you are already on the hospital grounds, you should remain with the man, make sure he does not move or attempt to move himself, and have someone else obtain skilled help to move him.

35. **(B)** The amount of notes taken during the course of an interview depends on the circumstances. In the situation given, the patient is anxious to avoid problems she experienced after the past operation. You should give her your entire attention. Both you and she will be disturbed if you take copious notes. Further, the actual amount of notes needed will probably be minimal since it is primarily a personality and factual situation not requiring specific detailed data, statistics, etc. Be sure to record pertinent data and impressions, problems, possible decision reached, etc., after the interview.

36. **(A)** A second interview is frequently a strained one since the patient has learned what will be expected of him or her, has had time to reconsider previous statements, and may not, for various reasons, have gained full confidence in or rapport with you, the Case Worker. The professional approach is for the Case Worker to review personal past actions, statements, attitudes, and feelings towards the patient and the situation to make certain that this second interview results in a more positive and productive relationship.

37. **(D)** In this fairly common situation, you have been assigned to overcome a diabetic patient's difficulty in injecting herself with the needed insulin. From the information given, there appears to be no age, mental, or medical reason for the problem. It would therefore be most appropriate to assume she does not fully understand or appreciate that it would be in her own best interest to learn how to inject herself. None of the wrong answers will solve the problem satisfactorily.

38. **(B)** In this situation, the possible medical reasons for the patient's past accidents are being studied by professional medical personnel. It is the Case Worker's role to explore possible nonmedical reasons for the repeated accidents. This *team* approach is the best method to solve the patient's problem.

39. **(B)** The situation presented is one of an adult so preoccupied with real or fancied problems that she neglects her medical problems. Your responsibility is to help her deal with these nonmedical problems so that she will be able to focus her attention on the medical ones. To do this you must discuss these nonmedical problems, determine their real importance, solvability, and any ways you can help her solve them or come to terms with them, so that she can be made to realize the need to keep the medical appointments.

40. **(C)** The primary goal of *all* hospital workers is to help the patient achieve the best health possible. The Case Worker's role is primarily one of making certain that emotional, family, and related social problems do not interfere with reaching that goal. To do this, the Case Worker must observe any signs of anxiety shown by the patient and to work with the patient to relieve such anxiety.

41. **(C)** In this situation, the Case Worker has a most important role: to help the young child to understand and cope with the frightening situation confronting him and to give him the assurance that there are adults around who care for his well-being and will help him with his problems.

42. **(B)** The client has many real and important problems, some of which may not be solv-

able. In order for you to be most helpful, you must help the client look at each problem, decide which can be solved and which must be accepted and accommodated, and attempt to find acceptable solutions. At the same time, you must assure the client you will help him to achieve these solutions to problems deemed solvable.

43. **(B)** As a Case Worker in a hospital setting, you are responsible for considering a patient's fears for her future well-being after she leaves the hospital since such fears may impede her recuperation. To that extent, the worker should offer to help the client obtain public assistance but must also emphasize the need for, and work with the patient to achieve, the independence needed to successfully cope on her own outside the hospital.

44. **(D)** A Case Worker in a government hospital *or* in any government welfare agency must *not* attempt to answer questions of a general public relations nature singlehandedly. All such questions should be referred to the office or individual responsible for such matters.

45. **(A)** All of us have problems similar in nature to those of other people and yet each individual has a unique set of circumstances and attitudes which may be sufficiently unique to result in a solution different from the one appropriate to another person. A good Case Worker knows that as much as possible must be learned about the individual client and his problem before attempting to work with that client towards finding an acceptable solution which may or may not be the same solution which was successfully utilized in other cases.

46. **(C)** The patient is ready for discharge and such discharge should not be delayed. There are several possible reasons for the occurrence, including the patient's subconscious fear of being discharged. Good case work practice requires you to help the patient leave the hospital as soon as possible by trying to find him shoes without cost to him and by following up on the actual situation with the ward nurse or with other appropriate hospital personnel.

47. **(A)** Most relatives are concerned about the patient care given to their loved ones. This is especially true when a child is hospitalized since the child is not able to verbalize complaints or fully understand what is happening. A good Case Worker must understand this and, knowing that the pediatric care is appropriate in this situation, should reassure the parents that the child is receiving proper nursing care.

48. **(A)** In this situation, the Case Worker's best approach would be to deal with the problem that is causing the patient to be distraught by pointing out that many paraplegics do marry. Only when the patient's primary cause of anxiety is allayed can the Case Worker hope to work with her to solve more immediate problems in a realistic manner.

49. **(C)** In this situation, the man knows his friend's condition. You have no idea why he is seeking your aid and your best approach is simply to ask in what way you can assist him.

50. **(C)** Even the most experienced Case Worker will sometimes miss part of what a client was saying. The best way to handle this is to admit your failure to listen and have the client repeat exactly what was said from the point where your mind began wandering. The new client will appreciate your concern to get the full story. The other solutions given in the wrong answers may result in your failure to grasp important details you will need in order to successfully work with this new client.

51. **(D)** Interviewers will often find that clients will stop in the middle of a discussion if another thought occurs to them about their topic. The best procedure is to give clients time to think thoughts through. Don't put words in a client's mouth (Answers A or B) or prompt. You may cause clients to omit something important.

52. **(D)** This situation calls for professional social work evaluation and action. A Case Worker should be aware of situations requiring *professional* help and is responsible for alerting the appropriate personnel of the need.

53. **(D)** Good case work procedure requires that the client, or in this case, the patient's mother, arrives at a decision she fully understands and accepts, and will take responsibility for any consequences resulting from *her* decision. Your role is to help her see alternatives and possible consequences and arrive at a decision that is right for her.

54. **(D)** Although the medication prescribed is *almost always* successful, it may not have been in this case. Further, you are not certain that the medication has been taken as prescribed. Your best procedure is to inform the doctor of the situation and suggest hospitalization for the child. If the medication is successful under the controlled conditions in the hospital, you will then have to work with the patient to insure that it is properly administered at home.

55. **(B)** In this situation, there is nothing to show that the patient is not benefiting from his wife's visits, and *his* welfare is *your* prime concern. Your best approach is to allow her to continue to visit but to concentrate on making her understand that hospital rules must be followed. Answers C and D may result in Mrs. Rodriguez's refusal to visit. Answer A will disrupt hospital routing, cause friction with the hospital staff, and cause possible resentment by other patients and their visitors.

56. **(B)** Study the glossary and other appropriate sections of this book. A hospital is the appropriate health facility for the care of an acutely ill person.

57. **(D)** Your study of the glossary will show you that an elderly person released from a hospital who can manage for herself but needs some supervision should be placed in a health-related facility.

58. **(C)** Your study of the glossary will teach you that a homemaker will be the best person to provide the all-day and perhaps all-night care for the children while the mother is hospitalized and the father works.

59. **(C)** Note that this situation does not require the client to have medical service and that housekeeping needs are minimal. The glossary will show you that a home attendant will solve the problem.

60. **(A)** Study the glossary to learn the differences between the services provided in the different facilities mentioned in the four possible answers. You will discover that a halfway house is the appropriate facility in this instance.

61. **(D)** This situation occurs frequently. Correct case work procedure requires that you obtain a release from the client/patient before forwarding confidential data to another governmental agency. In the situation described, the most expeditious way to process the referral is for you to obtain the release, give all the information you have available which will be needed by the other agency, and request an appointment for her. The other answers will delay or hinder correct and expeditious handling of the referral.

62. **(D)** One of the most important lessons a Case Worker must learn is when to refer a problem to a professional in another discipline. In this situation, the child's condition is becoming worse so that the recommending doctor must be alerted in order to expedite the proper referral/treatment. The wrong answers will all delay the receipt of immediate care.

63. **(B)** This situation is a serious one requiring skilled handling in order not to upset the existing good relationship between the grandmother and the child, which might result from the wrong solution (presented in Answer A). The child is not yet capable of mak-

ing her own decisions (as implied in Answer C). Nor should she be frightened as is implied in answer D. The worker should find positive "happy" reasons for the change as is possible under the procedure given in the correct answer.

Questions 64–69

As a Case Worker, you will frequently have to read other workers' case reports and treat a client accordingly. In answering questions 64–69, remember to respond *only* on the basis of information given, and base your answers on information given and on good case work reasoning.

64. **(C)** There is *no* indication given in this report that Answers A or B are true and there *is* indication that Answer D is contrary to the facts given. The correct answer is borne out by the facts given in the case report.

65. **(C)** Your client's well-being is your primary concern and it is most important that the heretofore good relationship between the sisters be maintained. The sister, Farlow, has come to you to assist her. Your best approach is to try to help Ms. Farlow understand her sister's feelings and work with her to either accept the client into her household or help you to convince the client that Ms. Farlow maintains her affection and support for the client even though she cannot bring her into her home.

66. **(B)** As noted above, a good relationship between the sisters is vital to your client's well-being. The ability of Ms. Farlow to visit her sister as frequently as possible is most important in helping your client, hitherto independent and self-sustaining, maintain a relationship with her family and with the world outside of the nursing home.

67. **(B)** The case record contains medical data which the Case Worker must understand in order to comprehend the client's physical limitations and the physical reasons behind her reactions and state of mind in order to be able to work with the client in resolving her problems and guilt feelings. The wrong answers will not help the Case Worker to carry out her primary role and are trivial reasons for understanding the medical terminology.

68. **(A)** The client has evidenced a poor attitude and a belief she is being punished for past sins. A good Case Worker must realize his or her own limitations in dealing with what may be deep psychological problems requiring expert psychological counseling. In this situation, the Case Worker should discuss the matter with the supervisor to determine the need for a psychiatric evaluation and possible psychological or psychiatric counseling for the client.

69. **(A)** The case record shows that the children are well and have no school problems. There is nothing in the record to indicate that the client's concern for the children is connected with anything other than her future ability to maintain the children's health and well-being.

70. **(A)** Based *solely* on the information given in the passage, the correct answer is clearly stated in the second paragraph. None of the other possible answers can be deduced from the passage.

71. **(C)** The passage *only* dictates that the recording process is a source of research. The other possible answers are *not* given in the passage as purposes of the recording process.

72. **(C)** The passage indicates the cost of research is considerable. There is *no* indication in the passage regarding the expenses incurred for the recording processes which are referred to in the other possible answers.

73. **(B)** The passage clearly implies that the author believes that the recording process is of limited ultimate usefulness.

74. **(C)** The passage clearly states that the advisory committee includes "a number of physicians who look after the interests of all private physicians who treat medical patients." From this, you can infer that private physicians on the committee would be less likely to be objective than the groups of persons indicated in the other possible answers.

75. **(B)** The passage indicates that in Midland City, administrators of the Medicaid program meet with representatives of the medical societies to gain their cooperation in informing citizenry where they can receive Medicaid. The correct answer can be inferred from that fact.

76. **(C)** The Governor's purpose in appointing an advisory committee is clearly stated in the first sentence of the passage. The correct answer paraphrases that sentence. The other possible answers cannot be inferred from the passage.

77. **(C)** Get the child to talk about his fears, then reassure him. The question emphasizes your first action: this is it. Further help that is needed, will follow.

78. **(A)** Records of interviews should be detailed enough so that anyone concerned with the client understands all problems. This will insure continuance if you are replaced by another Case Worker. It will also help other interested staff, including your supervisor and the client's physician, to understand the current situation if you are absent and thus to proceed knowledgeably with helping the client. It will enable your supervisor to review and correct your handling of the case. Records which are too detailed are wasteful of both the worker's and the reader's time and may result in your concentrating on writing a report instead of really listening to the client and helping to solve problems. Verbatim quotes are generally useful only in specific instances where they give real clues to the client's attitudes or beliefs or may be needed as definitive statements in response to a specific point (e.g., to your question, "Do you want to live with your brother?" Answer is "No.").

79. **(D)** The face sheet of a case record should give the essential facts in summary form. The case record itself and documents in it should contain the necessary details supporting this summary.

80. **(D)** A treatment plan prepared by a Case Worker requires utilization of the psychological and social problems of the patient, *not* the medical problems, so that the psychosocial summary would be a source of data for your treatment plan.

Answer Sheet For Practice Examination II

1. Ⓐ Ⓑ Ⓒ Ⓓ
2. Ⓐ Ⓑ Ⓒ Ⓓ
3. Ⓐ Ⓑ Ⓒ Ⓓ
4. Ⓐ Ⓑ Ⓒ Ⓓ
5. Ⓐ Ⓑ Ⓒ Ⓓ
6. Ⓐ Ⓑ Ⓒ Ⓓ
7. Ⓐ Ⓑ Ⓒ Ⓓ
8. Ⓐ Ⓑ Ⓒ Ⓓ
9. Ⓐ Ⓑ Ⓒ Ⓓ
10. Ⓐ Ⓑ Ⓒ Ⓓ
11. Ⓐ Ⓑ Ⓒ Ⓓ
12. Ⓐ Ⓑ Ⓒ Ⓓ
13. Ⓐ Ⓑ Ⓒ Ⓓ
14. Ⓐ Ⓑ Ⓒ Ⓓ
15. Ⓐ Ⓑ Ⓒ Ⓓ
16. Ⓐ Ⓑ Ⓒ Ⓓ
17. Ⓐ Ⓑ Ⓒ Ⓓ
18. Ⓐ Ⓑ Ⓒ Ⓓ
19. Ⓐ Ⓑ Ⓒ Ⓓ
20. Ⓐ Ⓑ Ⓒ Ⓓ

21. Ⓐ Ⓑ Ⓒ Ⓓ
22. Ⓐ Ⓑ Ⓒ Ⓓ
23. Ⓐ Ⓑ Ⓒ Ⓓ
24. Ⓐ Ⓑ Ⓒ Ⓓ
25. Ⓐ Ⓑ Ⓒ Ⓓ
26. Ⓐ Ⓑ Ⓒ Ⓓ
27. Ⓐ Ⓑ Ⓒ Ⓓ
28. Ⓐ Ⓑ Ⓒ Ⓓ
29. Ⓐ Ⓑ Ⓒ Ⓓ
30. Ⓐ Ⓑ Ⓒ Ⓓ
31. Ⓐ Ⓑ Ⓒ Ⓓ
32. Ⓐ Ⓑ Ⓒ Ⓓ
33. Ⓐ Ⓑ Ⓒ Ⓓ
34. Ⓐ Ⓑ Ⓒ Ⓓ
35. Ⓐ Ⓑ Ⓒ Ⓓ
36. Ⓐ Ⓑ Ⓒ Ⓓ
37. Ⓐ Ⓑ Ⓒ Ⓓ
38. Ⓐ Ⓑ Ⓒ Ⓓ
39. Ⓐ Ⓑ Ⓒ Ⓓ
40. Ⓐ Ⓑ Ⓒ Ⓓ

41. Ⓐ Ⓑ Ⓒ Ⓓ
42. Ⓐ Ⓑ Ⓒ Ⓓ
43. Ⓐ Ⓑ Ⓒ Ⓓ
44. Ⓐ Ⓑ Ⓒ Ⓓ
45. Ⓐ Ⓑ Ⓒ Ⓓ
46. Ⓐ Ⓑ Ⓒ Ⓓ
47. Ⓐ Ⓑ Ⓒ Ⓓ
48. Ⓐ Ⓑ Ⓒ Ⓓ
49. Ⓐ Ⓑ Ⓒ Ⓓ
50. Ⓐ Ⓑ Ⓒ Ⓓ
51. Ⓐ Ⓑ Ⓒ Ⓓ
52. Ⓐ Ⓑ Ⓒ Ⓓ
53. Ⓐ Ⓑ Ⓒ Ⓓ
54. Ⓐ Ⓑ Ⓒ Ⓓ
55. Ⓐ Ⓑ Ⓒ Ⓓ
56. Ⓐ Ⓑ Ⓒ Ⓓ
57. Ⓐ Ⓑ Ⓒ Ⓓ
58. Ⓐ Ⓑ Ⓒ Ⓓ
59. Ⓐ Ⓑ Ⓒ Ⓓ
60. Ⓐ Ⓑ Ⓒ Ⓓ

61. Ⓐ Ⓑ Ⓒ Ⓓ
62. Ⓐ Ⓑ Ⓒ Ⓓ
63. Ⓐ Ⓑ Ⓒ Ⓓ
64. Ⓐ Ⓑ Ⓒ Ⓓ
65. Ⓐ Ⓑ Ⓒ Ⓓ
66. Ⓐ Ⓑ Ⓒ Ⓓ
67. Ⓐ Ⓑ Ⓒ Ⓓ
68. Ⓐ Ⓑ Ⓒ Ⓓ
69. Ⓐ Ⓑ Ⓒ Ⓓ
70. Ⓐ Ⓑ Ⓒ Ⓓ
71. Ⓐ Ⓑ Ⓒ Ⓓ
72. Ⓐ Ⓑ Ⓒ Ⓓ
73. Ⓐ Ⓑ Ⓒ Ⓓ
74. Ⓐ Ⓑ Ⓒ Ⓓ
75. Ⓐ Ⓑ Ⓒ Ⓓ
76. Ⓐ Ⓑ Ⓒ Ⓓ
77. Ⓐ Ⓑ Ⓒ Ⓓ
78. Ⓐ Ⓑ Ⓒ Ⓓ
79. Ⓐ Ⓑ Ⓒ Ⓓ
80. Ⓐ Ⓑ Ⓒ Ⓓ

81. Ⓐ Ⓑ Ⓒ Ⓓ
82. Ⓐ Ⓑ Ⓒ Ⓓ
83. Ⓐ Ⓑ Ⓒ Ⓓ
84. Ⓐ Ⓑ Ⓒ Ⓓ
85. Ⓐ Ⓑ Ⓒ Ⓓ
86. Ⓐ Ⓑ Ⓒ Ⓓ
87. Ⓐ Ⓑ Ⓒ Ⓓ
88. Ⓐ Ⓑ Ⓒ Ⓓ
89. Ⓐ Ⓑ Ⓒ Ⓓ
90. Ⓐ Ⓑ Ⓒ Ⓓ
91. Ⓐ Ⓑ Ⓒ Ⓓ
92. Ⓐ Ⓑ Ⓒ Ⓓ
93. Ⓐ Ⓑ Ⓒ Ⓓ
94. Ⓐ Ⓑ Ⓒ Ⓓ
95. Ⓐ Ⓑ Ⓒ Ⓓ
96. Ⓐ Ⓑ Ⓒ Ⓓ
97. Ⓐ Ⓑ Ⓒ Ⓓ
98. Ⓐ Ⓑ Ⓒ Ⓓ
99. Ⓐ Ⓑ Ⓒ Ⓓ
100. Ⓐ Ⓑ Ⓒ Ⓓ

PRACTICE EXAMINATION II

Case Worker—Social Services

DIRECTIONS FOR ANSWERING QUESTIONS: Each question has four suggested answers, lettered A,B,C, and D. Decide which one is the best answer and on the sample answer sheet locate the question number and darken the area with a soft pencil which corresponds to the answer that you have selected.

TIME ALLOWED FOR ENTIRE EXAMINATION: 3½ HOURS

1. There is implicit in case work an acceptance of a client's value system which may be different from that of the Case Worker. Of the following, the most valid conclusion to be derived from this statement is that

   (A) clients do not have moral standards
   (B) the Case Workers' standards are always stricter than the clients' standards
   (C) cultural patterns have little effect on value systems of either clients or Case Workers
   (D) a Case Worker has no right to insist on conformity of a client's behavior with his or her own standards.

2. The establishment and maintenance of a professional relationship with a client is stressed in case work. This relationship should be

   (A) clear, businesslike and delimited by the agency function
   (B) permissive, friendly, and kindly, with the pace determined by the client
   (C) warm, enabling, and consciously controlled by the Case Worker
   (D) variable and unpredictable because of the fluctuations in client need.

3. There is great interest being shown currently in the possible merger of the child welfare and family case work fields, in private as well as public agencies. The best argument in support of such a merger is that

   (A) families with child care problems would not be broken up through placement of children
   (B) the taxpayers' and the voluntary contributors' money would be saved
   (C) through intensive work with children, prevention of the development of behavior problems would be possible
   (D) new techniques in family case work treatment and the development of new community resources would probably result.

4. There is general agreement among experts in the field that, when dealing with a client or handling a case, a Case Worker should

(A) place emphasis on the objective aspects, directing his or her work primarily to the physical factors in the client that indicate need for change
(B) place emphasis on the environmental factors, especially those surrounding the client which have caused him or her to be in this present state
(C) give attention not only to the environmental factors and social experiences, but also to the client's feelings about, and reactions to, his or her experiences
(D) consider each factor in the case as a separate unit after carefully distinguishing between the truly environmental and the truly emotional factors.

5. In case work practice, the unit of attention is generally considered to be the family, although in some agencies the client or patient is often viewed as being outside of the family. The trend in modern case work with respect to the family of a client is to

(A) involve the family wherever feasible in the total work process
(B) scientifically determine wherein the family is harmful to the client and try to make plans for the client to leave his or her family
(C) educate the public so that families of clients will not interfere with agency plans
(D) refer every member of the family for case work help.

6. John L., 15, was referred to a youth counseling agency by the principal of the high school he attends because he has been truant for the past six months. He is of above average intelligence, is in his sophomore year, and is currently failing 4 out 5 of his courses. His mother says that he frequently comes home after midnight and is friendly with two boys with court records. The family group consists of John and his mother who supports them by working as a secretary. Two sisters, 19 and 21, are married and out of the home. Mr. L. deserted when John was 3. The principal told John he had to go to the youth counseling agency or be brought into court by the truant officer. In beginning to work with John, the Case Worker should first

(A) recognize that since John did not come voluntarily he will refuse case work treatment
(B) establish himself or herself as an adult who will keep John in line
(C) secure more facts about John and his situation in order to determine further case activity
(D) promise that the agency will keep John from being sent to juvenile court.

7. A client tells the Case Worker that she is planning to leave her job as a junior executive trainee in a department store for a job as a laborer which will pay her a higher salary. After exploring the client's reasons for making this move, the Case Worker feels the plan is unwise, since the trainee position offers a considerably better future. In this situation, it would be best for the Case Worker to

(A) attempt to dissuade the client from making the job change, pointing out the reasons for the inadvisability of the move
(B) allow the client to change jobs, without attempting to dissuade or counsel her
(C) refuse to give the client permission to change jobs, without an attempt to dissuade or counsel her
(D) try to dissuade the client from making the job change without giving the real reasons for thinking the move undesirable.

8. Case work interviewing is always directed to the client and his or her situation. The one of the following which is the most accurate statement with respect to the proper focus of an interview is that the

(A) Case Worker limits the client to concentration on objective data
(B) client is generally permitted to talk about facts and feelings with no direction from the Case Worker
(C) main focus in case work interviews is on feelings rather than facts
(D) Case Worker is responsible for helping the client focus on any material which seems to be related to his or her problems or difficulties.

9. A Case Worker is faced with the problem of interviewing dull clients who give slow and disconnected case histories. The best of the following interviewing methods for the Case Worker to use in order to ascertain the facts is to

(A) ask the clients leading questions requiring yes or no answers
(B) request the clients to limit their narration to the essential facts so that the interview can be kept as brief as possible
(C) review the story with the clients, patiently asking simple questions
(D) tell the clients that unless they are more cooperative they cannot be helped to solve their problems.

10. A case record includes relevant social and psychological facts about the clients, the nature of their requests, their feelings about their situation, their attitudes towards the agency and their use of and reaction to treatment. In addition, it should always contain

(A) routine history
(B) complete details of personality development and emotional relationships
(C) detailed process accounts of all contacts
(D) data necessary for understanding the problem and the factors important to arriving at a solution.

11. The chief basis for the inability of a troubled client to express his or her problem clearly to the Case Worker is that the client

(A) sees his or her problem in complex terms and does not think it possible to give the Case Worker the whole picture
(B) has erected defenses against emotions that seem to him or her inadmissable or intolerable
(C) cannot describe how he or she feels about the problem
(D) views the situation as unlikely to be solved and is blocked in self-expression.

12. The one of the following statements which is most accurate in giving case work service to medically ill clients is that the Case Worker should

(A) understand the general aspects of medical treatment of the client's illness
(B) refrain from any involvement in the client's medical care or treatment routine
(C) be concerned only with problems directly relating to the client's illness
(D) consider problems of the client apart from the medical setting.

13. A 32-year-old wife and mother of two young children applies to a family counseling service because of her concern about the deterioration of her marriage of ten years' duration. In order to achieve optimum benefits from such counseling, it would be most desirable for the

(A) husband to be involved indirectly through counseling recommendations brought to him by his wife
(B) husband to participate directly in the counseling process along with his wife
(C) husband and the children to be involved directly in the counseling process
(D) wife only to receive counseling, without involving her husband.

14. A child has been temporarily removed from his household and given foster home care because of continued neglect and mistreatment at home. The one of the following which is the chief reason why it is important for case work therapy to be given to his parents is to

(A) bring them to a clearer realization of the undesirability of their conduct and the sad consequences to which their conduct had led
(B) help them to effect a change during the child's stay in foster care so that he can return to a more secure and satisfying relationship with his own family
(C) make them realize that it was their conduct alone that made the child act in an antisocial manner and precipitated the action to remove him from the household
(D) prevent them from degenerating further to a point where they too will become a more serious social problem and need possible institutionalization.

15. When a decision has been reached that a wayward child's needs can best be met by foster home placement, the best of the following approaches for the Case Worker assigned to the case to use order to break the news to the child is to

(A) inform the child that, although he is being punished in this manner for his bad conduct, he is being separated from his family only temporarily until home conditions are good enough for him to return
(B) point out to the child that he is being placed in a fine home with foster parents
(C) reassure the child that no punishment is involved in his separation from home and that efforts will be made to help him and his parents achieve the needed changes which will enable him to return home
(D) tell the child in a friendly but frank manner that he is being removed from the home because of his parents' inability and lack of intent to help him to become better adjusted.

16. A child who has been placed in a foster home runs away to the home of her mother and stepfather. A decision to place her in the custody of another relative is being considered. To return the child to foster care while this change is under consideration would be

(A) correct; no change should be made until a careful consideration of all the facts in the case will point to a final decision
(B) incorrect; since the child ran away from a foster home, she was unhappy there, and her desires should be of prime importance
(C) correct; since the child had been placed in a foster home earlier, the home of her mother must have been a less desirable place for her
(D) incorrect; no matter how bad her own home may be, it is definitely better for a child to be with her own relatives than with strangers.

17. In comparing the advantages of foster homes over institutional placement, it is generally agreed that institutional care is least advisable for children

(A) who cannot sustain the intimacy of foster family living because of their experiences with their own parents
(B) who are socially well-adjusted or have had considerable experience in living with a family
(C) who have need for special facilities for observation, diagnosis, and treatment
(D) whose natural parents find it difficult to accept the idea of foster home placement because of its close resemblance to adoption.

18. The school can play a vital part in detecting the child who displays overt symptomatic behavior indicative of social maladjustment chiefly because the teacher has the opportunity to

(A) assume a pseudoparental role in regard to discipline and punishment, thereby limiting the extent of the maladjusted child's antisocial behavior
(B) observe how the child relates to the group and what reactions are stimulated in him or her by peer relationships
(C) determine whether the adjustment difficulties displayed by the child were brought on by the teacher, or by the other students
(D) help the child's parents to resolve the difficulties in adjustment which are indicated by the child's reactions to the social pressures exerted by his or her peers.

19. A 9-year-old boy is living at home with his remarried, widowed mother, his stepfather and his 3-year-old half-sister. The boy is being neglected and often severely mistreated by his mother and stepfather. The stepfather resents the boy's presence in the home. After failing to correct the situation by discussions with the boy's mother and stepfather, the Case Worker should recommend for the boy's welfare,

(A) foster-home placement in order to prevent his further mistreatment while corrective educational therapy is used on the parents
(B) permanent separation of the boy from his family as the best means of preventing his continued exposure to the unsatisfactory pressures in the household
(C) placement of the boy outside the household and a stern warning to the parents that similar action will be taken on behalf of the younger child should the situation warrant it
(D) temporary placement of the boy with a foster family until such time as the stepfather is no longer in the household.

20. A deserted woman and her 13-year-old son have been receiving public assistance. The woman is drunk most of the time, is known to be consorting with men at all hours and has been unresponsive to case work treatment. The son has been involved in a few minor incidents which have brought him to the attention of the authorities. The best action for the Case Worker to take at this point in order to keep the son from becoming an outright delinquent is to recommend that

(A) the mother be arrested and jailed for contributing to the delinquency of a minor and the son be sent to a reformatory
(B) no action be taken against the mother because that will lower her status in the eyes of her son and will further weaken family controls
(C) the son be temporarily placed in a foster home and the mother given treatment for alcoholism
(D) the son be committed to a corrective school where his bad habits can be corrected, since the mother is apparently too sick to assume her responsibilities toward her son.

21. In visiting a school attended by children of a *hard-core* family under treatment by your agency it would generally be advisable to

(A) keep the school visit a secret from the family so as not to embarrass the children
(B) encourage the parents to obtain all necessary information themselves
(C) inform the family only if you have secured positive information from the school
(D) have the family fully accept the purpose of the visit beforehand.

22. In planning for the vocational rehabilitation of a physically handicapped person, the use of the sheltered workshop can be a very helpful resource. Of the following, the client for whom such service would be most appropriate is the one who

(A) will need a constructive way to spend his or her time for an indefinite period
(B) because of advanced age is unable to compete in the labor market
(C) needs a transitional experience between his or her medical care and undertaking a regular job
(D) has a handicap which permanently precludes any gainful employment.

23. Alcoholism may affect an individual client's ability to function as a spouse, parent, worker, and citizen. A Case Worker's main responsibility to a client with a history of alcoholism is to

(A) interpret to the client the causes of alcoholism as a disease syndrome
(B) work with the alcoholic's family to accept him or her and to stop trying to reform him or her
(C) encourage the family of the alcoholic to accept case work treatment
(D) determine the origins of his or her particular drinking problem, establish a diagnosis, and work out a treatment plan.

24. There is a trend to regard narcotic addiction as a form of illness for which the current methods of intervention have not been effective. Research on the combination of social, psychological, and physical causes of addiction would indicate that social workers should

(A) oppose hospitalization of addicts in institutions
(B) encourage the addict to live normally at home
(C) recognize that there is no successful treatment for addiction and act accordingly
(D) use the existing community facilities differentially for each addict.

25. The one of the following which is the chief danger of interpreting the delinquent behavior of a child in terms of morality alone when attempting to get at its causes is that

(A) this tends to overlook the likelihood that the causes of the child's actions are more than a negation of morality and involve varied symptoms of disturbance
(B) a child's moral outlook toward life and society is largely colored by that of the parents, thus encouraging parent-child conflicts
(C) too careful a consideration of the moral aspects of the offense and of the child's needs may often negate the demands of justice in a case
(D) standards of morality may be of no concern to the delinquent and he or she may not realize the seriousness of his or her offenses.

26. Assume that a Case Worker has been newly assigned to a caseload of about 70 cases. In order for him or her to be able to meet promptly the needs of the clients in this caseload, he or she should *first*

(A) arrange for each client to come to the office for a brief interview
(B) read the case history of each client to get a general understanding of the problems involved
(C) concentrate on those cases having the most serious problems
(D) make a short visit to the home of each client to determine immediate needs.

27. The two factors which are most likely to determine the size and cost of a public assistance program are the

(A) size of the staff and its degree of professionalism
(B) form of the grant and the method of disbursement
(C) number of clients accepted, and their previous standard of living
(D) conditions of eligibility and the standard of living deemed proper for relief recipients.

28. An increase in the size of the welfare grant may increase the cost of the welfare program not only in terms of those already on the public assistance rolls, but because it may result in an increase in the number of people on the rolls. The chief reason that an increase in the size of the grant may cause an increase in the number of people on the rolls is that the increased grant may

(A) induce low-salaried wage-earners to apply for assistance rather than continue at their menial jobs

(B) make eligible for assistance many people whose resources are just above the previous standard

(C) induce many people to apply for assistance who hesitated to do so because of meagerness of the previous grant

(D) make relatives less willing to contribute because the welfare grant can more adequately cover their dependent's needs.

29. All definitions of case work include certain major assumptions. Of the following, the one which is *not* considered a major assumption is that

(A) the individual and society are interdependent

(B) social forces influence behavior and attitudes, affording opportunity for self-development and contribution to the world in which we live

(C) reconstruction of the total personality and reorganization of the total environment are specific goals

(D) the client is a responsible participant at every step in the solution of his or her problems.

30. In order to provide those services to problem families which will help restore them to a self-maintaining status, it is necessary to *first*

(A) develop specific plans to meet the individual needs of the problem family

(B) reduce the size of those caseloads composed of multi-problem families

(C) remove them from their environment and provide them with the means of overcoming their dependency

(D) identify the factors causing their dependency and creating their problems.

31. When a client is faced with a new situation which he or she does not fully understand or know how to handle, the worker can help the client most by first

(A) sharing with the client his or her knowledge of how other people handled similar situations

(B) making the client aware of the facts and possibilities of the situation

(C) explaining to the client what steps he or she should take to correct the situation

(D) referring the client to that agency which is best equipped to aid him or her with his or her special problem.

32. From the point of view of the Case Worker in a public welfare agency, the assignment of welfare clients to different categories of assistance serves to

(A) establish uniform standards of need and factors of eligibility

(B) insure an adequate level of assistance by providing federal grants

(C) provide a source of statistical data from which plans for improved services can be drawn

(D) identify those social and health problems upon which case work services should be focused.

33. A significant factor in the United States economic picture is the state of the labor market. Of the following, the most important development affecting the labor market has been

   (A) an expansion of the national defense effort creating new plant capacity
   (B) the general increase in personal income as a result of an increase in overtime pay in manufacturing industries
   (C) the growth of manufacturing as a result of automation
   (D) a demand for a large number of new jobs resulting from new job applicants as well as displacement of workers by automation.

34. A working man becomes disabled and is unable to engage in any substantial gainful activity. He applies for benefits under the Social Security law. According to the Social Security regulations, his benefit payment would be based on

   (A) a prorated benefit for him and his dependents based on his current age
   (B) a monthly amount depending on the specific limb or bodily organ injured
   (C) the length of time he will probably be disabled
   (D) a monthly amount equal to the old age insurance benefit he would receive if he were 65.

35. According to the Social Security law, the eligible dependent wife of a man who is receiving old age benefits is entitled to receive

   (A) up to one-half of the husband's monthly benefit payment
   (B) a payment of ten percent less than her husband's monthly benefit payment
   (C) up to three-fourths of the husband's monthly benefit payment
   (D) a payment equal to her husband's monthly benefit payment.

36. When the purpose of a client-worker interview is to discuss the factors affecting his or her eligibility for public assistance, it would be *least* appropriate to attempt, at the same time, to

   (A) discuss with the applicant the reasons for his or her dependency and responsibility for his or her situation
   (B) assess with the applicant what he or she and his or her family can do about this immediate problem
   (C) assist the applicant to use his or her capacities to solve these problems
   (D) explore with the applicant views about his or her problems and about this situation.

37. At an intake interview, a client who seems very hesitant about seeking assistance, but who seems to be in need of help, makes several inconsistent statements about matters affecting eligibility for public assistance. You have attempted, unsuccessfully, to have inconsistencies clarified. Of the following, the best action for the worker to take in this situation is to

   (A) accept the case, but try to clear up the inconsistencies in subsequent interviews
   (B) attempt to clarify the statements through other sources before the next interview
   (C) overlook the inconsistencies, since the client may be frightened away by any attempt to probe
   (D) refuse further help to the client until he or she presents a more realistic picture of the situation.

38. A woman comes to the intake section of a Department of Social Services. The intake worker discovers, fairly early in the interview, that the applicant has come to the wrong

agency for the special help she needs. For the worker to continue the interview until the applicant has explained her need is

(A) advisable, mainly because the intake worker should create an atmosphere in which the client can talk freely
(B) inadvisable, mainly because the applicant will have to tell her story all over again to another agency's intake worker
(C) advisable, mainly because the proper referral cannot be made unless the worker has all the pertinent data
(D) inadvisable, the applicant should not be permitted to become too deeply involved in telling her story to an agency which cannot help her.

39. A man has been referred to a Department of Social Services by another agency. The intake worker has reviewed the detailed case history forwarded by the referring agency. When the client comes in for his initial interview, he proceeds to go into detail about his past situation. For the intake worker to allow the client to relate his history, at this point, is

(A) inadvisable, chiefly because allowing the client to give a detailed account of his past would allow him to control the course of the interview
(B) advisable, chiefly because the case history may not fully cover some essential areas
(C) inadvisable, chiefly because the facts are fully recorded and valuable time would be wasted in allowing the client to retell them
(D) advisable, chiefly because this will give the client the feeling that the worker is interested in him as an individual.

40. The type of case record to be used in a specific case depends on its purpose. If the case record is to serve as the document used to validate the kind of service or the amount and type of assistance to be granted, it is most important that the case record be

(A) chronological in form so that events can be seen in the proper perspective
(B) factual and not include the worker's evaluations
(C) organized so that information on continuing needs and services given is quickly available
(D) narrative in form so that the full history of the case can be recorded.

41. In handling a case, investigators should summarize the facts they have gathered and the observations they have made about the family and incorporate this material into a formal social study of the family. Of the following, the chief advantage of such a practice is that it will provide

(A) a picture of the family on the basis of which evaluations and plans can be made
(B) an easily accessible listing of the factors pertaining to eligibility
(C) a simple and uniform method of recording the family's social history
(D) an opportunity for the investigators to record their evaluation of the family's situation.

42. An applicant for public assistance tells the worker who is investigating his case that he has always supported himself by doing odd jobs. While attempting to verify the applicant's history of past maintenance, it is most important for the worker to determine, in addition,

(A) how the applicant was able to obtain a sufficient number of odd jobs to support himself
(B) what skills the applicant has that enabled him to obtain these jobs
(C) why the applicant never sought or kept a steady job
(D) whether such jobs are still available as a source of income for the applicant.

43. For a worker to make a collateral contact with a client's legally responsible relative when that relative is herself receiving public assistance is

    (A) advisable, mainly because the relative may be able to assist the client with needed services

    (B) inadvisable, mainly because the relative is in receipt of assistance and cannot assist the client financially

    (C) advisable, mainly because the worker may obtain information concerning the relative's eligibility for assistance

    (D) inadvisable, mainly because any information concerning the relative can be obtained from the other welfare center.

44. An applicant for public assistance tells the worker that her bank savings are exhausted. While a bank clearance can verify her statement, it is still important for the worker to see her bank book chiefly in order to

    (A) determine when the account was first opened and the amount of the initial deposit

    (B) correlate withdrawals and deposits with the applicant's story of past management

    (C) learn if the applicant had closed this account in order to open an account in another bank

    (D) verify that the last withdrawal was made before the applicant applied for assistance.

45. An unemployed father whose family is on public assistance has refused to take a job as a laborer because he has enrolled in a training course which will enable him to become an electrician's helper. He states that once he has completed the course he is sure that he can get a job and support his family. However, you learn that because of the long waiting list for this course, he cannot begin classes for four months. For his refusal to accept this laborer's job to be treated as a job refusal is

    (A) proper; there is no guarantee that he will be able to obtain employment when he has completed the course

    (B) improper; he should be encouraged to engage in a training program which will increase his job skills and earning capacity

    (C) proper; his working as laborer will not interfere with his starting the training course when he is reached on the waiting list

    (D) improper; he has a right to refuse a low-paying job in view of his potential skills.

46. Because of the heavy load of mail at Christmas time, a welfare family's check has not arrived on the expected date. The Investigator visits the family and finds that they are without food or funds. For the Investigator to ask the local grocer to extend credit to this family until their check arrives is

    (A) advisable, mainly because the family's needs will be met and there will be no need to duplicate assistance

    (B) inadvisable, mainly because the worker is sanctioning the family's use of credit buying and this might encourage them to make larger purchases on credit

    (C) advisable, mainly because this is the simplest and fastest way of meeting the family's needs, and the debt can be repaid when the check arrives

    (D) inadvisable, mainly because the family may not repay the debt when they receive their check, and the grocer might sue the worker.

47. When the case of an applicant who lives in a public housing project has been accepted, the authorities in charge of such projects should be notified of the case acceptance chiefly in order to insure that the

    (A) special services available to tenants in public housing projects are utilized

    (B) schedule of rents established for welfare recipients is used

    (C) family consists of only those people indicated on the welfare application

    (D) Housing Authorities are informed of the applicant's reduced income.

48. A client who is receiving supplementary assistance tells his Case Worker that he has been offered a higher paying job. He states, however, that he is not sure that he has the skill to handle the increased job responsibilities and asks the Case Worker for advice. The Case Worker should

(A) suggest that he take the job because he will then be able to support his family without help from the Department of Welfare

(B) allow the client to make his decision independently since only he can make such a decision

(C) help him to evaluate his level of skill and his ability to accept the new responsibilities

(D) recommend that the client refuse the job because he may not be able to keep it.

49. It has been suggested that all Case Workers be kept currently informed about general departmental actions taken, changes in other departmental work units, and new developments of general interest in their department. For a welfare department to put this suggestion into effect is generally

(A) inadvisable; Case Workers should perform the duties specifically assigned to them and not get involved in matters that do not concern them directly

(B) advisable; Case Workers may often need to know such information in order to coordinate their work properly with that of other work units

(C) inadvisable; changes in other work units have little effect on the work performed by Case Workers not assigned to these units

(D) advisable; broad knowledge of the activities in an agency tends to improve social work skills.

50. A training program for workers assigned to the intake section should include actual practice in stimulated interviews under stimulated conditions. The one of the following educational principles which is the chief justification for this statement is that

(A) the workers will remember what they see better and longer than what they read or hear

(B) the workers will learn more effectively by actually doing the act themselves than they would learn from watching others do it

(C) watching one or two simulated interviews will enable them to cope with the real situation with little difficulty

(D) a training program must employ methods of a practical nature if the workers are to find anything of lasting value in it.

51. The supervisor's main objective in holding an evaluation conference with a subordinate whose performance he or she must rate is to

(A) give the subordinate an opportunity to voice objections to the evaluation

(B) provide the supervisor with a basis for evaluating the subordinate's knowledge of his or her job

(C) provide an opportunity for the supervisor to discuss the subordinate's strengths and weaknesses

(D) enable the supervisor to train the subordinate in areas in which he or she is deficient.

52. In the evaluation process the employee who performs all or the greater portion of his or her job responsibilities in a satisfactory manner is considered standard in performance. Of the following, the factor which is not significant in choosing between a standard evaluation or a below-standard evaluation for a particular employee is

(A) growth potential in terms of his or her ability to handle duties which pertain to higher level position

(B) potential for improvement in areas where he or she is deficient

(C) the extent of supervision necessary for satisfactory performance

(D) work habits and adherence to the rules of the agency.

53. In a large city an intake worker determines that an applicant referred to his welfare center by the Homeless Women-Emergency Assistance Unit of the agency, although apparently in need of assistance, has been referred to the wrong welfare center. The worker should

(A) refer the applicant back to the Homeless Women-Emergency Assistance Unit after the case has been processed and the investigation completed

(B) process the referral and complete the investigation before transferring the case to the appropriate welfare center

(C) process the referral at his center only if the applicant is in need of emergency assistance, otherwise refer the case to the appropriate center

(D) refer the applicant back to the Homeless Women-Emergency Assistance Unit if she is in need of emergency assistance, otherwise refer her to the appropriate center.

54. When a restricted or indirect payment method is used by a local welfare agency, reimbursement by the federal government will be made only for

(A) medical care

(B) finder's fees

(C) security deposits

(D) utility payments.

55. Income resulting from a current court support order may be removed from the budget if the relative under court order ceases to make payments and if he

(A) presents verification to the investigator that he is now financially unable to assist

(B) has made no contribution under the court order for twelve consecutive months

(C) has disappeared and it is established that his whereabouts cannot be ascertained

(D) moves to another state and refuses to continue his contribution.

56. Assume that the total cost of the Public Assistance category decreases by 10% each year for the next three years after 1989, and that Midvale City continues to pay a portion of the costs. Then the total cost of the Public Assistance category for 1992 will be, most nearly,

(A) $11.5 million

(B) $12.7 million

(C) $14.1 million

(D) 14.5 million

MIDVALE CITY

Number of Persons Receiving Assistance and Cost of Assistance in 1988/1989

Category of Assistance	Monthly average number receiving assistance during		Total Cost for Year in Millions of Dollars		Cost Paid by Midvale City for Year in Millions of Dollars	
	1988	1989	1988	1989	1988	1989
PA	36,097	38,263	$19.2	$17.4	$9.7	$8.7
VA	6,632	5,972	2.5	1.6	1.3	.8
OAA	32,545	31,804	33.7	29.7	6.5	5.0
MAA	13,992	11,782	13.2	21.3	3.3	5.3
ADC	212,795	228,795	108.3	121.4	27.5	31.3

57. The category for which Midvale City paid the smallest percentage of the total cost was

(A) OAA in 1988

(B) OAA in 1989

(C) VA in 1988

(D) ADC in 1988

58. The monthly cost to Midvale City for each person receiving MAA during 1989 was, most nearly,

 (A) $67 more than in 1988
 (B) $26 less than in 1988
 (C) $20 more than in 1988
 (D) $18 more than in 1988

59. Assume that 40% of the number of persons receiving ADC in 1988 were adults caring for minor children, but Midvale City's contribution toward maintaining these adults was only 36% of its total contribution to the ADC program in 1988, then the amount paid by the city for each adult per month in 1988 is, most nearly,

 (A) $10
 (B) $14
 (C) $31
 (D) $36

60. Assume that 10% of the persons receiving OAA in 1989 will be transferred to MAA in 1990 and 6% of the persons receiving MAA in 1989 will no longer need any public assistance in 1990, then the percentage change from 1989 to 1990 in the monthly average number receiving MAA would be, most nearly,

 (A) an increase of 4%
 (B) an increase of 21%
 (C) an decrease of 6%
 (D) an increase of 27%

61. (This question is based only in part on the previous table.) The change from 1988 to 1989 in the monthly average number of persons stated in the table as receiving Old Age Assistance (OAA) may be best explained by the fact that the

 (A) number of aged persons in our population is on the increase
 (B) movement of population out of the city included more younger families than older single persons
 (C) number of persons receiving Social Security benefits and the amount of benefits have increased
 (D) cost of living for older persons is lower than that for the population as a whole.

Questions 62 through 68 are intended to test your ability to read and understand a series of paragraphs. It will be necessary for you to read each paragraph carefully because the questions are based only on the material contained therein.

Answer questions 62 through 64 solely on the basis of the following paragraph.

Toward the end of the 19th century, as social work principles and theories took form, areas of conflict between the responsibility of the social worker to the client group and to the status quo of social and economic institutions became highlighted. The lay public's attitude toward the individual poor was one of emphasis on betterment through the development of the individual's capacity for self-maintenance. They hoped to maintain this end both by helping the client to rely on his or her unused capacities for self-help and by facilitating his or her access to what were assumed to be the natural sources of help—family, relatives, churches, and other charitable associations. Professional social workers were fast becoming aware of the need for social reform. They perceived that traditional methods of help were largely inadequate to cope with the factors that were creating poverty and maladjustment for a large number of the population faster than the charity societies could relieve such problems through individual effort. The critical view, held by social workers, of the character of many social institutions was not shared by other groups in the community who had not reached the same point of awareness about the deficiencies in the functioning of these institutions. Thus, the views of the social worker were beginning to differ, sometimes radically, from the basic views of large sections of the population.

62. The social workers of the late 19th century found themselves in conflict with the status quo chiefly because they

(A) had become professionalized through the development of a body of theory and principles

(B) became aware that many social ills could not be cured through existing institutions

(C) felt that traditional methods of helping the poor must be expanded regardless of the cost to the public

(D) believed that the right of the individual to be self-determining should be emphasized.

63. It was becoming apparent, by the end of the 19th century, that in relation to the needs of the poor, existing social institutions

(A) did not sufficiently emphasize the ability of the poor to utilize their natural sources of help

(B) were using the proper methods of helping the poor, but were hindered by the work of social workers who had broken with tradition

(C) were no longer capable of meeting the needs of the poor because the causes of poverty had changed

(D) were capable of meeting the needs of the poor, but needed more financial aid from the general public since the number of people in need had increased.

64. Social workers at the end of the 19th century may be properly classified as

(A) growing in awareness that many social ills could be alleviated through social reform

(B) very perceptive individuals who realized that traditional methods of help were humiliating to the poor

(C) strong advocates of expanding the existing traditional sources of relief

(D) too radical, because they favored easing life for the poor at the expense of increased taxation to the public at large.

Answer questions 65 through 68 solely on the basis of the following paragraph.

Form W-280 provides a uniform standard for estimating family expenses, and is used as a basis for determining eligibility for the care of children at public expense. The extent to which legally responsible relatives can pay for the care of a child must be computed. The minimum amount of the payment required from legally responsible relatives shall be 50% of the budget surplus as computed on Form W-281, plus any governmental benefits, such as OASDI benefits, or Railroad Retirement benefits being paid to a family member for the child receiving care or services. Because of the kinds and quantities of service included in the budget schedule (W-280), and because only 50% of the budget surplus is required as payment, no allowances for special needs are made, except for verified payments into civil service pension funds, amounts paid to a garnishee, or amounts paid to another agency for the care of other relatives for whom the relative is legally responsible, or for other such expenses if approval has been granted after Form W-278 has been submitted. In determining the income of the legally responsible relative, income from wages, self-employment, unemployment insurance benefits, and any such portion of governmental benefits as is not specifically designated for children already receiving care is to be included. Should 50% of the family's surplus meet the child care expenses, the case shall not be processed. Form W-279, an agreement to support, shall be signed by the legally responsible relative when 50% of the surplus is $1.00 or more a week.

65. A family is required to sign an agreement to support
   (A) whenever they are legally responsible for the support of the child under care
   (B) before any care at public expense is given to the child
   (C) when their income surplus is at least $2 a week
   (D) when 50% of their income surplus meets the full needs of the child.

66. The reason for allowing a family to deduct only certain specified expenses when computing the amount they are able to contribute to the support of a child being cared for at public expense is that the family
   (A) should not be permitted to have a higher standard of living than the child being cared for
   (B) budget schedule is sufficiently generous and includes an allowance for other unusual expenses
   (C) may not be able to verify their extraordinary expenses
   (D) may meet other unusual expenses from the remainder of their surplus.

67. Mrs. B wishes to have her daughter Mary cared for at public expense. Her income includes her wages and OASDI benefits of $250 a month, of which $50 a month is paid for Mary, and $50 a month for another minor member of the family who is already being cared for at public expense. In order to determine the amount of Mrs. B's budget surplus, it is necessary to consider as income, her wages and
   (A) $50 of OASDI received by Mary
   (B) $150 of the OASDI benefits
   (C) $200 of the OASDI benefits
   (D) $200 of the OASDI benefits if she is legally responsible for the care of the other child in placement.

68. In order to determine a family's ability to contribute to the support of a child, the Case Worker should
   (A) have the legally responsible member sign Form W-279 agreeing to support the child, and then compute the family surplus on W-281 in accordance with public assistance standards
   (B) compute the family's income in accordance with the allowance included on Form W-280 and the expenses included on Form W-278 and have Form W-279 signed if necessary
   (C) use Form W-278 to work out a budget schedule for the family and compute their surplus on W-281 and then have them sign W-279 if necessary
   (D) compute income and expenses on Form W-281, based on Form W-280, and have Form W-279 signed if necessary.

69. Among the following needy persons, the one not eligible to receive veteran assistance is the
   (A) husband of a veteran, if living with the veteran
   (B) minor grandchild of a veteran, if living with the veteran
   (C) incapacitated child of a deceased veteran
   (D) non-veteran brother or sister of a veteran, if living with the veteran.

70. Under the Social Security Act, public assistance payments do not provide for
   (A) old-age assistance
   (B) care of children in foster homes
   (C) aid to the blind
   (D) aid to dependent children

71. The main difference between public welfare and private social agencies is that in public agencies

(A) case records are open to the public
(B) the granting of assistance cannot be sufficiently flexible to meet the varying needs of individual recipients
(C) only financial assistance may be provided
(D) all policies and procedures must be based upon statutory authorizations.

72. Of the following items in the standard budget of a Department of Social Services, the one for which actual expenditures would be most constant throughout the year is

(A) fuel
(B) housing
(C) medical care
(D) clothing.

73. Foster home placement of children is often advocated in preference to institutionalization primarily because

(A) the law does not provide for local supervision of children's institutions
(B) institutions furnish a more expensive type of care
(C) the number of institutions is insufficient compared to the number of children needing care
(D) foster homes provide a more normal environment for children.

74. An interview is best conducted in private primarily because

(A) the person interviewed will tend to be less self-conscious
(B) the interviewer will be able to maintain his or her continuity of thought better
(C) it will insure that the interview is "off the record"
(D) people tend to "show off" before an audience.

75. Interviewers will be better able to understand the person interviewed and his or her problems if they recognize that much of the person's behavior is due to motives

(A) which are deliberate
(B) of which he or she is unaware
(C) which are inexplicable
(D) which are kept under control

76. When an applicant for public assistance is repeatedly told that "everything will be all right," the effect that can usually be expected is that he or she will

(A) develop overt negativistic reactions toward the agency
(B) become too closely identified with the interviewer
(C) doubt the interviewer's ability to understand and help with his or her problems
(D) have greater confidence in the interviewer.

77. While interviewing a client, it is preferable that the Case Worker

(A) take no notes in order to avoid disturbing the client
(B) focus primary attention on the client while the client is talking
(C) take no notes in order to impress upon the client the worker's ability to remember all the pertinent facts of the case
(D) record all the details in order to show the client that what is being said is important

78. During an interview, a curious applicant asks several questions about the Case Worker's private life. As the interviewer, you should

   (A) refuse to answer such questions

   (B) answer the questions fully

   (C) explain that your primary concern is with his or her problems and that discussion of your personal affairs will not be helpful in meeting his or her needs

   (D) explain that is the responsibility of the interviewer to ask questions and not to answer them.

79. An interviewer can best establish a good relationship with the person being interviewed by

   (A) assuming casual interest in the statements made by the person being interviewed

   (B) asking questions which enable the person to show pride in his or her knowledge

   (C) taking the point of view of the person interviewed

   (D) showing a genuine interest in the person.

80. "An interviewer's attention must be directed toward himself or herself as well as toward the person interviewed." This statement means that the interviewer should

   (A) keep in mind the extent to which his or her own prejudices may influence his or her judgment

   (B) rationalize the statements made by the person interviewed

   (C) gain the respect and confidence of the person interviewed

   (D) avoid being too impersonal.

81. More complete expression will be obtained from a person being interviewed if the interviewer can create the impression that

   (A) the data secured will become part of a permanent record

   (B) official information must be accurate in every detail

   (C) it is the duty of the person interviewed to give accurate data

   (D) the person interviewed is participating in a discussion of his or her own problems.

82. The practice of asking leading questions should be avoided in an interview because the

   (A) interviewer risks revealing his or her attitudes to the person being interviewed

   (B) interviewer may be led to ignore the objective attitudes of the person interviewed

   (C) answers may be unwarrantedly influenced

   (D) person interviewed will resent the attempt to lead him or her and will be less cooperative.

83. A good technique for the interviewer to use in an effort to secure reliable data and to reduce the possibility of misunderstanding is to

   (A) use casual undirected conversation, enabling the person being interviewed to talk about himself or herself and thus secure the desired information

   (B) adopt the procedure of using direct questions regularly

   (C) extract the desired information from the person being interviewed by putting him or her on the defensive

   (D) explain to the person being interviewed the information desired and the reason for needing it.

84. As a Case Worker interviewing applicants for public assistance, your attitude toward their veracity should be that the information they have furnished you is

   (A) untruthful until you have had an opportunity to check the information

   (B) truthful only insofar as verifiable facts are concerned

   (C) untruthful because clients tend to interpret everything in their own favor

   (D) truthful until you have information to the contrary.

85. As a Case Worker conducting the first interview with a new public assistance client you should

(A) ask questions requiring "yes" or "no" answers in order to simplify the interview
(B) rephrase several of the key questions as a check on his previous statements
(C) let him tell his own story while keeping him to the relevant facts
(D) avoid showing any sympathy for the applicant while he is revealing his personal needs and problems.

86. An aged person who is unable to produce immediate proof of age has made an application for old-age assistance. He states that it will take about a week to obtain the necessary proof and that he does not have enough money to provide meals for himself until then. If it appears that he is in immediate need, he should be told that

(A) the law requires proof of age before any assistance can be granted
(B) temporary assistance will be provided pending the completion of the investigation
(C) a personal loan will be made to him from a revolving fund
(D) he should arrange for a small loan from private sources.

87. Of the sources through which a social service agency can seek information about the family background and economic needs of a particular client, the most important consists of

(A) records and documents covering the client
(B) interviews with the client's relatives
(C) the client's own story
(D) direct contacts with former employers.

88. The one of the following sources of evidence which would be most likely to give information needed to verify residence is

(A) family affidavits
(B) medical and hospital bills
(C) an original birth certificate
(D) rental receipts.

89. In public assistance agencies, vital statistics are a resource used by the workers mainly to

(A) help establish eligibility through verification of births, deaths, and marriages.
(B) help establish eligibility through verification of divorce proceedings
(C) secure proof of unemployment and eligibility for unemployment compensation
(D) secure indices of the cost of living in the larger cities.

90. Case records should be considered confidential in order to

(A) make it impossible for agencies to know each other's methods
(B) permit workers to make objective rather than subjective comments
(C) prevent recipients from comparing amounts of assistance given to different families
(D) protect clients and their families.

91. Because Social Case Workers generally are not trained psychiatrists, they should, when encountering psychiatric problems in the performance of their departmental duties

(A) ignore such problems because they are beyond the scope of their responsibilities
(B) inform the affected persons that they recognize their problems personally but will take no official cognizance of them
(C) ask to be relieved of the cases in which these problems are met and recommend that they be assigned to a psychiatrist.
(D) recognize such problems where they exist and make referrals to the proper sources for treatment.

Answer questions 92 through 94 based solely on the information contained in the following passage.

The problem of homelessness is not unique to the nation's largest cities. Rather, it is a growing national problem. The causes of homelessness are deeply rooted in underlying social and economic ills—ills which are pushing more and more formerly normal, well-adjusted, self-sufficient people out of the mainstream of American life. Even the most prosperous cities have only limited ability to address the problem of the homeless. They can only partly ameliorate the situation with the limited moneys and resources at their command. In every city, there is a chronic and ever-growing shortage of housing which poor families can afford. There are inadequate facilities for the mentally ill who have been released from institutions, without any adequate community-based facilities for their utilization. The homeless problem is only one of the manifestations of a larger one. It is the rapidly changing and complex economic and social structure in the United States that has been the primary cause for an ever-increasing number of families and individuals exhibiting not just housing difficulties but also many other social problems. The recent fiscal and social retrenchment policies of the federal government have further exacerbated these problems.

92. According to the passage, homelessness

   (A) could be eliminated if federal funds were extended to build public housing
   (B) is largely the fault of the cities' failure to properly utilize their resources to provide affordable housing for the poor
   (C) is increased by the large number of people moving to the cities from rural areas to improve their economic conditions
   (D) is one face of the large problem of increased inability of many people to cope with the ills prevalent in today's society.

93. Assume that a family, hitherto self-supporting, has applied for supplementary public assistance because they cannot meet their needs. They are in danger of becoming homeless because they cannot pay the interest on their mortgaged home. Based on the passage, the reason for their monetary problems is probably

   (A) the result of poor management of their funds
   (B) due to the current practice of mortgage holders to charge exorbitant rates of interest
   (C) the inability of the father to command a higher salary
   (D) a combination of social and economic factors existing in the United States.

94. Assume that the manager of a hotel to which mentally ill persons are released by institutions comes to you, a Case Worker at the nearby public assistance office. He states that one of the residents receives SSI but frequently tells the manager he has insufficient funds to pay his rent. Based on the passage, it can be inferred that

   (A) SSI has incorrectly determined the amount the individual's grant should be
   (B) an attempt should be made to inform SSI or a locally based community organization of the help the individual may need in managing his money properly
   (C) someone else in the hotel, staff or resident, is probably appropriating part of the man's monthly check
   (D) the rent payment should be sent directly to the hotel by the SSI office.

Answer questions 95 through 97 solely on the basis of information contained in the following passage.

Various laws in New York City and New York State protect the rights of people with AIDS or with AIDS Related Complex (ARC). These laws prohibit discrimination against people who have disabilities and AIDS is considered to be a disability. A person with AIDS or ARC cannot be fired from his or her job unless he is incapable of satisfactorily performing it, nor can an employer dismiss a person because he is a homosexual and, therefore, in a high-risk group with respect to AIDS susceptibility, since such action would mean the employer is perceiving the individual to have a disability. In New York City, the law further prohibits any discrimination in employment because of sexual orientation, without reference to AIDS or ARC.

The city and state laws also protect AIDS/ARC victims from eviction provided they pay their rent from a rent-stabilized or rent-controlled apartment. Tenants in a boarding home where the landlord also resides, however, are not protected from eviction under these laws. Failure to pay rent owed the landlord may result in eviction. An AIDS/ARC victim may be unable to work and, therefore, cannot meet his or her financial obligations. If a diagnosis of such inability is obtained, the person may be eligible for financial aid through federal entitlement programs. During the time an application for such assistance is being processed, the city's welfare department may intervene to pay back rent if the rent is reasonable.

95. Assume you are a Case Worker in Bloomstown, Arkansas. A male client who has been receiving supplementary assistance to augment his weekly salary reports that he has lost his job because his employer has learned that he has AIDS. Based on the passage, you should

(A) advise the client to file an anti-discrimination suit since firing a person because of AIDS is illegal

(B) personally talk to the employer and try to convince her or him that a person with AIDS can still perform meaningful work

(C) refer the client for application for a federal entitlement program

(D) research appropriate material regarding the legality of the employer's actions in your city or state.

96. A man applying for public assistance in New York City shows you, the Case Worker, a letter of eviction from his landlord. The applicant complains the landlord is pursuing this action because the applicant is a homosexual. Based on the passage, you should *first* determine whether the applicant

(A) has filed an anti-discrimination suit

(B) has AIDS or ARC

(C) has paid his rent each month

(D) is a bona fide resident of New York City

97. A young female client on supplementary public assistance in Owegee, New York, has a work history of frequent changes in employment. She comes to you, her Case Worker, to report that she has just lost her job as a file clerk in a large company because the personnel office of the company has discovered she is a lesbian. Based on the passage, you should

(A) urge her to file an anti-discrimination suit

(B) inform her that her work history shows she is unable to hold a job because of reasons other than her sexual preferences and that you cannot accept her reasons for losing her current job

(C) obtain more information from her and from the employer regarding the reasons for her dismissal

(D) refer her for possible employment elsewhere without discussing her previous work pattern, since she is able and willing to work.

Answer questions 98 through 100 based solely on the information contained in the following passage.

AIDS is caused by a virus called HIV (Human Immunodeficiency Virus). The virus attacks a person's immune system, leaving the body susceptible to a large number and variety of life-threatening infections, as well as certain types of cancer. The HIV virus is found in blood, semen, and certain other body fluids such as saliva, tears, and vaginal secretions.

Although the diseases caused by HIV can be devastating, it has been determined that the virus itself is very fragile outside of the human body. Thus, if it is not inhabiting human tissue, it does not survive for a long period of time. It can be inactivated by exposure to drying, chlorine bleach, heat, household disinfectants, and other chemicals used in sterilization.

98. According to the paragraph, HIV

   (A) causes certain types of cancer.
   (B) causes AIDS
   (C) is a dangerous infection affecting the bodily fluids
   (D) can survive for long periods of time within a household.

99. From the passage, it can be inferred that a person with AIDS

   (A) is susceptible to many life-threatening infections
   (B) will be very likely to succumb to the diseases
   (C) can be cured if the virus is outside his or her body
   (D) will not contract certain types of cancer.

100. Assume that a suitable, completely vacant apartment has been found for an AFDC family. The apartment has been vacant for several months. The mother comes to you, the Case Worker for her case, and expresses fear because the previous tenant of the apartment had died of AIDS. Based on the passage, you should

   (A) immediately require that the family member be examined for AIDS
   (B) immediately remove the family from the apartment
   (C) assure the woman that sufficient time has expired so that there is no danger to the family
   (D) advise the woman to thoroughly disinfect the kitchen and bathroom facilities to make certain no HIV virus remains in the apartment as a precautionary measure.

Correct Answers for Practice Examination II

1. D	21. D	41. A	61. C	81. D
2. C	22. C	42. D	62. B	82. C
3. D	23. D	43. A	63. C	83. D
4. C	24. D	44. B	64. A	84. D
5. A	25. A	45. C	65. C	85. C
6. C	26. B	46. D	66. D	86. B
7. A	27. D	47. B	67. B	87. C
8. D	28. B	48. C	68. D	88. D
9. C	29. C	49. B	69. D	89. A
10. D	30. D	50. B	70. B	90. D
11. B	31. B	51. C	71. D	91. D
12. A	32. D	52. A	72. B	92. D
13. B	33. D	53. B	73. D	93. D
14. B	34. D	54. A	74. A	94. B
15. C	35. A	55. C	75. B	95. D
16. A	36. A	56. B	76. C	96. C
17. B	37. B	57. B	77. B	97. C
18. B	38. C	58. D	78. C	98. B
19. A	39. D	59. A	79. D	99. A
20. C	40. C	60. B	80. A	100. D

Explanations of Correct Answers for Practice Examination II

1. **(D)** The correct answer is the only one which can be derived from the statement given in the preamble. It states a *basic* premise which all Case Workers must fully understand and follow in working with their clients.

2. **(C)** A professional relationship between the Case Worker and the client requires that a sympathetic atmosphere be created by the Case Worker so that the client feels able to trust and therefore to confide in the worker. At the same time, the Case Worker must maintain control of the relationship and not allow the client to digress or pursue areas which are not directly related to the worker's responsibility. Nor must the worker permit the relationship to become a friendship which may hinder the worker's maintenance of objectivity and ability to help the client successfully resolve problems.

3. **(D)** Of the possible arguments given in support of the merger of welfare and family case work fields, the best one is that new techniques and new community resources may become available to both fields which previously were used only by or known to only one of the fields, or which are discovered because of the new combination of people and knowledge available as a result of the merger. Other possible answers are either irrelevant to the question asked (Answers A and C) or possibly not true (B).

4. **(C)** Most social work experts believe the best case work practice requires that attention be given both to the physical, environmental, and social factors involved in the situation and to the client's reactions to these factors and to his or her own life experiences.

5. **(A)** Modern case work theory tends to believe the family unit is of great importance in

solving a client's problems and will try to involve them whenever possible. In many instances, the family relationship *is* a central reason for the problem or is the problem. In any event, members of the family, and the family as a whole, should be aware of the problem, help to solve it if possible, accept the solutions arrived at, and help to carry out these solutions successfully.

6. **(C)** In this situation, the Case Worker merely knows that John is intelligent, is in his proper year in high school, has become a truant, and has been ordered by the school principal to go to youth counselling. You, the Case Worker in the youth counseling agency, must *first* learn considerably more about John—what he does during the hours he is not at school, who his friends are, the financial and social scene at home, etc. Only when you have a more complete picture of these factual matters can you properly begin to explore with John his attitudes and the reasons for his relatively sudden change in behavior.

7. **(A)** A fundamental principle in good case work procedure is that the worker must help the client understand a given situation and reach the conclusions that feel best for him or her. In the situation given, the Case Worker should attempt to help the client understand the pros and cons of changing jobs and try to obtain the client's acceptance of the worker's viewpoint.

8. **(D)** You are given a statement that is a *basic* premise in all good case work interviewing in that it requires a particular focus on the client's actual situation. The correct answer amplifies this basic premise.

9. **(C)** Even with the best intentions, some clients are either too dull or too inarticulate to give the Case Worker a crisp, connected story. Good case work requires that in these instances you retain your patience, ask simple questions requiring straightforward responses, and frequently review with the client what you think he or she has said to be sure you understand the response. *Never* ask leading questions since they may confuse the client or prompt him or her to give what *for them* is the wrong answer but which they think is the answer *you* want.

10. **(D)** The passage gives you most of the main points that should ordinarily be included in a case record but *neglects* the vital need that a case record must contain sufficient data for understanding the client's actual problem as well as sufficient information about factors that *must* be known in order for a solution to be reached. Without such data, a case record will not be of any real use.

11. **(B)** It would be extremely difficult for a "troubled client" to achieve the degree of confidence in the Case Worker necessary to reveal true feelings during the interview. Therefore, the client is likely to hide such feelings especially in areas where the client believes the Case Worker is unlikely to believe and respond properly.

12. **(A)** The Case Worker's role is to help the client cope with problems. In working with a sick client, the worker must know and understand enough about the medical condition, limitations, and prognosis to intelligently discuss with the client the specific problems, including the medical problems that will affect the resolution of other problems. Note that while Answer B may be a correct statement of fact, it does *not* answer the question posed.

13. **(B)** In this situation, the 32-year-old mother is concerned about the deterioration of her marriage. To be of most help, the husband should be a direct participant in the counseling service, and they should meet with the Case Worker in trying to solve what is, in effect, a joint problem.

14. **(B)** A foster home, no matter how good it is, may not be the best long-run solution in

the case of a neglected, mistreated child. The best solution from the taxpayer's, child's, and parent's viewpoints is to attempt to remedy the home situation so that the child can return to the family and to a normal environment.

15. **(C)** There is nothing in the passage to indicate the home life is anything but a normal, *good* one. A positive approach is the most useful one for the Case Worker to take. The child must be made aware that while he is not being punished, his actions have been such that temporary removal to a foster home will help him and his family achieve changes which will benefit him and enable him to go home.

16. **(A)** No information is given to explain why the child ran away from the foster home to the home of the mother and stepfather and there is no indication that the foster home was unsuitable. The reasons for the initial temporary placement in the foster home must be considered as still valid. It would, therefore, be correct case work procedure to return the child to the foster home while long-term custody in a relative's home is being considered. While Answer C is a correct statement, it is not the best reason for returning the child to the foster home since it refers to the *original* placement and not to the present situation. The child's *desire* is not of primary importance (Answer B) but rather the child's *welfare* and that of the mother and stepfather, and the original decision to remove the child from their home has not changed. Answer D is irrelevant in this situation and is not always true.

17. **(B)** Case work students have found that socially well-adjusted children and/or those accustomed to living with a family, either their own or in a foster home, fare better in a foster home placement rather than in an institution which lacks the intimate relationships familiar to the children with which they have successfully coped in the past. The children needing strong discipline or with social and psychological problems needing professional help should be placed in an institutional setting. **Note:** Answer A is the *opposite* of the question being asked.

18. **(B)** A teacher plays a vital role in spotting the child who doesn't "fit in" with the appropriate peer group and is responsible for discussing the matter with the school social worker and/or the child's parents to obtain needed professional help for the child.

19. **(A)** In this situation, discussion with the parents has not improved the boy's home life and he is being mistreated. Foster home placement is indicated until the parents are able to accept and properly care for him. Solutions presented in the other possible answers are not indicated (Answer B), not warranted by the facts (Answer C), or not possible according to the facts given (Answer D).

20. **(C)** Foster home placement is the correct procedure to be utilized in this instance. Commitment to a correctional facility will not be mandated because the boy has not perpetrated an actual crime. The mother should continue to be urged to receive treatment for her alcoholism so that her son can ultimately be returned to her.

21. **(D)** Good case work procedure mandates that the family always be aware of and fully accept the need for the worker's specific actions. In this situation, the worker should let the family know of the reasons for such a personal visit to the school. A *hard-core* family is one that has continuously or for a long "on-and-off" period been on public assistance or social work treatment. Frequently, such families cannot be relied on to make the school visit or to ask the pertinent questions, or will not receive the full proper answers needed.

22. **(C)** Vocational rehabilitation means work training for a person expected to be employable after completion of such training. A sheltered workshop is a specifically designed facility geared to training persons with physical or mental handicaps to compete in the

labor market. The wrong answers refer to persons who are *not* potential candidates for vocational rehabilitation.

23. **(D)** In this situation, the Case Worker must concentrate on working with the alcoholic client in the direct, positive fashion indicated in the correct answer. The other answers will not help resolve the client's special problem which, as noted in the first sentence, must be solved.

24. **(D)** You are told that research shows there are many different social, psychological, and physical reasons for addiction and no one cure for all cases. Accordingly, community facilities dealing with addiction and related problems must be utilized on a differentiated basis, depending on the individual client's background—social, economic, education, physical condition, etc. Thus, one addict may be best treated at home, one in a hospital, another in a group facility, etc.

25. **(A)** This question is asking what the danger is in interpreting a child's delinquent behavior merely in terms of being moral or immoral, i.e., "right" or "wrong." A moralistic approach may prevent the Case Worker from discovering the more important true cause of the delinquency. Thus, for example, a child who is always stealing cannot just be labelled delinquent or immoral. He or she may be displaying behavior that is symptomatic or have other, deeper disturbances which a good Case Worker must explore, or, if need be, refer the child for professional psychological help.

26. **(B)** Your best approach in this situation is to first get an overview of all 70 cases in order to learn which ones will need immediate attention, which can be delayed, and which will require deep study before any action can be taken. Study each case record to set your priorities and to obtain an overview of the problems that face you.

27. **(D)** The size of and cost for the total public assistance payroll depends largely on both the number of eligible people receiving such assistance and the amount of money granted to each of these people. The conditions for eligibility enable the agency to forecast how many people are likely to be on assistance in a given period of time. The standard of living deemed proper for relief recipients will largely determine the amount of money that will be needed for each of these recipients.

28. **(B)** As explained in Answer 27, the number of people on public assistance and the amount of each person's grant are the important factors in determining the cost of a welfare program. If the size of the grant is increased, the standard of eligibility will go down, allowing people who have resources just at or just below the previous standard to be eligible for public assistance.

29. **(C)** Case work theory and practice concentrates on solving *individual* and family behavior problems and attitudes, on obtaining *individual* and family participation in the solution of problems affecting their lives, and on helping to change their environments for the welfare of client(s). It is *not* generally concerned with attempts to reconstruct *total* personalities or *total* environments. All the wrong answers *are* major case work assumptions.

30. **(D)** The *first* step that must be taken to help restore a family to self-maintaining status is to learn *why* the family is dependent. Only after the *cause* is determined can plans be made to reduce or eliminate the dependency on problem assistance.

31. **(B)** Good case work practice requires that the worker help the client understand the facts of new problems, offer possible alternative solutions, identify the problems involved with each solution, and work with the client in determining the best solution.

32. **(D)** The Case Worker's point of view is primarily one of helping the client. By dividing the cases into different categories, the worker can see a commonality with other clients

of similar problems (e.g., problems of disability of age, etc.) and can draw knowledge and possible solutions from these other cases. The wrong answers are reasons for dividing cases by category from an administrative, policy-making point of view, but *not* from the Case Worker's primary responsibility or concern.

33. **(D)** The demands of the labor market have resulted in the increase in the number of unskilled or semi-skilled persons looking for jobs because automation and computerization have made their former jobs obsolete. At the same time, the need has grown for persons with specialized skills required by the newly computer-automated industries. The influx of women into the job market has further increased the number of job applicants.

34. **(D)** Self-explanatory. If disability is expected to last a minimum of 12 months and the worker was employed within the last five years in covered employment, Answer D is appropriate.

35. **(A)** The wife of a husband declared disabled and receiving benefits under the Social Security law can receive no more than one half of her husband's payments. This can work the other way: if the wife is disabled and covered by disability payments the husband can also collect up to one-half of the amount involved.

36. **(A)** In the situation presented, the only appropriate topics to discuss are those related to the establishment of current eligibility for public assistance. The three wrong answers *are* appropriate topics for discussion. Note that the question asks for the *least* appropriate subject for discussion.

37. **(B)** Case Workers frequently encounter clients who, because of language difficulties, excitement, fear, or many other reasons, appear to be inconsistent in their statements. The best way to handle this is to obtain other more official information. Thus, a client may say he has no bank account and later mentions he did have one. A check with the bank will clarify the matter. The Case Worker must neither assume the client is lying nor trust that future interviews may reveal that the client has resources and that the case should never have been accepted.

38. **(C)** A Case Worker in a public agency cannot afford to give a considerable amount of time to a situation which is known not to be the concern of the agency. Nevertheless, good case work and public relations procedure mandate that the worker listen to enough about the problem to determine what agency can help the woman and to direct her to it, e.g., a blind woman coming to a public assistance agency may actually be looking for a medical facility, not a public assistance agency. Only by talking to her can the worker be of assistance.

39. **(D)** While Case Workers in public agencies have limited time to spend on a client, it is *most* important that good rapport be established. By taking the time to hear the client's story, even if it repeats data given in the case record of the referring agency, the client will become comfortable with the new agency, will feel that her individual interests are going to be considered and that she is not merely a "statistic" being transferred from one agency to another.

40. **(C)** To be most useful for validating the kinds of service granted and the amount and type of assistance granted, pertinent data should be placed in the case record where it is most accessible. Such pertinent data would include information regarding continuing needs and services.

41. **(A)** The ultimate purpose of a formal social study in a public assistance case is to help evaluate the needs of the family, and to plan how to meet those needs.

42. **(D)** The first aim of the Case Worker in this situation is to prevent the family from

having to go on public assistance or to achieve a degree of self-support which will necessitate their receiving only supplementary assistance. The worker should, therefore, not only verify past work history but also determine if there is the possibility of employment now or in the near future at the client's previous places of employment. The other wrong answers are useful steps to be taken after it has been determined that public assistance is needed.

43. **(A)** The proposal to contact the client's legally responsible relative in this situation is a good one. Although the relative is on public assistance and not able to offer financial assistance, upon direct contact with the relative you may be able to have this relative provide other services your client needs (e.g., in helping your client clean the house or mind the children while your client has to go to clinics). Note that Answer C is unacceptable because the relative's inability to give financial help has been established and is not yet your concern.

44. **(B)** A Case Worker must examine a client's closed bank book to determine past management. Thus, a closed account showing steady withdrawals for many months prior to closing the account at "zero" amount of money will help establish the lack of present income and that the client had been living on the amount in the bank. A steady addition of small amounts before the withdrawals will help verify that the client had a job at one time, etc. The bank book may also show the withdrawal of a substantial amount of money just prior to application for public assistance. Explanation and proof of the use of that amount would be required prior to acceptance of the case.

45. **(C)** A client may refuse to accept a job which might give him and his family assistance only for good and sufficient reasons. In the situation presented, the reasons stated are not sufficient to warrant acceptance of the client's job refusal because the laborer position *now* will not interfere with enrolling in the training course several months from now.

46. **(D)** It is not good public policy for the worker to request extension of credit in this instance. If the family is in dire need, an emergency check can be issued and the original check stopped at the bank. There is no guarantee that the client will pay the money owed to the grocer and possible ensuing problems may be avoided both by the worker, agency, client, and grocer by following the correct procedure.

47. **(B)** Special rent schedules are utilized for persons on public assistance who live in housing projects.

48. **(C)** Good case work procedure requires you to work with the client to help reach an acceptable decision. In this instance, the Case Worker must help the client determine whether he can really handle the new job he has been offered both in terms of the skills needed and the higher level of responsibilities involved.

49. **(B)** A public welfare agency, especially in a large city, is generally organized on a functional basis with separate units handling specialized matters such as housing, resource evaluation, legal matters, etc. A Case Worker must be aware of all changes in these areas which might affect how these cases should be handled.

50. **(B)** A basic training principle is that learning by doing is the most effective way to learn something new. The utilization of simulated interviews in which the new worker is an active participant is a good learning device for workers whose main activity is conducting actual interviews.

51. **(C)** An evaluation procedure can be most effective if it also contains a frank discussion between the supervisor and the subordinate about the worker's good points and problems, including suggestions on how to improve performance in specific areas. Although

it gives the subordinate the opportunity to object to the evaluation, its main objective is to help the worker to understand the areas in need of improvement. The conference *may* result in a decision to give the worker more training *after* the conference.

52. **(A)** An evaluation is of an employee's actual performance for the period covered, and one is evaluated against the agency's or unit's standards of performance. It generally does *not* cover future performance or growth potentiality. In determining an individual's potentiality for promotion to a higher level job, past evaluations may be considered, but that is not the question being asked.

53. **(B)** Here is an area in which an apparent error has been made by a worker from Social Services. Therefore, it should be corrected without further inconveniencing the client and in a manner that will not reduce the confidence of the client in the operation of the agency as a whole. If a client mistakenly walks in to the wrong unit of the agency, he or she should be directed to the proper unit even if it is some distance away. However, if the client has been sent to the wrong location by a social services worker, proper corrective measures should be instituted at once.

54. **(A)** This is a factual question. The federal government will *not* reimburse restricted payments for finder's fees, security deposits, or utility payments, but *will* reimburse restricted payments for medical expenses. (See the Glossary for definition of restricted payment.)

55. **(C)** The client's budget provides that under a court order the client receive a degree of financial support from the relative. Agency policy generally provides that the amount remain in the budget unless the court removes or modifies its order or the agency is certain the order will not be followed and the client will not be receiving that amount of money. Answers A and B do not provide that assurance. When the relative moves to another state, as in wrong Answer D, there are reciprocal agreements between states. to provide that the court-ordered amount of money will still be made available for the client. Only when a relative has disappeared and an exhaustive search for his or her whereabouts has proved unsuccessful can the income from the relatives be removed from the budget.

56. **(B)** 1. $17.4 million in 1989.
    2. 10% less in 1990 = $15,660,000.
    3. 10% less in 1991 = $14,094,00
    4. 10% less in 1992 = $12,680,000.

57. **(B)** Answer A: Cost of OAA to Midvale City in 1988 = $6.5 million. Total cost of OAA in 1988 = $33.7 million.

Percent paid by Midvale City in 1988 $= \dfrac{6.5m}{33.7m} = $ 19.29%

Answer B: Cost of OAA to Midvale City in 1989 = $5 million. Total cost of OAA in 1989 = $29.7 million.

Percent paid by Midvale City in 1989 $= \dfrac{5.0m}{29.7m} = $ $16.48%

Answer C: Cost of VA to Midvale City in 1988 = $1.3 million. Total cost of VA in 1988 = 2.5 million.
Percent paid by Midvale City $=$ 52%

Answer D: Cost of ADC to Midvale City in 1988 = $27.5 million. Total cost of ADC in 1988 = 108.3 million.
Percent paid by Midvale City in 1988 $=$ 25%

58. **(D)**

    1988 $3,300,000 \div 13,992 = \$235.85$
    1989 $5,300,000 \div 11,782 = \$449.84$
    $\$449.84 - \$235.85 = \$213.99$
    $213.99 \div 12 = \$ 17.83$

    Most nearly $18

59. **(A)** Number of persons on ADC per month in 1988 = 212,795. 40% adults = 85,118 per month. Midvale total contribution to ADC in 1988 = $27.5 million per year. 36% of Midvale contribution per month to ADC in 1988 $= \dfrac{27.5 \text{ m}(.36)}{12} = 825,000.$

    $\dfrac{825,000}{85,118} = 9.69.$

60. **(B)** Number of persons per month on OAA in 1989 = 31,804. 10% of 31,804 = 3,180 = number transferred per month in 1989. So, 14,962 = number otherwise on MAA per month in 1990 (11,782 + 3,180 = 14,962). But, 6% of 11,782 per month will not be on public assistance in 1990 = 706.92 fewer (707). 14,962 − 707 = 14,255. 14,255 will be on MAA in 1990. 14,255 − 11,782 = 2,473 increase (i.e., $\dfrac{2,473}{11,782} = 21\%$ increase).

61. **(C)** The table shows you that the monthly average of persons on MAA has *decreased* from 1988 to 1989. Answer A is known to be true and, therefore, cannot be the answer for a *decrease* on persons on MAA. Answer B has no relevance to the question being asked. While Answer D may be a true statement, it would not by itself affect the number of persons eligible for MAA which depends on the resources of the elderly person *and* his living expenses. Answer C is correct both in the facts given and the deduction you can make from those facts. Social Security is a financial resource and since *more* people are receiving it, many of those persons will now have sufficient funds to no longer need OAA. Further, if the amount of a benefit increases, the amount of their financial resources also increases, so that persons who would have heretofore been eligible for OAA would no longer be eligible.

62. **(B)** The paragraph clearly states that the social workers began to view the character of many social injustices with a critical eye and were becoming aware of the deficiencies in these institutions in curing these injustices.

63. **(C)** The paragraph clearly states that professional social workers were becoming aware of the need for social reform because the traditional means of helping the poor (e.g., private charitable institutions, families, etc.) were inadequate to cope with the new factors "that were creating poverty and maladjustment."

64. **(A)** The whole tenor of the passage shows that social workers were becoming aware that social reform was needed. None of the wrong answers can be deduced or inferred from the passage.

65. **(C)** The last sentence of the passage states that an agreement to support form is signed by the legally responsible when 50% of the weekly surplus is at least $1.00 a week.

66. **(D)** The paragraph clearly states that no allowance for special needs is made, except for the certain instances also spelled out in the paragraph, "because only 50% of the budget surplus is required as payment for support of the child or children being cared for at public expense." There is nothing *in the paragraph* to indicate the other possible answers are correct.

67. **(B)** Mrs. B's OASDI benefits are $250 a month. The paragraph states that, in determin-

ing a legally responsible relative's income, "any portion of a government benefit not specifically designated for children already receiving care" is included as income. Accordingly, the $50 paid for Mary's care and the $50 paid for the other minor's care are deducted from Mrs. B's OASDI benefits from OASDI and must be considered in determining her budget surplus.

68. **(D)** The paragraph indicates Form W280 is used to compute family expenses. Form W281 is used to compute income and budget surplus. If the "bottom line" on Form W281 (i.e., income as given on Form 281 *minus* expenses as given on Form W280) indicates a surplus of at least $2.00 a week, Form W279 must be signed.

69. **(D)** Most cities and states, if providing for veteran assistance, do *not* consider nonveteran brothers or sisters, living with the veteran who is eligible for such assistance, as eligible for that form of assistance.

70. **(B)** This is a factual question. Care for children in foster homes is not provided for under the Federal Social Security Act and is, therefore, completely a local or state expense.

71. **(D)** The chief difference between public welfare and private social work agencies is that all major policies and procedures pursued by public agencies have their basis in statutes passed by the legislature of the governmental jurisdiction concerned and are signed by the head of that jurisdiction.

72. **(B)** Fuel and clothing items are all budgeted differently depending on the season of the year, and medical care is budgeted on an "as needed" basis. The cost of housing will generally not change during the year for a family on public assistance since most of them pay rent which will be the same amount each month.

73. **(D)** Good child welfare theory is that a child thrives best if his environment is similar to that provided children in their own homes. In the absence of such care, the best care for a well-adjusted child is a foster home since such care is closer to a normal home environment than is institutionalization.

74. **(A)** An interview with a client generally concerns specific information pertaining to eligibility for public assistance or to a client's problems or needs. It is best conducted in an atmosphere where the client will feel unselfconscious and free to give pertinent information of a private nature which he or she may not want others to hear and should, therefore, generally be conducted with only the Case Worker present. Note: Interviews are not "off the record" in public welfare agencies (Answer C).

75. **(B)** A client, especially if being interviewed in connection with personal or family problems, is often not aware or not fully aware of the reasons for particular actions and beliefs. It is the Case Worker's role to be aware of and to try to make the client understand the underlying reasons for such behavior in order to help the client decide on the best solutions.

76. **(C)** Applicants for public assistance, like most of the rest of us, have problems which we know to be real and complex. By telling a client "everything will be all right," you are misleading and making the client doubt your ability to understand the complexity of the problem and the difficulty in solving it, and may result in a loss of confidence in your interest and competence.

77. **(B)** The extent of note-taking needed while interviewing depends upon the nature of the discussion and the experience of the worker. In all cases, primary attention must be paid to what the client is saying, in order to maintain a dialogue with the client and not allow note-taking to interfere with the client's confidence in your ability to help and your interest in the problem.

78. **(C)** The best way to handle the situation presented is merely to remind the client that together you are focusing *solely* on his or her problems. A discussion of your personal affairs will not be useful in resolving any of these problems.

79. **(D)** A good relationship with a client requires that the Case Worker show genuine interest and concern in what the client believes to be real problems and in the client as a person. This requires you to understand the client's point of view but not necessarily agree with it. While it may be feasible in some instances to ask questions which allow the client to display knowledge, this technique exclusively, if overused, will not result in progress, and the relationship will deteriorate as the client begins to doubt your ability to help.

80. **(A)** The quotation reminds the Case Worker that personal attitude and beliefs, unless understood and accounted for, may distort finding a solution of the client's problems which will be acceptable to the client although not necessarily to the worker.

81. **(D)** A basic rule in good case work interviewing is that the client must be aware of being involved in the development and implementation of all decisions regarding any problems and their solutions. Only in this way will all facets of the problem and all pertinent information, including matters otherwise unknown to the interviewer, be considered before the solution is determined.

82. **(C)** In situations requiring interviews, research experience has shown that interviewees often tend to take the path of least resistance and give the interviewer the answers believed to be sought which may not be the real answers. Answers A and C may also occur with some clients, but the best answer has been found to be more universally true.

83. **(D)** The best way to obtain reliable information and lessen the chance of misunderstandings in case work interviewing is to make sure that the client understands both the reasons for the question and how the truthful, accurate answer will help solve problems or establish eligibility for public assistance. Other answers may result in misunderstandings (Answer A), prevarication (Answer B), or resentment (Answer C).

84. **(D)** *Basic* case work interviewing in a public setting requires that the worker generally assume that information the client furnishes is truthful unless reliable information or documentation to the contrary is in the worker's possession at the time the interview is being conducted or unless the client's information is so contrary to common sense that its truthfulness must be explored. This does *not* mean that certain required basic data to establish eligibility must be left unverified (e.g., age must be verified in determining eligibility for OASDI).

85. **(C)** The first interview with an applicant for public assistance is most important in obtaining facts that will be either accepted at face value or explored and verified in order to establish eligibility for public assistance. This first interview is also important in establishing a good relationship between the client and agency case worker. Asking questions requiring "yes" or "no" answers and allowing the client to tell his or her story while keeping the client to relevant facts is the best way to do this. To obtain the more basic data needed to establish eligibility is useful and insures uniformity and completeness of such data, but it is not as helpful in establishing the real reasons for a problem, the need for public assistance, or the good relationship required for an ongoing rapport. (Read the chapter entitled "Investigation Process" later in this book.)

86. **(B)** According to SSI, they *do not* give any money in this situation.

87. **(C)** The primary source for information about the family background and economic needs of a client is simply the client. Relatives, friends, records, employers, etc., are

secondary sources and may be consulted to verify certain information given by the client, but it is only from the client that the complete picture can be obtained.

88. **(D)** Residence verification is best obtained by the perusal of rent receipts. The other answers give no information and/or no verification of current residence.

89. **(A)** Vital statistics are kept by a local or state government agency and provide official record of births, deaths, and marriages in that locality. Such official information is vital in giving proof of age, parentage of a child, etc., which are often needed in establishing eligibility for certain types of public assistance.

90. **(D)** A case record contains the client's needs, problems, and other personal data which a client is often willing to impart only to the Case Worker. To give such information to other persons without first obtaining the permission of the client would make rapport with the client very difficult. It may result in the client's failure to give the worker information that is very important to a successful working relationship. Further, it may result in actual harm to the client if such data is seen without the client's permission by persons outside the agency.

91. **(D)** A good Case Worker must know when the help of a professional in another discipline is needed—medical, psychiatric, legal, etc.—and refer the client to this other source. At the same time, the worker must remain responsible for the entire case and coordinate activities with the other professional.

92. **(D)** This choice succinctly states the main point contained in this passage.

93. **(D)** This choice enunciates the socioeconomic problems that exist in this society, which could lead to the predicament this family now finds itself in.

94. **(B)** Of the choices given, this is the only one that presents a direct attempt at the solution of the problem. The three other choices contain facts that do not appear in the preamble of the question. They cannot be therefore given serious consideration.

95. **(D)** This is a tricky question since the passage states the laws in the State and City of New York. The passage therefore does not apply and the problem therefore should be researched consistent with laws existing in the locality given in the preamble of the question. Note that there is no indication that the person cannot find other work; and the inability to work is usually a primary factor in all localities to determine eligibility for public assistance.

96. **(C)** The passage states that eviction can never be considered discrimination when it is for nonpayment of rent. Therefore, the Case Worker must verify and determine the real reason for the eviction before proper action can be taken.

97. **(C)** The passage clearly indicates discrimination because of sexual preferences is illegal in New York State. Given the poor work history of the client, the reason for dismissal given by the client should be verified in order to determine if an antidiscrimination suit is appropriate in this instance. Note that the facts given in the question warrant a frank discussion with the client regarding her work habits and attitudes before advising her to file suit.

98. **(B)** Refer to the first sentence in the passage.

99. **(A)** Refer to the second sentence of the first paragraph. The other choices contain facts not included in the passage and therefore should not be considered.

100. **(D)** This choice of action not only represents all that one can do concerning this problem, but it is also likely to reassure the woman.

Answer Sheet for Practice Examination III

1. Ⓐ Ⓑ Ⓒ Ⓓ	21. Ⓐ Ⓑ Ⓒ Ⓓ	41. Ⓐ Ⓑ Ⓒ Ⓓ	61. Ⓐ Ⓑ Ⓒ Ⓓ	81. Ⓐ Ⓑ Ⓒ Ⓓ
2. Ⓐ Ⓑ Ⓒ Ⓓ	22. Ⓐ Ⓑ Ⓒ Ⓓ	42. Ⓐ Ⓑ Ⓒ Ⓓ	62. Ⓐ Ⓑ Ⓒ Ⓓ	82. Ⓐ Ⓑ Ⓒ Ⓓ
3. Ⓐ Ⓑ Ⓒ Ⓓ	23. Ⓐ Ⓑ Ⓒ Ⓓ	43. Ⓐ Ⓑ Ⓒ Ⓓ	63. Ⓐ Ⓑ Ⓒ Ⓓ	83. Ⓐ Ⓑ Ⓒ Ⓓ
4. Ⓐ Ⓑ Ⓒ Ⓓ	24. Ⓐ Ⓑ Ⓒ Ⓓ	44. Ⓐ Ⓑ Ⓒ Ⓓ	64. Ⓐ Ⓑ Ⓒ Ⓓ	84. Ⓐ Ⓑ Ⓒ Ⓓ
5. Ⓐ Ⓑ Ⓒ Ⓓ	25. Ⓐ Ⓑ Ⓒ Ⓓ	45. Ⓐ Ⓑ Ⓒ Ⓓ	65. Ⓐ Ⓑ Ⓒ Ⓓ	85. Ⓐ Ⓑ Ⓒ Ⓓ
6. Ⓐ Ⓑ Ⓒ Ⓓ	26. Ⓐ Ⓑ Ⓒ Ⓓ	46. Ⓐ Ⓑ Ⓒ Ⓓ	66. Ⓐ Ⓑ Ⓒ Ⓓ	86. Ⓐ Ⓑ Ⓒ Ⓓ
7. Ⓐ Ⓑ Ⓒ Ⓓ	27. Ⓐ Ⓑ Ⓒ Ⓓ	47. Ⓐ Ⓑ Ⓒ Ⓓ	67. Ⓐ Ⓑ Ⓒ Ⓓ	87. Ⓐ Ⓑ Ⓒ Ⓓ
8. Ⓐ Ⓑ Ⓒ Ⓓ	28. Ⓐ Ⓑ Ⓒ Ⓓ	48. Ⓐ Ⓑ Ⓒ Ⓓ	68. Ⓐ Ⓑ Ⓒ Ⓓ	88. Ⓐ Ⓑ Ⓒ Ⓓ
9. Ⓐ Ⓑ Ⓒ Ⓓ	29. Ⓐ Ⓑ Ⓒ Ⓓ	49. Ⓐ Ⓑ Ⓒ Ⓓ	69. Ⓐ Ⓑ Ⓒ Ⓓ	89. Ⓐ Ⓑ Ⓒ Ⓓ
10. Ⓐ Ⓑ Ⓒ Ⓓ	30. Ⓐ Ⓑ Ⓒ Ⓓ	50. Ⓐ Ⓑ Ⓒ Ⓓ	70. Ⓐ Ⓑ Ⓒ Ⓓ	90. Ⓐ Ⓑ Ⓒ Ⓓ
11. Ⓐ Ⓑ Ⓒ Ⓓ	31. Ⓐ Ⓑ Ⓒ Ⓓ	51. Ⓐ Ⓑ Ⓒ Ⓓ	71. Ⓐ Ⓑ Ⓒ Ⓓ	91. Ⓐ Ⓑ Ⓒ Ⓓ
12. Ⓐ Ⓑ Ⓒ Ⓓ	32. Ⓐ Ⓑ Ⓒ Ⓓ	52. Ⓐ Ⓑ Ⓒ Ⓓ	72. Ⓐ Ⓑ Ⓒ Ⓓ	92. Ⓐ Ⓑ Ⓒ Ⓓ
13. Ⓐ Ⓑ Ⓒ Ⓓ	33. Ⓐ Ⓑ Ⓒ Ⓓ	53. Ⓐ Ⓑ Ⓒ Ⓓ	73. Ⓐ Ⓑ Ⓒ Ⓓ	93. Ⓐ Ⓑ Ⓒ Ⓓ
14. Ⓐ Ⓑ Ⓒ Ⓓ	34. Ⓐ Ⓑ Ⓒ Ⓓ	54. Ⓐ Ⓑ Ⓒ Ⓓ	74. Ⓐ Ⓑ Ⓒ Ⓓ	94. Ⓐ Ⓑ Ⓒ Ⓓ
15. Ⓐ Ⓑ Ⓒ Ⓓ	35. Ⓐ Ⓑ Ⓒ Ⓓ	55. Ⓐ Ⓑ Ⓒ Ⓓ	75. Ⓐ Ⓑ Ⓒ Ⓓ	95. Ⓐ Ⓑ Ⓒ Ⓓ
16. Ⓐ Ⓑ Ⓒ Ⓓ	36. Ⓐ Ⓑ Ⓒ Ⓓ	56. Ⓐ Ⓑ Ⓒ Ⓓ	76. Ⓐ Ⓑ Ⓒ Ⓓ	96. Ⓐ Ⓑ Ⓒ Ⓓ
17. Ⓐ Ⓑ Ⓒ Ⓓ	37. Ⓐ Ⓑ Ⓒ Ⓓ	57. Ⓐ Ⓑ Ⓒ Ⓓ	77. Ⓐ Ⓑ Ⓒ Ⓓ	97. Ⓐ Ⓑ Ⓒ Ⓓ
18. Ⓐ Ⓑ Ⓒ Ⓓ	38. Ⓐ Ⓑ Ⓒ Ⓓ	58. Ⓐ Ⓑ Ⓒ Ⓓ	78. Ⓐ Ⓑ Ⓒ Ⓓ	98. Ⓐ Ⓑ Ⓒ Ⓓ
19. Ⓐ Ⓑ Ⓒ Ⓓ	39. Ⓐ Ⓑ Ⓒ Ⓓ	59. Ⓐ Ⓑ Ⓒ Ⓓ	79. Ⓐ Ⓑ Ⓒ Ⓓ	99. Ⓐ Ⓑ Ⓒ Ⓓ
20. Ⓐ Ⓑ Ⓒ Ⓓ	40. Ⓐ Ⓑ Ⓒ Ⓓ	60. Ⓐ Ⓑ Ⓒ Ⓓ	80. Ⓐ Ⓑ Ⓒ Ⓓ	100. Ⓐ Ⓑ Ⓒ Ⓓ

PRACTICE EXAMINATION III

Case Worker—Social Services

DIRECTIONS: Each Question has four suggested answers, lettered A,B,C, and D. Decide which one is the best answer and on the sample answer sheet locate the question number and darken the area with a soft pencil which corresponds to the answer that you have selected.

TIME ALLOWED FOR ENTIRE EXAMINATION: 3½ HOURS

1. The primary function of any Department of Social Services is to

(A) refer needy persons to legally responsible relatives for support
(B) enable needy persons to become self-supporting
(C) refer ineligible persons to private agencies
(D) grant aid to needy eligible persons.

2. A public assistance program objective should be designed to

(A) provide for eligible persons in accordance with their individual requirements and with consideration of the circumstances in which they live
(B) provide for eligible persons at a standard of living equal to that enjoyed while they were self-supporting
(C) make sure that assistance payments from public funds are not too liberal
(D) guard against providing a better living for persons receiving aid than is enjoyed by the most frugal independent families.

3. It is often stated that it would be better to abolish the need for relief rather than to extend the existing public assistance programs. This statement suggests that

(A) attempts should be made to eradicate those forces in our social organization which cause poverty
(B) public assistance should be limited to institutional care for rehabilitative purposes
(C) the support of needy persons should be the responsibility of their own families and relatives rather than that of the government
(D) the existing criteria used to determine "need" for public assistance are too liberal and should be modified to include a "work test."

4. The one of the following types of public assistance which is frequently described as a "special privilege" is

(A) veteran assistance
(B) emergency assistance
(C) aid to dependent children
(D) vocational rehabilitation of the handicapped.

91

5. The first form of *state* Social Security legislation developed in the United States was

   (A) health insurance
   (B) unemployment compensation
   (C) workmen's compensation
   (D) old age insurance.

6. Census Bureau reports show certain definite social trends in our population. One of these trends which was a major contributing factor in the establishment of the federal old age insurance system is the

   (A) increased rate of immigration to the United States
   (B) rate at which the number of Americans living to 65 years of age and beyond is increasing
   (C) increasing amounts spent for categorical relief in the country as a whole
   (D) number of states which have failed to meet their obligations in the care of the aged.

7. Reports show that more men than women are physically handicapped mainly because

   (A) men are more likely to be exposed to hazardous conditions
   (B) men are more likely to have congenital deformities
   (C) women tend to seek surgical remedies because of greater concern about personal appearance
   (D) men have less ability to recover from injury.

8. Of the following home conditions, the one most likely to cause emotional disturbances in children is

   (A) being the only child
   (B) disrupted family relationships
   (C) lower family income than that of neighbors
   (D) overcrowded living conditions.

9. Casual unemployment, as distinguished from other types of unemployment, is traceable most readily to

   (A) a decrease in the demand for labor as a result of scientific progress
   (B) more of less haphazard changes in the demand for labor in certain industries
   (C) periodic changes in the demand for labor in certain industries
   (D) disturbances and disruptions in industry resulting from international trade barriers.

10. Labor legislation, although primarily intended for the benefit of the employee, may aid an employer by

    (A) increasing his or her control over the immediate labor markets
    (B) prohibiting government interference with operating policies
    (C) protecting the employer, through equalization of labor costs, from being undercut by other employers
    (D) transferring to the general taxpayer the principal costs of industrial hazards of accident and unemployment.

11. When employment and unemployment figures both decline, the most probable conclusion is that

    (A) the population has reached a condition of equilibrium
    (B) seasonal employment has ended
    (C) the labor force has decreased
    (D) payments for unemployment insurance have been increased.

12. In evaluating the adequacy of an individual's income, a Case Worker should place primary emphasis on
    (A) its value in relation to the average income
    (B) the source of the income
    (C) its relation to the earning capacity of the individual
    (D) its purchasing power.

13. An individual with an I.Q. of 100 may be said to have demonstrated
    (A) superior intelligence
    (B) absolute intelligence
    (C) substandard intelligence
    (D) approximately average intelligence.

14. If a state passed a law in a field under Congressional jurisdiction and if Congress subsequently passed contrary legislation, the state provision would be
    (A) regarded as never having existed
    (B) valid until the next session of the state legislature, which would be obliged to repeal it
    (C) superseded by the federal statute
    (D) still operative in the state involved.

Questions 15 through 24 are based on the following table.

WELFARE CENTER CASELOAD SUMMARY, June–September 1988

	June	July	August	September
Total Cases under Care at End of Month	13,790	11,445	13,191	12,209
Home relief	4,739	2,512	6,055	5,118
Old-age assistance	5,337	b	5,440	2,265
Aid to dependent children	3,487	1,621	1,520	4,594
Aid to the blind	227	251	176	232
Net Change during Month	− 344	c	1,746	− 982
Applications Made during Month	1,542	789	3,153	1,791
Total Cases Accepted during Month	534	534	2,879	982
Home relief	278	213	342	338
Old-age assistance	43	161	1,409	f
Aid to dependent children	195	153	1,115	307
Aid to the blind	18	7	13	14
Total Cases Closed during Month	878	d	1,133	1,964
To private employment	326	1,197	460	870
To unemployment insurance	96	421	126	205
Reclassified	176	326	178	399
All other reasons	280	935	e	490
Total Cases Carried Over to Next Month	a	11,455	13,191	12,209

15. The number which should be placed in the blank indicated by a is

(A) 12,912
(B) 13,466
(C) 13,790
(D) None of the foregoing.

16. The number which should be placed in the blank indicated by b is

(A) 7,061
(B) 7,601
(C) 8,933
(D) None of the foregoing.

17. The number which should be placed in the blank indicated by c is

(A) −2,345
(B) −344
(C) 344
(D) None of the foregoing.

18. The number which should be placed in the blank indicated by d is

(A) 2,789
(B) 2,345
(C) 7,601
(D) None of the foregoing.

19. Of the total number of cases closed during the month of August, the percentage closed for reasons other than reclassification or receipt of unemployment insurance is approximately

(A) 13.8%
(B) 73.17%
(C) 26.83%
(D) 40.60%.

20. In comparing June and July, the figures indicate that with respect to the total cases under care at the end of each month

(A) the percentage of total cases accepted during the month was lower in June
(B) the percentage of total cases accepted during the month was higher in June
(C) the percentage of total cases accepted during both months was the same
(D) there is insufficient data for comparision of the total cases under care at the end of each month.

21. The total number of cases accepted during the entire period in the category in which most cases were accepted was

(A) 1,409
(B) 1,936
(C) 1,770
(D) 4,929.

22. In comparing July and September, the figures indicate that

(A) more cases were closed in September because of private employment
(B) the total number of cases accepted during the month consisted of a greater proportion of home relief cases in September
(C) in one of these months, there were more total cases under care at the end of the month than at the beginning of the month
(D) none of the foregoing is correct.

23. The total number of applications made during the four-month period was

(A) more than four times the number of cases closed because of private employment during the same period
(B) less than the combined totals of aid-to-dependent-children cases under care in June and July
(C) 4,376 more than the total number of cases accepted during August
(D) 5,916 less than the total number of cases carried over to September.

24. The ratio of old age assistance cases accepted in August to the total number of such cases under care at the end of that month is expressed with the greatest degree of accuracy by the figures

(A) 1:4
(B) 1:25
(C) 4:1
(D) 10:39.

25. The term *mores* refers to

(A) English meadows
(B) bribery
(C) social customs
(D) telegraphic code.

26. *Disparity* refers most directly to

(A) difference
(B) argument
(C) low wages
(D) separation.

27. The technical term used to express the ratio between mental and chronological age is called the

(A) mentality rating
(B) intelligence quotient
(C) psychometric standard
(D) achievement index.

28. In social case work, the disorganizing factors in a personal or familial situation which prevent or hinder rehabilitation are called

(A) median deviations
(B) transference situations
(C) rank correlations
(D) liabilities.

29. The period in the life of some persons when mental abilities begin to deteriorate is known as

(A) puberty
(B) antiquity
(C) gerontology
(D) senility.

Questions 30 through 32 are based on the following passage:

Aid to dependent children shall be given to a parent or other relative as herein specified for the benefit of a child or children under sixteen years of age or of a minor or minors between sixteen and eighteen years of age if in the judgment of the administrative agency: (1) the granting of an allowance will be in the interest of such child or minor, and (2) the parent or other relative is a fit person to bring up such child or minor so that his physical, mental, and moral well-being will be safeguarded, and (3) aid is necessary to enable such parent or other relative to do so, and (4) such child or minor is a resident of the state on the date of application for aid, and (5) such minor between sixteen and eighteen years of age is regularly attending school in accordance with the regulations of the department. An allowance may be granted for the aid of such child or minor who has been deprived of parental support or care by reason of death, continued absence from the home, or physical or mental incapacity of parent, and who is living with his father, mother, grandfather, grandmother, brother, sister, stepfather, stepmother, stepbrother, stepsister, uncle, or aunt. In making such allowances, consideration shall be given to the ability of the relative making application and of any other relatives to support and care for or to contribute to the support and care of such child or minor. In making all such allowances, it shall be made certain that the religious faith of the child or minor shall be preserved and protected.

30. The preceding passage is concerned primarily with

    (A) the financial ability of persons applying for public assistance
    (B) compliance on the part of applicants with the "settlement" provisions of the law
    (C) the fitness of parents or other relatives to bring up physically, mentally, or morally delinquent children between the ages of sixteen and eighteen
    (D) eligibility for aid to families with dependent children.

31. On the basis of the preceding passage, the most accurate of the following statements is

    (A) Mary Doe, mother of John, age 18, is entitled to aid for her son if he is attending school regularly
    (B) Evelyn Stowe, mother of Eleanor, age 13, is not entitled to aid for Eleanor if she uses her home for immoral purposes.
    (C) Ann Roe, cousin of Helen, age 14, is entitled to aid for Helen if the latter is living with her.
    (D) Peter Moe, uncle of Henry, age 15, is not entitled to aid for Henry if the latter is living with him.

32. The preceding passage is probably an excerpt from a

    (A) City's Administrative Code
    (B) State's Social Welfare Law
    (C) Federal Security Act
    (D) City's Charter.

33. The length of residence required to make a person eligible for the various forms of public assistance available in the United States

    (A) is the same in all states but is different among different public assistance programs in a given state
    (B) is the same in all states and among different public assistance programs in a given state
    (C) is the same in all states for different categories
    (D) varies among states and among different assistance programs in a given state.

34. Social Welfare Law often requires that whenever an applicant for aid to dependent children resides in a place where there is a central index or a social services exchange, the public welfare official shall register the case with such index or exchange. This requirement is for the purpose of

(A) preventing duplication and coordinating the work of public and private agencies
(B) establishing prior claims on the amounts of assistance furnished when repayments are made
(C) having the social service exchange determine which agency should handle the case
(D) providing statistical data regarding the number of persons receiving grants for aid to dependent children.

35. A person who knowingly brings a needy person from one state into another state for the purpose of making him or her a public charge is generally guilty of

(A) violation of the Displaced Persons Act
(B) violation of the Mann Act
(C) a felony
(D) a misdemeanor.

36. Generally pauperization, or loss of initiative and interest in self-help as a result of an experience as a welfare recipient,

(A) will not occur if assistance is only sufficient to cover bare necessities
(B) occurs if dependency continues over a long period
(C) occurs in communities in which wages are low
(D) occurs in periods in which there is not lack of goods, but of jobs.

37. Of the several activities of our government that contribute to the general welfare of our national community, the one *not* generally conceded to be available to the individual as a matter of right is

(A) public health services
(B) public education
(C) public parks, playgrounds, and adult recreation centers
(D) public assistance.

38. Adoption laws tend to place increased emphasis upon

(A) informal signing of adoption papers
(B) lowered residence requirements for adoption
(C) establishment of the child's inheritance rights
(D) social investigation of the home before adoption.

39. Any person or organization soliciting donations in public places in New York City is required to have a license issued by the

(A) Police Department
(B) Department of Sanitation
(C) Division of Labor Relations
(D) Department of Social Services.

40. A person who, though himself or herself in good health, harbors disease germs which may be passed on to others, is called

(A) an instigator
(B) a carrier
(C) an incubator
(D) an inoculator.

41. Diseases most commonly caused by certain working environments or conditions are known as

    (A) infectious diseases
    (B) contagious diseases
    (C) occupational diseases
    (D) hereditary diseases.

42. The process of destroying microorganisms which cause disease or infection is called

    (A) contamination
    (B) immunization
    (C) inoculation
    (D) sterilization.

43. Proper utilization of the term *carious* would involve reference to

    (A) teeth
    (B) curiosity
    (C) shipment of food packages to needy persons in Europe
    (D) hazardous or precarious situations.

44. The chemical agent which has been used extensively to control the spread of syphilis infection is

    (A) cortisone
    (B) penicillin
    (C) D.D.T.
    (D) ephedrine.

45. The medical term for "hardening of the arteries" is

    (A) carcinoma
    (B) arthritis
    (C) thrombosis
    (D) arteriosclerosis.

46. A set of symptoms which occur together is called a

    (A) sympathin
    (B) syncope
    (C) syndrome
    (D) synecdoche.

47. If the characteristics of a person were being studied by competent observers, it would be expected that their observations would differ most markedly with respect to their evaluation of the person's

    (A) intelligence
    (B) height
    (C) temperamental characteristics
    (D) weight.

48. If there are evidences of dietary deficiency in families where cereals make up a major portion of the diet, the most likely reason for this deficiency is that

    (A) cereals cause absorption of excessive water
    (B) persons who concentrate their diet on cereals do not chew their food properly
    (C) carbohydrates are deleterious
    (D) other essential food elements are omitted.

49. Although malnutrition is generally associated with poverty, dietary studies of population groups in the United States reveal that

(A) malnutrition is most often due to a deficiency of nutrients found chiefly in high-cost foods

(B) there has been overemphasis of the causal relationship between poverty and malnutrition

(C) malnutrition is found among people with sufficient money to be well fed

(D) a majority of the population in all income groups is undernourished.

50. A medically trained person who treats mental diseases is called

(A) a psychologist

(B) a sociologist

(C) a psychiatrist

(D) a physiologist.

51. The organization which has as one of its primary functions the mitigation of suffering caused by famine, fire, floods, and other national calamities is the

(A) National Safety Council

(B) Salvation Army

(C) Public Administration Service

(D) American Red Cross.

52. In the welfare system of any state the broad policies and patterns of social services are laid down by

(A) the people of each state through its legislature

(B) the state's board of Social Welfare

(C) the state's Department of Social Welfare

(D) each of the local city, county, or town public welfare districts for their respective jurisdictions.

53. A recipient of public assistance in New York City who is in need of the services of an attorney but is unable to pay the customary fees, should generally be referred to the

(A) Small Claims Court

(B) Legal Aid Society

(C) New York County Lawyers Association

(D) New York City Corporation Counsel.

54. An injured worker should attempt to obtain compensation through the state's

(A) Labor Relations Board

(B) Division of Placement and Unemployment insurance

(C) Industrial Commission

(D) Workers' Compensation Board.

55. Anything concerned with the art of healing or with remedies for disease is described as

(A) therapeutic

(B) thereputic

(C) therapetic

(D) theraputic.

56. The most frequent cause of "broken homes" is attributed to the

(A) temperamental incompatibilities of parents and in-laws

(B) extension of the system of children's courts

(C) death of one or both spouses

(D) institutionalization of one of the spouses.

57. In rearing children, the problems of the widower are traditionally greater than those of the widow, largely because of the

(A) tendency of widowers to impose excessively rigid moral standards
(B) increased economic hardship
(C) added difficulty of maintaining a desirable home
(D) possibility that a stepmother will be added to the household.

58. After interviewing a client who complains about the inadequate size of his living quarters, the one of the following words which the Case Worker might properly use in the record of the interview is

(A) spaceal
(B) spaciel
(C) spatial
(D) spatiel.

59. One of the most common characteristics of the chronic alcoholic is

(A) low intelligence level
(B) wanderlust
(C) psychosis
(D) egocentricity.

60. Of the following factors leading toward the cure of the alcoholic, the most important is thought to be

(A) removal of all alcohol from the immediate environment
(B) development of a sense of personal adequacy
(C) social disapproval of drinking
(D) segregation from former companions.

61. Paul R., age 19, is employed and, as a member of a household in which public assistance is received, he is expected to contribute a major share of his earnings to the family. His mother requests an increase in her allowance because Paul will not make his proper contribution and threatens to leave home altogether. As the Case Worker in this case, you should

(A) tell the mother it is her responsibility to see that Paul does his share, and no increase can be granted
(B) give the increase because, if Paul leaves home, it will cost the local department of welfare more in the long run
(C) try to determine the character of Paul's relationship with the members of his family, their attitudes towards money in general and his money and his behavior in particular, and work out a solution with him and them
(D) see Paul alone and interpret the law and eligibility requirements so that he will understand and conform with them.

62. An individual suffering from a mental disorder characterized by some eccentricity or emotional instability is frequently found to be

(A) psychopatic
(B) psycopatic
(C) psycopathic
(D) psychopathic.

63. Because circumstances under which applications are made to a Department of Welfare are so often the result of financial conditions, the nature of home relief assistance is usually

(A) monetory
(B) monetary
(C) monitory
(D) monitary.

64. Another way of expressing a financial relationship is by describing it as

(A) pecuniary
(B) pecuniory
(C) pecunary
(D) picuniary.

65. An unfortunate occurrence which threatens to happen immediately is one that is

(A) immanent
(B) immenent
(C) imminent
(D) omenent.

66. A Case Worker assigned to the child welfare program would occasionally mention in his or her reports the science which treats the hygiene and diseases of children. Of the following, the word which should be used is

(A) pidiatrics
(B) pediatrics
(C) pideatrics
(D) pedeatrics.

67. Strabismus is usually associated with

(A) hearing
(B) sight
(C) blood pressure
(D) bone structure.

68. The Rorschach Test is best described as a type of

(A) reading scale
(B) loyalty investigation
(C) achievement profile
(D) personality test.

69. A type of neurotic impulse which manifests itself in a desire to steal without any economic motive is known as

(A) neurasthenia
(B) introversion
(C) kleptomania
(D) recidivism.

70. The science having to do with the betterment of living conditions to secure more efficient human beings is

(A) euthenics
(B) economics
(C) eugenics
(D) genetics.

71. A personality restraint imposed upon one psychical activity by another, which is harmful and may lead to mental illness, is known as

(A) expression
(B) transference
(C) symbiosis
(D) inhibition.

72. The ophthalmic professions are concerned principally with problems affecting
    (A) eyesight
    (B) drugs
    (C) prognostication
    (D) weather control.

73. When a public assistance agency assigns its most experienced interviewers to conduct initial interviews with applicants, the most important reason for its action is that
    (A) experienced workers are always older, and therefore command the respect of applicants
    (B) the applicant may be given a complete understanding of the procedures to be followed and the time involved in obtaining assistance payments
    (C) applicants with fraudulent intentions will be detected and prevented from obtaining further services from the agency
    (D) the applicant may be given an understanding of the purpose of the assistance program and of the bases for granting assistance in addition to the routine information.

74. Responsibility for fully informing the public about the availability of public assistance can most successfully be discharged by
    (A) local public assistance agencies
    (B) social service exchanges
    (C) community chest organizations
    (D) councils of social agencies.

75. In closing the case of a client, the Case Worker should attempt to give the client
    (A) a feeling of being rejected by the agency as a worthy person
    (B) an idea of the progress of similar cases being handled by the agency
    (C) an understanding that his or her case could be reopened for full assistance if necessary, but not for emergency assistance
    (D) an explanation of the conditions upon which he or she might make reapplication

76. One of the major purposes of the federal Social Security insurance system for unemployment compensation and old age and survivors insurance is to
    (A) lessen the need for public assistance because it is degrading for the individual
    (B) provide maintenance of income for the people deprived of such, in order to keep the economy in balance
    (C) make certain that no one goes hungry in this land of abundance
    (D) bring order out of the chaos of 50 state laws.

77. Of the following public welfare services, the one *not* carried as a direct responsibility of the New York government is
    (A) treatment and custodial care of the mentally ill
    (B) care, training, and treatment of the mentally deficient
    (C) institutional care and training of the physically handicapped
    (D) care, training, and support of dependent children in foster care.

78. Chronological old age is usually accompanied by recognizable characteristics. Of the following, the one not generally characteristic of old age is
    (A) lessening of the affectional contribution in a relationship
    (B) lessening of the capacity for sustained work
    (C) chronic and progressive illness of a disabling nature
    (D) lessening of physical adequacy.

79. An emotionally mature adult is a person who has

(A) no need to be dependent on others and who is proud of his or her independence and ability to help others who are dependent on him or her
(B) little need for satisfaction from social relationships and who is able to live comfortably alone
(C) insight into and understanding of his or her emotional needs and strengths
(D) considerable need to depend on others and to be loved and cared for.

80. An essential part of the Case Worker's job is recording the facts of a client situation, the client's activity in self-help, and the Worker's activity in the client's behalf. Of the several methods of recording a case history, the topical summary

(A) is best because it contains only pertinent information, and is most economical of time for writer and readers
(B) has value only for certain types of interviews because it does not reflect, where necessary, the client's movement and the Case Worker's activity
(C) is a good method because it is easiest for the new and inexperienced Case Worker to use
(D) in not a good method because it tends to make the Case Worker follow the outline in the interviews as well as in the recording.

81. In making a social study of an application for service, a thorough review of the previous history of a family's contacts with the Department of Social Service, contained in the Department's case records, is

(A) not important because current eligibility is based on contemporary facts and these will have to be secured and verified anew
(B) important because the Case Worker can anticipate whether he or she will have trouble with the family in determining their eligibility by learning how they behaved in the past
(C) important but should not be made until after the Case Worker has formed his or her own opinion in personal contact, because previous Workers' opinions may prejudice him or her
(D) important so that current investigation can be focused on such additional information as is needed, with a minimum of time and effort and in a manner that will be of help to the family.

82. "It is recognized that many workers choosing public welfare as their field of professional activity have done so out of readiness to live beyond themselves, out of their liking and concern for people." This quotation suggests that these workers

(A) have no personal needs to be realized in their work
(B) have readiness to understand and some capacity to deal with their own personal needs
(C) have a neurotic basis for their choice of vocation
(D) have a tendency to reform their clients.

83. "The fact that an individual receives his means of support from an assistance agency rather than from wages or other recognized income is a fact of difference from his neighbors that cannot be denied or dismissed lightly. There is a deeply rooted tradition in this country that the person who is 'anybody' supports himself by his own efforts, that there is something wrong about getting one's support from a source created by the whole. Thus the individual who gets his support from a social agency is considered in a group apart and different from his neighbours." Relating this statement to his or her practice, the Case Worker should

(A) recognize the client as different and give such case work service as will enable him to become a member of the self-supporting community as soon as possible

(B) explain to each client that he or she understands the difficulties of asking for and receiving help, and there is no need to be self-conscious with him or her

(C) analyze his or her own feelings towards the particular clients to secure some insight into how he or she personally relates to this cultural pattern and to them, and what his or her own attitudes towards dependency are

(D) make strenuous efforts to change the cultural pattern of the community, which is harmful to so large a part of it.

84. "No piece of social legislation, no matter how worthy its objectives, is any better than its administration. And yet, simultaneously, it must be recognized that administration is the servant of social objectives, never the master." The application of this principle to practice means that the Case Worker should

(A) not help to have the law improved until administration catches up with the philosophy of the current law

(B) not have to feel any responsibility toward the function he or she represents

(C) handle each on an individual basis, making such exceptions to general policy as are indicated by the need of the client

(D) always work within the existing limitations of agency function, however narrow and punitive it may seem to him or her in relation to a particular case.

85. Mr. W. comes to a Department of Social Services to request assistance. He matter-of-factly presents his situation, methodically submits bills, receipts, and other verification documents, and then asks how much help he will get and how soon he may expect it. This behavior should indicate to an alert Case Worker that Mr. W.

(A) is probably a relatively secure adult with considerable strength and capacity for independence

(B) is probably a chronically dependent person who has been through this routine so often before that he has the procedure memorized

(C) is a naturally aggressive individual accustomed to sweeping everything before him in the accomplishment of his purpose

(D) has probably prepared a fictitious story in order to hide his real situation and "beat" the eligibility requirements.

86. Ms. L., an unmarried mother, has applied for temporary placement of her half-year-old baby until she "gets back on her feet." Her financial resources are almost exhausted. In making the investigation the Case Worker learns that the baby was born strong and well-developed, but is now pale and thin. He is not taken regularly to a "well baby" clinic. He cries a great deal, particularly when his mother picks him up. She handles him roughly, complaining about her loss of sleep because the baby is spoiled and cranky. He has a feeding problem and, the Case Worker observes, if he refuses the first offer of food, it is withdrawn immediately. In this case the Case Worker should

(A) refer Ms. L. for Aid to Families with Dependent Children, because regular income may make her more comfortable and more patient with the baby, and babies are better off with their own mothers

(B) discuss the possibilities for and encourage a decision to place the baby for adoption, since there are indications of the mother's emotional rejection of the baby in his and her behavior

(C) go along with the mother's plan since she knows her situation best

(D) refer Ms. L. to a psychiatric clinic since her behavior is definitely pathological.

Questions 87 through 92 are based on the following table:

Distribution of Welfare Households in Yaggerstown by Number of Public Assistance Recipients January 1985 and December 1987

Number of Recipients in Household	Thousands of Households		Percentage Change 1985–1987	Percentage Distribution	
	Jan. 1985	Dec. 1987		Jan. 1985	Dec. 1987
1	119.4	164.6	37.9	37.3	39.2
2	97.8	134.9	37.9	30.5	32.1
3	61.3	76.0	24.0	19.2	?
4	?	29.8	10.4	8.4	7.1
5	6.4	6.5	1.6	2.0	1.6
6	8.3	7.8	6.0	2.6	1.9
TOTAL	320.3	419.8	?	100.0	100.0

Distributions may not add exactly to totals because of rounding.

87. The number of households having four or more recipients in the household in January 1985 was most nearly

(A) 2,700
(B) 27,000
(C) 4,200
(D) 42,000

88. The total percentage change in the distribution of welfare households in 1985-1987 is

(A) 186.5%
(B) 180.5%
(C) 24%
(D) 31.1%

89. The % change during 1985-1987 for households with 6 or more recipients is

(A) 5%
(B) 6%
(C) .93%
(D) 1.17%

90. The average percentage change between July 1985 and December 1987 is most nearly

(A) 37.9%
(B) 19.63%
(C) 23.56%
(D) 117.8%

91. The percentage distribution of households having three recipients in the household in December 1987 is most nearly

(A) 13.7%
(B) 16.4%
(C) 18.1%
(D) 81.9%

92. In January 1985, the percentage of households that contain six recipients receiving public assistance was most nearly

(A) 26%
(B) 2½%
(C) 4%
(D) 6%

Answer questions 93 through 95 only on the basis of the information contained in the following passage.

The Medicaid program is designed to aid low-income people who cannot pay for their own medical care. In order to be eligible, an individual must meet certain income and assets limitations. The program is directly administered by local social services agencies throughout the United States under the overall supervision of each state's Department of Social Services in accordance with both federal and state regulations. The eligibility rules may differ somewhat in each state but are similar and follow guidelines.

If you are found eligible for Medicaid, your medical bills will be paid in whole or in part. In New York State, you must be a resident of the state, a citizen of the United States, or an alien admitted for lawful permanent residence in the United States, or have resided in the state continuously since June 30, 1948. In New York State, you meet the financial requirements for Medicaid eligibility if you receive public assistance or Supplementary Security Income (SSI). You may also be eligible for Medicaid depending on your income and assets (property and/or money) you possess, and on the extent of your medical expenses. You may also be found qualified for Medicaid if you meet the criteria for disability which are given in the Federal Social Security Act and if your assets (money and property) and medical expenses warrant it. You may also be eligible if you received both Social Security and Supplementary Security Income (SSI) at the same time but were later found ineligible for SSI.

93. Based on the passage, medical bills may be paid through the Medicaid program and administered by New York State if the individual meets the income and assets requirements and is

(A) a citizen of France visiting New York City and becomes ill
(B) a U.S. citizen and resident of New Jersey working in New York and becomes hospitalized in New York City
(C) a naturalized American residing in New York State for five years
(D) a Brazilian youth residing in New York on a student visa.

94. Assume that you are a Case Worker in the public assistance division of a social services center in Badgerville, New York. After investigation, you determine that you must deny the application for supplementary assistance of an obviously ill man and his family because he works on a part-time basis which puts his funds just above the income level allowed for such assistance. He complains bitterly that just because he works, even though he is frequently ill, his family cannot get assistance and he cannot afford to visit the doctor to cure his chronic bronchitis. You should

(A) make an exception in this case and approve the family's application for public assistance
(B) deny the application but suggest the man apply for Medicaid for himself and his family
(C) deny the application and explain the importance of finding full-time work so that he can take proper care of his health
(D) deny his application and inform him that he can probably get free medical assistance from a municipal health or hospital clinic.

95. A middle-aged severely disabled woman living in New York City complains to you, the worker in a public assistance center, that she must have assistance in paying the medical bills she has been receiving from her private doctor. She formerly received SSI as well as Social Security, but due to a recent slight increase in the amount of her monthly Social Security check, she has been found ineligible for continued SSI. You should

(A) have her apply for supplementary public assistance
(B) refer her to the state office handling SSI for reconsideration of her case
(C) refer her to the nearest municipal hospital
(D) refer her to possible acceptance on Medicaid.

Answer questions 96 through 100 based solely on the information contained in the following passage.

One of the problems involved in living to an older age is the increasing possibility of becoming homeless. Because both pensions and Social Security benefits have not kept up with rising inflation and with rent costs, many elderly persons find it impossible to pay their rent and upkeep of their apartments or homes. Most homeowners over 65 have homes which predate the 1920s and, therefore, require higher costs for maintenance than most elderly couples or individuals can afford. In addition, the elimination of federally funded housing projects and the lack of transitional shelters have resulted in an urban-wide increase in homelessness in which the elderly are just one more group seeking places to live.

The problem is further exacerbated by the fact that many homeless elderly people are former mental patients who have recently been released from institutions. While an institution is not the best place for rehabilitation and healthy living, the decision to deinstitutionalize many of these persons without first providing adequate alternate community mental health care programs for them in our communities has resulted in increased numbers of homeless and has broadened the scope of the problem of homelessness. Many of these individuals, both young and old, are disoriented and unable to cope with the decisions they must make in their daily lives. Since many of the elderly deinstitutionalized homeless have spent a large period of their lives in institutions, this unsupervised discharge into general community life has been particularly traumatic.

96. According to the passage, the elimination of federal funds for housing projects has resulted in

(A) the inability of a number of elderly homeless people to move into housing projects
(B) an exacerbated conflict between the elderly and the young people seeking apartments in housing projects
(C) severe trauma among elderly people who prefer the safety and security of living in housing projects to living in other types of living quarters
(D) no special problem to elderly people who as a whole prefer to live in their own homes.

97. Based on the passage, in comparison with younger people returned to the community from mental institutions, elderly people in the same situation

(A) are more able to cope with homelessness since they have more life experience than do younger people
(B) are more disadvantaged because many of them have spent a large part of their lives in a sheltered environment
(C) frequently must be returned to the mental institution because they cannot find places to live
(D) frequently are ill-treated or abused by the community-at-large because of their inability to cope with normal people.

98. In a few large cities, rent increases on certain apartments are controlled or stabilized if the tenants are elderly. It can be inferred from the passage that this practice

(A) makes the homeless problem for the elderly in such cities nonexistent

(B) would not affect the mentally ill elderly since they are returned to the institution if they cannot pay their rent

(C) would not affect most of the elderly since they own their own homes

(D) would result in those elderly people being able to remain in the same apartments in which they have been domiciled

99. Based on the passage, of the following, a major cause for homelessness among the elderly is the

(A) inability to properly manage their funds

(B) ineligibility of many elderly persons for Social Security or pension funds

(C) failure of the amount of monthly received Social Security funds to meet rising housing and general living costs

(D) inability of elderly people to compete with younger, more aggressive people for vacant apartments

100. According to the paragraph, the need for many elderly people to abandon their private homes is due to

(A) poor management on the part of these elderly people

(B) preference of such elderly people to live in apartment houses when they can no longer cope with the management of a home

(C) the rising costs of maintenance of their homes

(D) their inability to continue to pay the high interest on the mortgages on their homes

Correct Answers for Practice Examination III

1. D	21. B	41. C	61. C	81. D
2. A	22. D	42. D	62. D	82. B
3. A	23. D	43. A	63. B	83. C
4. A	24. D	44. B	64. A	84. C
5. C	25. C	45. D	65. C	85. A
6. B	26. A	46. C	66. B	86. B
7. A	27. B	47. C	67. B	87. D
8. B	28. D	48. D	68. D	88. D
9. B	29. D	49. C	69. C	89. B
10. C	30. D	50. C	70. A	90. B
11. C	31. B	51. D	71. D	91. C
12. D	32. B	52. A	72. A	92. B
13. D	33. D	53. B	73. D	93. C
14. C	34. A	54. D	74. A	94. B
15. C	35. D	55. A	75. D	95. D
16. A	36. B	56. C	76. B	96. A
17. A	37. D	57. C	77. D	97. B
18. D	38. D	58. C	78. A	98. D
19. B	39. D	59. D	79. C	99. C
20. A	40. B	60. B	80. A	100. C

Explanations of Correct Answers for Practice Examination III

1. **(D)** The chief duty of a public welfare agency is to investigate the eligibility of a person or family applying for public assistance and to grant such assistance to those found eligible.

2. **(A)** The level of assistance granted an individual or family by a public agency should enable the recipients to have the standard of living established under the appropriate statutes of that community or state. The amount of actual money required depends on the individual circumstances. Thus, for example, if housing is available to the client, no rent is included in their budget. Standard amounts of money are provided for basic necessities, e.g., x amount of dollars for food for y number of persons on assistance, but special individual needs may also be provided (e.g., for purchase of special food if the client has medical need, etc.).

3. **(A)** The correct answer suggests that attempts should be made to eradicate the forces in society that cause poverty. This is an extension of the statement given in the question. Other possible answers cannot be deduced from the statement given.

4. **(A)** Public assistance accorded to a group deemed to be worthy of special attention (like veterans of the armed forces) is generally referred to as a "special privilege" category.

5. **(C)** This is a factual question, the answer to which should be part of a Case Worker's general knowledge. Workman's compensation is granted to anyone, regardless of financial status, who is injured during working hours at the place of or in the pursuit of employment, and can provide the injured person with funds while unable to work.

6. **(B)** A major reason for the passage of the Federal Age Insurance System (Social Security) legislation was the ever-growing rate of increase in the number of persons who live beyond the age of 65. It became evident that a method was needed to insure that such persons should continue to live in an acceptable manner after they could no longer successfully compete in the labor market. Personal savings from prior years' employment was often insufficient, as people continued to live to older and older ages.

7. **(A)** Employee health and accident statistics show that many occupations traditionally reserved to males are more hazardous than those in which both males and females or just females are employed. Service in the armed forces, especially during wartime, also increased the number of males who are physically handicapped.

8. **(B)** Social work and psychological studies have shown that children brought up in homes where family relationships are disrupted are more likely to have emotional problems than children living under the conditions described in the wrong answers.

9. **(B)** Casual unemployment, i.e., frequent periods of unemployment between the same type of job or the same job, results from the irregular demand for workers in a particular industry, e.g., a factory or industry where the demand for unskilled help fluctuates haphazardly.

10. **(C)** Labor legislation may be helpful to employers because it forces all employers in the same industry to pay at least the same minimum wages, provide the same workman's compensation, disability insurance, etc. This equalizes much of the labor costs in an industry and lessens the ability of the company to cut labor costs and thus sell the product being manufactured at a lower price than competitors.

11. **(C)** When there are both fewer employees and fewer unemployed, the labor force, i.e., the number of persons available for work, has decreased.

12. **(D)** The purchasing power of the dollar, i.e., the monetary cost of purchasing goods and services, varies from one locale to another and differs due to economic conditions in that locale. The public assistance individual's income, therefore, must be evaluated in terms of its purchasing power. The same dollar amount the client possesses in times of depression which enables self-sufficiency, for example, may be insufficient in periods of inflation.

13. **(D)** An IQ of 100 is demonstrative of average intelligence. IQs below the 100 mark are demonstrative of varying degrees of substandard intelligence. IQs above 100 are demonstrative of varying degrees of superior intelligence.

14. **(C)** Basic constitutional law in the United States provides that a federal law supersedes a state law. Note: Answer A is wrong because the state law is in effect *until* federal law supersedes it.

15. **(C)** You are asked the number of cases carried over from June to July 1988. This would be the same number appearing on the first line of the chart which is labelled "Total Cases under Care at End of Month," i.e., 13,790.

16. **(A)** You are asked for the total number of OAA cases at the end of July.
    Total number of Public Assistance cases at the end of July = 11,445
    Total number of Public Assistance cases *except* for OAA at the end of July = 4,384
    Therefore, the number of OAA cases = 11,445 − 4,384 = 7,061

17. **(A)** You are asked to give the net change in the number of cases between the end of June and the end of July.
    Total number of cases at the end of June =   13,790
    Total number of cases at the end of July =   11,445

    Answer =   2,345

18. **(D)** You are asked for the total number of cases closed in July. You are given four categories comprising case closings and the numbers of cases closed in each category. The total of those numbers equals the total number of cases closed, i.e., 1,197 + 421 + 326 + 935 = 2,879. This number is *not* given as any of the possible answers.

19. **(B)** Find the number of cases closed in August for "all other reasons."
    Total number of cases closed in August = 1,113
    Total number of cases closed in August except for other reasons = 829
    The percentage of (2) above, i.e., 829 to the total number of cases closed, 1,113 = 73.17% (829 ÷ 1,113)

20. **(A)** Number of total cases accepted in June = 534
    Total cases in June = 13,790. 534 ÷ 13,790 = .038%
    Number of total cases accepted in July = 534
    Total cases in July = 11,145. 534 ÷ 11,445 = .05%

21. **(B)** First you must determine what (F) is (i.e., the number of Old Age Assistance cases accepted in September). It is 323.
    Total number of cases accepted in September = 982
    Total number of non-OAA cases accepted in September = 659
    Total number of OAA cases accepted in September = 323
    Inspection will show you that HR cases and AB cases can be eliminated.
    Total number of OAA cases accepted in four months = 43 + 161 + 1,409 + 323 = 1,936
    Total number of AD cases accepted in four months = 195 + 153 + 1,115 + 307 = 1,770
    Therefore, the 1,936 cases accepted in the OAA category is the correct answer.

22. **(D)** You must test possible answers A, B, and C to see which, if any, are correct: A is wrong. Private employment resulted in case closing of 870 cases in September and 1,197 cases in July. Answer B is wrong. In September 338 HR cases were accepted out of a total of 982 cases accepted that month, 34.42% In July, 213 Home Relief cases out of a total of 534 cases were accepted = 39.89%. Answer C is wrong. In July, the total number of cases under care at the end of the month = 13,790 − 11,445 = 2,345 *fewer* cases. In September, 13,191 − 12,209 = 1,981 *fewer* cases.

23. **(D)** Total number of applications made = 1,542 in June + 789 in July + 3,153 in August + 1,791 in September = 7,275 applications made in four months. Test each possible answer:
    In Answer A, the total number of cases closed by private employment = 326 + 1,197 + 460 + 870 = 2,853. The number of cases closed by employment, 7,275, is *not* four times 2,853. Thus, Answer A is wrong. In Answer B, ADC cases under care in June and July = 3,487 + 1,621 = 5,108. 7,275 is more than 5,108. So, Answer B is also wrong. In Answer C, the total number of cases accepted in August = 2,879. 7,275 − 2,879 = 4,396 cases. So, Answer C is wrong as well. In Answer D, the total number of cases carried over to September = 13,191. 13,191 − 7,275 = 5,916. This is the correct answer.

24. **(D)** In ratio and proportion problems, you establish a relationship between the two variables.
    1409:5440 = .259
        10/39 = .256
    Answer D is the most accurate of the choices given.

25. **(C)** A *more* is a social custom.

26. **(A)** Disparity refers to difference.

27. **(B)** An intelligence quotient is derived by dividing the mental age of the individual being tested by his/her chronological age:

$$\frac{\text{level of intelligence per test}}{\text{chronological age of testee}} = \frac{1,500}{15} = 100 \text{ IQ}$$

28. **(D)** This is a factual question. Answers A and C are mathematical/statistical terms. Transference situations (Answer B) refer to psychological situations.

29. **(D)** Senility is the technical word for the condition which may occur in a person's life when his/her mental abilities begin to deteriorate.

30. **(D)** The paragraph concerns the facts that must be considered and the rules which must apply in establishing eligibility in the category of public assistance called Aid to Families with Dependent Children.

31. **(B)** The paragraph clearly states that eligibility for AFDC is conditioned upon whether the parent of other relatives applying for the assistant is a "fit" person to bring up such a child so that his "physical, mental, or moral well-being will be safeguarded." Such a situation is not indicated in the situation described in the correct answer. Note that Answer A is incorrect because the child is 18 years of age. Answers C and D are not true according to the paragraph.

32. **(B)** The paragraph concerns the legal requirements for eligibility for the Aid to Families With Dependent Children's category of public assistance. This program is a state-wide program, and the statutes governing such a program would be found in the state's welfare laws.

33. **(D)** The correct answer is self-explanatory.

34. **(A)** A central index or a social service exchange will contain information about all families who have sought or are seeking social services and/or financial aid. Registration of all such cases and study of the cases listed by other agencies will prevent duplication of effort and will help coordinate activities concerned with the children and family.

35. **(D)** In most states, the action indicated in the sentence would make the person who committed such action guilty of a misdemeanor. None of the other answers are appropriate to the action described.

36. **(B)** Social welfare studies have determined that if dependency on public assistance continues for a long period of time, the recipients often lose their desire to be financially independent or to make their own decisions. Thus, it is important to require recipients to seek and accept employment if the physical, social, and family conditions enable them to do so, and to make their own final decisions to the solutions of their problems.

37. **(D)** *All* of us are entitled, as a right, to use of public health, public education, and public parks/recreation facilities. All of us have a right to *apply* for public assistance, but it is granted only if eligibility requirements are met.

38. **(D)** Experts in the theory and practice of adoption have found that prior knowledge of the proposed adoptive parent's home life through home investigations leads to a more successful adoption.

39. **(D)** The social service agency in most localities is responsible for validating charities within its areas.

Questions 40-46 require knowledge of medical terms which social case workers may encounter in their work. It is suggested that you consult your dictionary if you are unfamiliar with any of the terms listed right or wrong.

40. **(B)**

41. **(C)**

42. **(D)**

43. **(A)**

44. **(B)**

45. **(D)**

46. **(C)**

47. **(C)** Height and weight are easily and accurately measured. Standardized tests result in marks which measure intelligence with sufficient accuracy so that most experts utilizing such tests will come out with the same evaluation of a person's intelligence. Observance of temperamental characteristics are *not* scientifically measured, and experts frequently differ in their evaluations depending on the tests used, the expert's own biases, the situation surrounding the observations, etc.

48. **(D)** While cereals can provide many nutritional benefits, a diet made up largely of cereal will result in a deficiency of the essential food elements not found in cereal.

49. **(C)** Dietary studies, especially in the United States, show that many of us, although affluent enough to feed ourselves properly, suffer from malnutrition because we prefer to eat foods lacking in nutritional value ("junk food") rather than nutritive foods and/or diet-conscious but not diet-wise foods.

50. **(C)** A good Case Worker should know the meanings of all four of these occupations. Consult your dictionary if you have difficulties with the meaning of any of these occupations.

51. **(D)** This is a factual question. Case Workers should be aware of the functions and purposes of the American Red Cross.

52. **(A)** The broad policies and patterns of social services in the United States are determined by each state legislature elected by the voters of that state. The individual state's Board or Department of Social Services administers the social services programs and promulgates rules and regulations to implement the broad policies and may also administer/audit programs. Local, city, county, or town public welfare agencies actually carry out public welfare activities subject to review by the state authorities.

53. **(B)** The Legal Aid Society may also be known as the public defender in other localities.

54. **(D)** Compensation for work-related injuries is provided through a State Workers' Compensation Board. A state's Labor Relations Board is generally concerned with matters dealing with employer (industry)/worker (union) relations. A Department of Placement and Unemployment Insurance administers the granting of money and attempts to find employment for people who lose their jobs and are unable to find other employment on their own. A State Industrial Commission is generally not concerned with individual workers.

55. **(A)** The correct spelling is *therapeutic*.

56. **(C)** A broken home is one in which one of the parents is no longer living in the home. Of the possible answers, the most frequent cause of a broken home is the death of one of the spouses.

57. **(C)** Traditionally, a widower has more trouble in raising children because he has been the breadwinner and must continue to be away from the home for a good part of the day, leaving the care of the house and children to relatives or paid helpers.

58. **(C)** The correct spelling of the word is *spatial*.

59. **(D)** Studies of chronic alcoholics show many such individuals to be concerned with and unwilling or unable to focus on problems outside of their own immediate concern.

60. **(B)** The three wrong answers are only temporary deterrents to continuance of alcoholism. The cure must be linked to a personality change. The alcoholic must be convinced of personal worth, of the ability to resist alcohol, and of the ability to resume a worthwhile place in society.

61. **(C)** In the situation described, the 19-year-old working son is, according to the mother, not making his proper financial contribution to the household and is threatening to leave the home. The mother is, therefore, requesting an increase in the public assistance allowance currently received. The budget for the family *cannot* be changed as long as the boy is working and lives in the household (wrong Answer B). The best thing to do is to meet with the boy and the family and after full discussion, as given in the correct answer, determine with them how best to resolve the problem. Answers A and D may result in the boy leaving home, causing both loss of his income to the family and a serious deterioration of the familial relationships.

Questions 62 through 66 are an exercise in evaluating one's knowledge of the spelling of terms often used in Case Work.

62. **(D)**

63. **(B)**

64. **(A)**

65. **(C)**

66. **(B)**

67. **(B)** Strabismus is a disorder of vision due to the inability of one or both eyes to turn from the normal position. Therefore, both eyes cannot be directed at the same point or object at the same time (i.e. squint or cross-eye).

68. **(D)** The Rorschach Test is a standardized personality test. The person being tested is asked to explain what he "sees" in each of two series of ink blots. A trained psychologist is able to interpret personality factors from the test-taker's responses.

69. **(C)** The neurotic condition described is called kleptomania. Case Workers should be familiar with the meaning of the wrong answers. Consult your dictionary if you are unsure of their meanings.

70. **(A)** The correct answer is euthenics. Look up the meanings of the wrong answers if you are unsure of them.

71. **(D)** Inhibition is the correct word for the mental process that restrains an action. Look up the meanings of the words given in the wrong answers to be sure you understand their psychological and scientific meanings.

72. **(A)** Ophthalmic professions are concerned with eye problems. Note: You should know the differences between optometrists, ophthalmologists, and opticians. Use your dictionary.

73. **(D)** At the initial interview with an applicant for public assistance, the purpose of the programs, the basic rules for eligibility, and the responsibilities in proving eligibility must be explained and understood. The ability to impart this data to a new applicant and to set the proper tone for future relations between the applicant and the agency requires skills which are best taught by experience. For further information about intake procedures, read "The Investigative Process" chapter later in this book.

74. **(A)** Only a governmental agency may be assigned the responsibility under the law to inform the public at large of the availability of public assistance. This is ordinarily done by the local social service agency.

75. **(D)** Good social case work policy in a public welfare agency requires that the client whose case is being closed knows the reason(s) for the closing and the conditions under which future acceptance for public assistance may be possible. Thus, if a case is closed because, for example, employment has been obtained which pays sufficient money to meet all needs on public assistance standards, the client must know reapplication and public acceptance for public assistance is possible if the employment is terminated.

76. **(B)** Answer B is entirely correct because of the stated and implied purpose of the function. Choice A is incorrect because the process may be degrading to some, but it is not degrading to all its beneficiaries. This choice is too positive. If people have money, they will spend it and the businesses dependent on this spending will not suffer. Thus, the economy will stay in balance.

77. **(D)** Self-explanatory. New York State is responsible for the other categories listed. The category in Answer A is assumed by local government.

78. **(A)** Every profession has its jargon, and social work is no exception. Don't be put off by the language of the correct answer. It is typical of some of the material you may have read. Old age does *not* affect one's ability to love others. It does frequently have the characteristics given in the wrong answers.

79. **(C)** One who is emotionally mature knows himself or herself, including any emotional weaknesses and strengths and, to an extent, their reasons. The wrong answers may be true of some emotionally mature people, but these characteristics do not differentiate them from emotionally immature individuals.

80. **(A)** A topical summary of a case situation will give both the reader and the worker a quick concise picture of the important elements in the case, including the problems and the steps being taken towards their solutions.

81. **(D)** A Case Worker should thoroughly examine case records concerning a family's past contacts with the agency under the circumstances described because it will avoid duplication of investigation verification. Further, discussion which has been thoroughly investigated and verified can then lead to concentration on current problems and/or changes in the situations, e.g., the death of the father of a family need not be discussed if previously verified.

82. **(B)** The quotation states many public welfare workers do so "out of readiness to live beyond themselves, out of their liking and concern for people." Such persons are able to understand their own needs and then go beyond concentration on such personal needs to think about and have concern for others. None of the other answers are implied in the quotation.

83. **(C)** The quotation concerns the fact that society in general feels that people on public assistance are somehow set apart and are different from the rest of society. It is *most* important that a Case Worker in a public agency examine personal attitudes and prejudices towards public assistance in general and his or her own case load in particular in

order to be able to relate objectively to them as individuals able to be understood and assisted.

84. **(C)** The Case Worker who follows the principle stated in the quotation will handle each client as an individual with individual problems and will try to obtain exceptions to general policy and rules if such exceptions are needed to realize the individual's social objectives.

85. **(A)** In this situation, the applicant, Mr. W, displays ideal client behavior, and it can be deduced that he is a relatively secure individual with the strength of character needed to remain independent and possibly to become self-supporting again.

86. **(B)** The course of action indicated in Answer B would at least serve to determine the mother's feelings towards the adoption of her child who is apparently causing her difficulties. After ascertaining the mother's feelings along these lines, appropriate action can then be taken. Money alone (Answer A) is not likely to solve the problem. Answers C and D are also faulty because obviously the mother is not doing what is best for the child at the present time, and the determination that the mother is pathological is not supported by the evidence given in the preamble of the question.

87. **(D)** Add all figures which are given in column one; total 293.2. Subtract this figure, 293.2, from 320.3 to obtain the missing number, 27.1. Then add 27.1 plus 6.4 plus 8.3 = 41.8. Multiply 41.8 by 1000 = 41,800 (most nearly).

88. **(D)** 419.8 minus 320.3 = 99.5
    99.5 divided by 320.3 = 31.1%

89. **(B)** This answer is a gift. Read it right from the table. The percentage change from 1985 to 1987 in a 6 recipient household is 6%.

90. **(B)** Add all of the changes in percents which are given for period 1985-1987. The total is 117.8. Obtain the average by dividing by 6. Answer 19.63%.

91. **(C)** Add all percent distributions given for December 1987. Total 81.9. Subtract 81.9% from 100% = 18.1%

92. **(B)** Divide 8.3 by 320.3. The answer is .0259, which is closest to 2½%.

93. **(C)** The passage clearly indicates a citizen residing in New York State must be eligible.

94. **(B)** Regulations must be adhered to; however, the suggestion that Medicaid benefits might solve his problem is the only course you, as a Case Worker, might take.

95. **(D)** The paragraph clearly indicates the strong possibility that this woman too might qualify for medicaid benefits.

96. **(A)** The passage implies that because of the curb on the building housing projects, and the withholding of federal funds for that purpose, the elderly among others have a reduced opportunity to move into housing projects. The other choices contain statements which may or may not be true. However, they cannot by implied from the information contained in the passage.

97. **(B)** Refer to the last sentence of the passage.

98. **(D)** The passage indicates tha the inability of the elderly to pay increased rents because they are on fixed incomes is alleviated in some large cities by rent control laws.

99. **(C)** Second sentence of first paragraph.

100. **(C)** Second sentence of first paragraph.

Answer Sheet for Practice Examination IV

1. Ⓐ Ⓑ Ⓒ Ⓓ
2. Ⓐ Ⓑ Ⓒ Ⓓ
3. Ⓐ Ⓑ Ⓒ Ⓓ
4. Ⓐ Ⓑ Ⓒ Ⓓ
5. Ⓐ Ⓑ Ⓒ Ⓓ
6. Ⓐ Ⓑ Ⓒ Ⓓ
7. Ⓐ Ⓑ Ⓒ Ⓓ
8. Ⓐ Ⓑ Ⓒ Ⓓ
9. Ⓐ Ⓑ Ⓒ Ⓓ
10. Ⓐ Ⓑ Ⓒ Ⓓ
11. Ⓐ Ⓑ Ⓒ Ⓓ
12. Ⓐ Ⓑ Ⓒ Ⓓ
13. Ⓐ Ⓑ Ⓒ Ⓓ
14. Ⓐ Ⓑ Ⓒ Ⓓ
15. Ⓐ Ⓑ Ⓒ Ⓓ
16. Ⓐ Ⓑ Ⓒ Ⓓ
17. Ⓐ Ⓑ Ⓒ Ⓓ
18. Ⓐ Ⓑ Ⓒ Ⓓ
19. Ⓐ Ⓑ Ⓒ Ⓓ
20. Ⓐ Ⓑ Ⓒ Ⓓ

21. Ⓐ Ⓑ Ⓒ Ⓓ
22. Ⓐ Ⓑ Ⓒ Ⓓ
23. Ⓐ Ⓑ Ⓒ Ⓓ
24. Ⓐ Ⓑ Ⓒ Ⓓ
25. Ⓐ Ⓑ Ⓒ Ⓓ
26. Ⓐ Ⓑ Ⓒ Ⓓ
27. Ⓐ Ⓑ Ⓒ Ⓓ
28. Ⓐ Ⓑ Ⓒ Ⓓ
29. Ⓐ Ⓑ Ⓒ Ⓓ
30. Ⓐ Ⓑ Ⓒ Ⓓ
31. Ⓐ Ⓑ Ⓒ Ⓓ
32. Ⓐ Ⓑ Ⓒ Ⓓ
33. Ⓐ Ⓑ Ⓒ Ⓓ
34. Ⓐ Ⓑ Ⓒ Ⓓ
35. Ⓐ Ⓑ Ⓒ Ⓓ
36. Ⓐ Ⓑ Ⓒ Ⓓ
37. Ⓐ Ⓑ Ⓒ Ⓓ
38. Ⓐ Ⓑ Ⓒ Ⓓ
39. Ⓐ Ⓑ Ⓒ Ⓓ
40. Ⓐ Ⓑ Ⓒ Ⓓ

41. Ⓐ Ⓑ Ⓒ Ⓓ
42. Ⓐ Ⓑ Ⓒ Ⓓ
43. Ⓐ Ⓑ Ⓒ Ⓓ
44. Ⓐ Ⓑ Ⓒ Ⓓ
45. Ⓐ Ⓑ Ⓒ Ⓓ
46. Ⓐ Ⓑ Ⓒ Ⓓ
47. Ⓐ Ⓑ Ⓒ Ⓓ
48. Ⓐ Ⓑ Ⓒ Ⓓ
49. Ⓐ Ⓑ Ⓒ Ⓓ
50. Ⓐ Ⓑ Ⓒ Ⓓ
51. Ⓐ Ⓑ Ⓒ Ⓓ
52. Ⓐ Ⓑ Ⓒ Ⓓ
53. Ⓐ Ⓑ Ⓒ Ⓓ
54. Ⓐ Ⓑ Ⓒ Ⓓ
55. Ⓐ Ⓑ Ⓒ Ⓓ
56. Ⓐ Ⓑ Ⓒ Ⓓ
57. Ⓐ Ⓑ Ⓒ Ⓓ
58. Ⓐ Ⓑ Ⓒ Ⓓ
59. Ⓐ Ⓑ Ⓒ Ⓓ
60. Ⓐ Ⓑ Ⓒ Ⓓ

61. Ⓐ Ⓑ Ⓒ Ⓓ
62. Ⓐ Ⓑ Ⓒ Ⓓ
63. Ⓐ Ⓑ Ⓒ Ⓓ
64. Ⓐ Ⓑ Ⓒ Ⓓ
65. Ⓐ Ⓑ Ⓒ Ⓓ
66. Ⓐ Ⓑ Ⓒ Ⓓ
67. Ⓐ Ⓑ Ⓒ Ⓓ
68. Ⓐ Ⓑ Ⓒ Ⓓ
69. Ⓐ Ⓑ Ⓒ Ⓓ
70. Ⓐ Ⓑ Ⓒ Ⓓ
71. Ⓐ Ⓑ Ⓒ Ⓓ
72. Ⓐ Ⓑ Ⓒ Ⓓ
73. Ⓐ Ⓑ Ⓒ Ⓓ
74. Ⓐ Ⓑ Ⓒ Ⓓ
75. Ⓐ Ⓑ Ⓒ Ⓓ
76. Ⓐ Ⓑ Ⓒ Ⓓ
77. Ⓐ Ⓑ Ⓒ Ⓓ
78. Ⓐ Ⓑ Ⓒ Ⓓ
79. Ⓐ Ⓑ Ⓒ Ⓓ
80. Ⓐ Ⓑ Ⓒ Ⓓ

81. Ⓐ Ⓑ Ⓒ Ⓓ
82. Ⓐ Ⓑ Ⓒ Ⓓ
83. Ⓐ Ⓑ Ⓒ Ⓓ
84. Ⓐ Ⓑ Ⓒ Ⓓ
85. Ⓐ Ⓑ Ⓒ Ⓓ
86. Ⓐ Ⓑ Ⓒ Ⓓ
87. Ⓐ Ⓑ Ⓒ Ⓓ
88. Ⓐ Ⓑ Ⓒ Ⓓ
89. Ⓐ Ⓑ Ⓒ Ⓓ
90. Ⓐ Ⓑ Ⓒ Ⓓ
91. Ⓐ Ⓑ Ⓒ Ⓓ
92. Ⓐ Ⓑ Ⓒ Ⓓ
93. Ⓐ Ⓑ Ⓒ Ⓓ
94. Ⓐ Ⓑ Ⓒ Ⓓ
95. Ⓐ Ⓑ Ⓒ Ⓓ
96. Ⓐ Ⓑ Ⓒ Ⓓ
97. Ⓐ Ⓑ Ⓒ Ⓓ
98. Ⓐ Ⓑ Ⓒ Ⓓ
99. Ⓐ Ⓑ Ⓒ Ⓓ
100. Ⓐ Ⓑ Ⓒ Ⓓ

PRACTICE EXAMINATION IV

Eligibility Specialist

DIRECTIONS: Each question has four suggested answers, lettered A,B,C, and D. Decide which one is the best answer and on the sample answer sheet locate the question number and with a soft pencil darken the area which corresponds to the answer that you have selected.

TIME ALLOWED FOR THE ENTIRE EXAMINATION: 3½ HOURS

1. As an Eligibilty Specialist you find that an applicant for public assistance is hesitant about showing you some required personal material and documents. Your initial reaction to this situation should be to

   (A) quietly insist that the applicant give you the required materials
   (B) make an exception in this case to avoid making the applicant uncomfortable
   (C) suspect that the applicant may be trying to withold evidence
   (D) understand that the applicant is in a stressful situation and may feel ashamed to reveal such information

2. An applicant has just given an Eligibilty Specialist a response which does not seem clear. Of the following, the best course of action to take in order to check his or her understanding of the applicant's response is to

   (A) ask the question again during a subsequent interview with this applicant
   (B) repeat the applicant's answer in the applicant's own words and ask if that is what the applicant means
   (C) later in the interview, repeat the question that led to this response
   (D) repeat the question that led to this response, but say it more forcefully.

3. While speaking with applicants for public assistance, an Eligibility Specialist may find that there are times when an applicant will be silent for a short while before answering questions. In order to gather the best information from the applicant, the interview should generally treat these silences by

   (A) repeating the same question to make the applicant stop hesitating
   (B) rephrasing the question in a way that the applicant can answer it faster
   (C) directing an easier question to the applicant so that he or she can gain confidence in answering
   (D) waiting patiently and not pressuring the applicant into quick undeveloped answers.

4. In dealing with members of different ethnic and religious groups among the applicants he or she interviews, the Eligibility Specialist should give

   (A) individuals the services to which they are entitled
   (B) less service to those he or she judges to be more advantaged
   (C) better service to groups with which he or she sympathizes most
   (D) better service to groups with political "muscle."

5. As an Eligibility Specialist you must be sure that, when interviewing an applicant, you phrase each question carefully. Of the following, the most important reason for this is to insure that

(A) the applicant will phrase each of his or her responses carefully
(B) you use correct grammar
(C) it is clear to the applicant what information you are seeking
(D) you do not word the same questions differently for different applicants.

6. When given a form to complete, a client hesitates, tells you that he cannot fill out forms too well and that he is afraid he will do a poor job. He asks you to do it for him. You are quite sure, however, that he is able to do it himself. In this case, it would be most advisable for you, as an Eligibility Specialist to

(A) encourage him to try filling out the application as well as he can
(B) fill out the applications for him
(C) explain to him that he must learn to accept responsibility
(D) tell him that if others can fill out an application he can too.

7. Assume that an applicant for public assistance whom you are interviewing has made a statement that is obviously not true. Of the following, the best course of action for you, an Eligibility Specialist, to take at this point in the interview is to

(A) ask the applicant if he or she is sure about this statement
(B) tell the applicant that this statement is incorrect
(C) question the applicant further to clarify his or her response
(D) assume that the statement is correct.

8. Assume that you, an Eligibility Specialist, are conducting an initial interview with an applicant for public assistance. Of the following, the most advisable questions for you to ask at the beginning of this interview are questions that

(A) can be answered in one or two sentences
(B) have nothing to do with the subject matter of the interview
(C) are most likely to reveal any hostility on the part of the applicant
(D) the applicant is most likely to be willing and able to answer.

9. When interviewing a particularly nervous and upset applicant for public assistance, the one of the following actions which you should take first is to

(A) inform the applicant that, to be helped, he or she must cooperate
(B) advise the applicant that proof must be provided for statements he or she makes
(C) assure the applicant that every effort will be made to provide him or her with whatever assistance applicants are entitled to
(D) tell the applicant he or she will have no trouble obtaining public assistance so long as he or she is truthful.

10. Assume that, as an Eligibility Specialist, it is part of your job to prepare a monthly report for your unit head that eventually goes to the director of your Welfare Center. The report contains information on the number of applicants you have interviewed that have been approved for different types of public assistance and the number of applicants you have interviewed that have been turned down. Errors on such reports are serious because

(A) you are expected to be able to prove how many applicants you have interviewed each month
(B) accurate statistics are needed for effective management of the department
(C) they may not be discovered before the report is transmitted to the Welfare Center director
(D) they may result in a loss of assistance to the applicants left out of the report.

11. During interviews, people give information about themselves in several ways. Which of the following usually gives the least amount of information about the person being questioned?

(A) their spoken words
(B) their tones of voice
(C) their facial expressions
(D) their body positions.

12. Suppose a male applicant, while being interviewed about his eligibility for public assistance, becomes angered by your questioning and begins to use sharp, uncontrolled language. Which of the following is the best way for you to react to him?

(A) Speak in his style to show him that you are neither impressed nor upset by his speech.
(B) Interrupt him and tell him that you are not required to listen to this kind of speech.
(C) Lower your voice and slow the rate of your speech in an attempt to set an example that will calm him.
(D) Let him continue in his way but insist that he answer your questions directly.

13. You have been informed that no determination has yet been made on the eligibility of an applicant for public assistance. The decision depends on further checking. Her situation, however, is similar to that of many other applicants whose eligibility has been approved. The applicant calls you, quite worried, and asks you whether her application has been accepted. What would be best for you to do under these circumstances? Tell her

(A) that her application is being checked and you will let her know the final result as soon as possible
(B) that a written request addressed to your supervisor will probably get faster action for her case
(C) not to worry since other applicants with similar backgrounds have already been accepted
(D) since there is no definite information and you are very busy, you will call her back.

14. Suppose that you have been talking with an applicant for public assistance. You have the feeling from the latest things the applicant has said that some of his or her answers to earlier questions were not totally correct. You guess that he or she might have been afraid or confused earlier but that your conversation has now put him or her in a more comfortable frame of mind. In order to test the reliability of information received from the earlier questions, the best thing for you to do now is to ask new questions that

(A) allow the applicant to explain why he or she deliberately gave false information to you
(B) ask for the same information, although worded differently from the original questions
(C) put pressure on the applicant so that he or she personally wants to clear up the facts in the earlier answers
(D) indicate to the applicant that you are aware of his or her deceptiveness.

15. Assume that you are an Eligibility Specialist. While providing you with required information, an applicant for public assistance informs you that she does not know who is the father of her child. Of the following, the most advisable action for you to take at this time is to

(A) ask her to explain further
(B) advise her about birth control facilities
(C) express your sympathy for the situation
(D) go on to the next item of information.

16. If, in an interview, you wish to determine a client's usual occupation, which one of the following questions is most likely to elicit the most useful information?

(A) Did you ever work in a factory?
(B) Do you know how to do office work?
(C) What kind of work do you do?
(D) Where are you working now?

17. Assume that, as an Eligibility Specialist, you are approached by a clerk from another office who starts questioning you about one of the clients you have just interviewed. The clerk says that she is a relative of the client. According to departmental policy, all matters discussed with clients are to be kept confidential. Of the following, the best course of action for you to take in this situation would be to

(A) check to see whether the clerk is really a relative before you make any further decision
(B) explain to the clerk why you cannot divulge the information
(C) tell the clerk that you do not know the answers to her questions
(D) tell the clerk that she can get from the client any information the client wishes to give.

18. Which of the following is usually the best technique for you, as an interviewer, to use to bring an applicant back to subject matter from which the applicant has strayed?

(A) Ask the applicant a question that is related to the subject of the interview.
(B) Show the applicant that his or her response is unrelated to the question.
(C) Discretely remind the applicant that there is a time allotment for the interview.
(D) Tell the applicant that you will be happy to discuss the extraneous matters at a future interview.

19. Assume that, as an Eligibility Specialist, you notice that your co-worker has accidentally pulled the wrong form to give to her client. Of the following, the best way for you to handle this situation would be to tell

(A) the other Eligibility Specialist about her error, and precisely describe the problems that will result
(B) the other Eligibility Specialist about her error in an understanding and friendly way
(C) the other Eligibility Specialist about her error in a humorous way and tell her that no real damage was done
(D) your supervisor that Eligibility Specialists need more training in the use and application of departmental forms.

20. Of the following characteristics, the one which would be most valuable to an Eligibility Specialist when helping an angry client to understand why he has received less assistance than he believes he is entitled to, would be the ability to

(A) state the rules exactly as they apply to the applicant's problem
(B) cite examples of other cases where the results have been similar
(C) remain patient and understanding of the person's feelings
(D) remain completely objective and uninvolved in individual personal problems.

21. Of the following, the most reasonable implication of the preceding question is that an Eligibility Specialist should, when speaking to a client, control and use his or her voice to

(A) simulate a feeling of interest in the problems of the client
(B) express emotions directly and adequately
(C) help produce in the client a sense of comfort and security
(D) reflect his or her own true personality.

22. Suppose you are writing a report on an interview you have just completed with a particularly hostile applicant for public assistance. Which of the following best describes what you should include in this report?

   (A) What you think caused the applicant's hostile attitude during the interview.
   (B) Specific examples of the applicant's hostile remarks and behavior.
   (C) The relevant information uncovered during the interview.
   (D) A recommendation that the applicant's request be denied because of his or her hostility.

23. When including recommendations in a report to your supervisor, which of the following is most important for you to do?

   (A) Provide several alternate courses of action for each recommendation.
   (B) First present the supporting evidence, then the recommendations.
   (C) First present the recommendations, then the supporting evidence.
   (D) Make sure the recommendations arise logically out of the information in the report.

24. It is often necessary that the writer of a report present facts and sufficient arguments to gain acceptance of the points, conclusions, or recommendations set forth in the report. Of the following, the least advisable step to take in organizing a report, when such argumentation is the important factor, is

   (A) an elaborate expression of personal belief
   (B) a businesslike discussion of the problem as a whole
   (C) an orderly arrangement of convincing data
   (D) a reasonable explanation of the primary issues

Answer questions 25 through 33 on the basis of the information in the following passage.

The establishment of a procedure whereby the client's rent is paid directly by the Social Service agency has been suggested recently by many people in the Social Service field. It is believed that such a procedure would be advantageous to both that agency and the client. Under the current system, clients often complain that their rent allowances are not for the correct amount. Agencies, in turn, have had to cope with irate landlords who complain that they are not receiving rent checks until much later than their due date.

The proposed new system would involve direct payment of the client's rent by the agency to the landlord. Clients would not receive a monthly rent allowance. Under one possible implementation of such a system, special rent payment offices would be set up in each of the five boroughs in Midvale City, and staffed by Social Service clerical personnel. Each office would handle all work involved in sending out monthly rent payments. Each client would receive monthly notification from the Social Service agency that the rent has been paid. A rent office would be established for every three Social Service centers in each borough. Only in cases where the rental exceeds $350 per month would payment be made and records kept by the Social Service center itself rather than a special rent office. However, clients would continue to make all direct contacts through the Social Service center.

Files in the rent offices would be organized on the basis of client rental. All cases involving monthly rents up to, but not exceeding, $150 would be placed in salmon-colored folders. Cases with rents from $151 to $250 would be placed in buff folders and those with rents exceeding $250 but less than $350 would be filed in blue folders. If a client's rental changed he or she would be required to notify the center as soon as possible, so that this information could be brought up-to-date in the folder and the color of the folder changed if necessary. Included in the information needed, in addition to the amount of rent, are the size of the apartment, the type of heat, and the number of flights of stairs to climb if there is no elevator.

Discussion as to whether the same information should be required of clients residing in City housing projects was resolved with the decision that the identical system of filing and updating of files should apply to such project tenants. The basic problem that might arise from the institution of such a program is that clients would resent being unable to pay their own rent. However, it is likely that such resentment would be only a temporary reaction to change and would disappear after the new system became standard procedure. It has been suggested that this program first be experimented with on a small scale to determine what problems may arise and how the program can be best implemented.

25. According to the passage, there are a number of complaints about the current system of rent payments. Which of the following is a complaint expressed in the passage?

   (A) Landlords complain that clients sometimes pay the wrong amount for their rent.
   (B) Landlords complain that clients sometimes do not pay their rent on time.
   (C) Clients say that the Social Service agency sometimes does not mail the rent out on time.
   (D) Landlords say that they sometimes fail to receive a check for the rent.

26. Assume that there are 15 Social Service centers in one borough of Midvale City. According to the passage, the number of rent offices that should be established in that borough under the new system is

   (A) 1
   (B) 3
   (C) 5
   (D) 15

27. According to the passage, a client under the new system would receive

   (A) a rent receipt from the landlord indicating that Social Services has paid the rent
   (B) nothing, since the rent has been paid by Social Services
   (C) verification from the landlord that the rent was paid
   (D) notices of rent payment from the Social Service agency.

28. According to the passage, a case record involving a client whose rent has changed from $155 to $270 per month should be changed from a

   (A) blue folder to a salmon-colored folder
   (B) buff folder to a blue folder
   (C) salmon-colored folder to a blue folder
   (D) yellow folder to a buff folder.

29. According to the passage, if a client's rental is lowered because of violations in his or her building, he or she would be required to notify the

   (A) building department
   (B) landlord
   (C) rent payment office
   (D) Social Service center.

30. Which of the following kinds of information about a rented apartment is not mentioned in the passage as being necessary to include in the client's folder?

   (A) The floor number, if in an apartment house with an elevator
   (B) the rental, if in a City Housing project apartment
   (C) the size of the apartment, if in a two-family house
   (D) The type of heat, if in a City Housing project apartment.

31. Assume that the rent payment proposal discussed in the passage is approved and ready for implementation in the City of Midvale. Which of the following actions is most in accordance with the proposal described in the passage?

    (A) Change over completely and quickly to the new system to avoid the confusion of having clients under both systems.
    (B) Establish rent payment offices in all of the existing Social Service centers.
    (C) Establish one small rent payment office in one of the boroughs for about six months.
    (D) Set up an office in each borough and discontinue issuing rent allowances.

32. According to the passage, it can be inferred that the most important drawback of the new system would be that once a program is started clients might feel

    (A) they have less independence than they had before
    (B) unable to cope with problems that mature people should be able to handle
    (C) too far removed from Social Service personnel to successfully adapt to the new requirements
    (D) too independent to work with the system.

33. The passage suggests that the proposed rent program be started as a pilot program rather than be instituted immediately throughout the City of Midvale. Of the following possible reasons for a pilot program, the one which is stated in the passage as the most direct reason is that

    (A) any change made would then be only on a temporary basis
    (B) difficulties should be determined from small-scale implementation
    (C) implementation on a wide scale is extremely difficult
    (D) many clients might resent the new systems.

34. Suppose you receive a phone call from an applicant about a problem which requires that you look up the information and call her back. Although the applicant had given you her name earlier and you can pronounce the name, you are not sure that you can spell it correctly. Asking the applicant to spell her name is

    (A) good, because this indicates to the applicant that you intend to obtain the information she requested
    (B) poor, because she may feel you are making fun of her name
    (C) good, because you will be sure to get the correct name
    (D) poor, because she will think you have not been listening to her.

35. A report is often revised several times before final preparation and distribution in an effort to make certain the report meets the needs of the situation for which it is designed. Which of the following is the best way for the author to be sure that a report covers the areas he or she intended?

    (A) Obtain a co-worker's opinion.
    (B) Compare it with a content checklist.
    (C) Test it on a subordinate.
    (D) Check the bibliography.

36. Visual aids in a report may be placed either in the text material or in the appendix. Deciding where to put a chart, table, or any such aid should depend on the

    (A) title of the report
    (B) purpose of the visual aid
    (C) title of the visual aid
    (C) length of the report.

37. In which of the following situations is an oral report preferable to a written report? When

    (A) a recommendation is being made for a future plan of action
    (B) a department head requests immediate information
    (C) a long-standing policy change is made
    (D) an analysis of complicated statistical data is involved.

38. When an applicant is approved for public assistance, the Eligibility Specialist must fill in standard forms with certain information. The greatest advantage of using standard forms in this situation rather than having the Eligibility Specialist write the report as he or she sees fit is that

    (A) the report can be acted on quickly
    (B) the report can be written without directions from a supervisor
    (C) coded information is less likely to be left out of the report.
    (D) information that is written up this way is more likely to be verified.

39. In some types of reports, visual aids add interest, meanings, and support. They also provide an essential means of effectively communicating the message of the report. Of the following, the selection of the suitable visual aids to use with a report is least dependent on the

    (A) nature and scope of the report
    (B) way in which the aid is to be used
    (C) aids used in other reports
    (D) prospective readers of the report.

40. He wanted to *ascertain* the facts before arriving at a conclusion. The word *ascertain* means most nearly

    (A) disprove
    (B) determine
    (C) correct
    (D) provide.

41. Did the supervisor *assent* to her request for annual leave? The word *assent* means most nearly

    (A) allude
    (B) protest
    (C) agree
    (D) refer.

42. The new Case Worker was fearful that the others would *rebuff* her. The word *rebuff* means most nearly

    (A) ignore
    (B) forget
    (C) copy
    (D) snub.

43. The supervisor of that office does not *condone* lateness. The word *condone* means most nearly

    (A) mind
    (B) excuse
    (C) punish
    (D) remember.

44. Each employee was instructed to be as *concise* as possible when preparing a report. The word *concise* means most nearly

(A) exact
(B) sincere
(C) flexible
(D) brief.

45. Despite many requests for them, there was a *scant* supply of new blotters. The word *scant* means most nearly

(A) adequate
(B) abundant
(C) insufficient
(D) expensive.

46. Did they *replenish* the supply of forms in the cabinet? The word *replenish* means

(A) straighten up
(B) refill
(C) sort out
(D) use.

47. Employees may become bored unless they are assigned *diverse* duties. The word *diverse* means most nearly

(A) interesting
(B) different
(C) challenging
(D) enjoyable.

48. During the probation period, the worker proved to be *inept*. The word *inept* means most nearly

(A) incompetent
(B) insubordinate
(C) satisfactory
(D) uncooperative.

49. The *putative* father was not living with the family. The word *putative* means most nearly

(A) reputed
(B) unemployed
(C) concerned
(D) indifferent.

Answer questions 50 through 53 on the basis of the information in the passage below.

Some authorities have questioned whether the term "culture of poverty" should be used since "culture" means a design for living which is passed down from generation to generation. The culture of poverty is, however, a very useful concept, if it is used with care, with recognition that poverty is a subculture, and with avoidance of the "cookie-cutter" approach. With regard to the individual, the cookie-cutter view assumes that all individuals in a culture turn out exactly alike, as if they were so many cookies. It overlooks the fact that, at least in our urban society, every individual is a member of more than one subculture; and which subculture most strongly influences his or her response in a given situation depends on the interaction of a great many factors, including his or her individual make-up and history, the specifics of the various subcultures to which he or she belongs, and the specifics of the given situation. It is always important to avoid the cookie-cutter view of culture, with regard to the individual and to the culture or subculture involved.

With regard to the culture as a whole, the cookie-cutter concept again assumes homogeneity and consistency. It forgets that within any one culture or subculture there are conflicts and contradictions, and that at any given moment an individual may have to choose, consciously or unconsciously, between conflicting values or patterns. Also, most individuals, in varying degrees, have a dual set of values—those by which they live and those they cherish as best. This point has been made and documented repeatedly about the culture of poverty.

50. The "cookie-cutter" approach assumes that
   (A) members of the same "culture" are all alike
   (B) "culture" stays the same from generation to generation
   (C) the term "culture" should not be applied to groups who are poor
   (D) there are value conflicts within most "cultures."

51. According to the passage, every person in our cities
   (A) is involved in the conflicts of urban culture
   (B) recognizes that poverty is a subculture
   (C) lives by those values to which he or she is exposed
   (D) belongs to more than one subculture.

52. The passage emphasizes that a culture is likely to contain within it
   (A) one dominant set of values
   (B) a number of contradictions
   (C) one subculture to which everyone belongs
   (D) members who are exactly alike.

53. According to the passage, individuals are sometimes forced to choose between
   (A) cultures
   (B) subcultures
   (C) different sets of values
   (D) a new culture and an old culture.

Answer questions 54 through 57 solely on the basis of the passage given below.

There are approximately 33 million poor people in the Unites States; 14.3 million of them are children, 5.3 million are old people, and the remainder are in other categories. Altogether 6.5 million families live in poverty because the heads of the households cannot work; they are either too old or too sick or too severely handicapped, or they are widowed or deserted mothers of young children. There are the working poor; the low-paid workers, and the workers in seasonal industries. There are the underemployed: those who would like full-time jobs but cannot find them, those employees who would like year-round work but lack the opportunity, and those who are employed below their level of training. There are the nonworking poor: the older men and women with small retirement incomes and those with no income, the disabled, the physically and mentally handicapped, and the chronically sick.

54. According to the passage, approximately what percent of the poor people in the United States are children?
   (A) 33
   (B) 16
   (C) 20
   (D) 44

55. According to the passage, people who work in seasonal industries are likely to be classified as

(A) working poor
(B) underemployed
(C) nonworking poor
(D) low-paid workers.

56. According to the passage, the category of nonworking poor includes people who

(A) receive unemployment insurance
(B) cannot find full-time work
(C) are disabled or mentally handicapped
(D) are single mothers.

57. It can be inferred from the preceding passage, among the underemployed are those who

(A) can find only part-time work
(B) are looking for their first job
(C) are inadequately trained
(D) depend on insufficient retirement incomes.

Answer questions 58 through 67 solely on the basis of the information given in the following charts.

CHILD CARE SERVICES 1985-1989

CHILDREN IN FOSTER HOMES AND VOLUNTARY INSTITUTIONS, BY TYPE OF CARE, IN BERGERSVILLE AND UPSTATE*

| Year End | FOSTER FAMILY HOMES | | | | Total in Voluntary Institutions | Total in Other | Total Number of Children |
	Boarding Homes	Adoptive or Free Homes	Wage, Work or Self-Supporting	Total in Foster Family Homes			
Bergersville							
1985	12,389	1,773	33	14,195	7,187	1,128	22,510
1986	13,271	1,953	42	15,266	7,277	1,237	23,730
1987	14,012	2,134	32	16,178	7,087	1,372	24,637
1988	14,558	2,137	29	16,724	6,717	1,437	24,778
1989	14,759	2,241	37	17,037	6,777	1,455	25,264
Upstate							
1985	14,801	2,902	90	17,793	3,012	241	21,046
1986	15,227	2,943	175	18,345	3,067	291	21,703
1987	16,042	3,261	64	19,367	2,940	273	22,580
1988	16,166	3,445	60	19,671	2,986	362	23,121
1989	16,357	3,606	55	20,018	3,024	485	23,527

* "Upstate" is defined as all of the state, excluding Bergersville

NUMBER OF CHILDREN, BY AGE, UNDER FOSTER FAMILY CARE
IN BERGERSVILLE IN 1989

Borough	Children's Ages					
	One Year or Younger	Two Years	Three Years	Four Years	Over Four Years	Total All Ages
Manto	1,054	1,170	1,060	1,325	445	5,070
Johnston	842	1,196	1,156	1,220	484	4,882
Kiley	707	935	470	970	361	?
Appleton	460	555	305	793	305	2,418
Richardson	274	505	160	173	112	1,224
Total All Boroughs	3,337	4,361	3,151	4,481	?	17,037

58. According to the table of Child Care Services, 1985–1989, the number of children in Bergersville boarding homes was at least twice the number of children in Bergersville voluntary institutions in

(A) only one of the five years
(B) only two of the five years
(C) only three of the five years
(D) all of the five years.

59. If the number of children cared for in voluntary institutions in the entire state increased from 1989 to 1990 by exactly the same number as from 1988 to 1989, then the 1990 year-end total of children in voluntary institutions in the state would be

(A) 3,062
(B) 6,837
(C) 7,494
(D) 9,899

60. If the total number of children under Child Care Services in Bergersville in 1985 was 25% more than in 1984, then the 1984 Bergersville total was most nearly

(A) 11,356
(B) 11,647
(C) 16,883
(D) 18,008

61. From 1985 through 1989, the average number per year of children in Child Care Services classified as "other" is most nearly

(A) 330
(B) 728
(C) 1,326
(D) 1,650

62. Of all the children under foster family care in Johnston in 1989 the percentage who were one year of age or younger is most nearly

(A) 16%
(B) 17%
(C) 18%
(D) 19%

63. Suppose that upstate, the "wage, work or self-supporting" type of foster family care is given only to children between the ages of 14 and 18, and that, of the children in "adoptive or free home" foster care in each of the five years listed, only one percent each year are between the ages of 14 and 18. The total number of 14- to 18-year-olds under foster family care upstate exceeded 95 in

(A) each of the five years
(B) four of the five years
(C) three of the five years
(D) two of the five years.

64. The average number of two-year-olds under foster family care in each of Bergersville's five boroughs in 1989 is most nearly

(A) 872
(B) 874
(C) 875
(D) 882

65. The difference between the total number of children of all ages under foster family care in Kiley in 1989, and the total number under foster care in Richardson that year is

(A) 1,224
(B) 2,219
(C) 3,443
(D) 4,667

66. Suppose that by the end of 1990 the number of children one year or younger under foster family care in Appleton was twice the 1989 total, while the number of two-year-olds was four-fifths the 1989 total. The 1990 total of children two years or younger under foster family care in Appleton was

(A) 2,418
(B) 1,624
(C) 1,364
(D) 1,015

67. The total number of children over four years of age under foster care in Bergersville in 1989 was

(A) 1,607
(B) 1,697
(C) 1,707
(D) 1,797

68. At the start of a year, a family was receiving a public assistance grant of $191 twice a month, on the 1st and 15th of each month. On March 1 their rent allowance was decreased from $75 to $71 a month, since they had moved to a smaller apartment. On August 1 their semi-monthly food allowance, which had been $40.20, was raised by 10%. In that year, the total amount of money disbursed to this family was

(A) $2,272.10
(B) $3,290.70
(C) $4,544.20
(D) $4,584.20

69. It is discovered that a client has received double public assistance for two months by having been enrolled at two service centers of Department of Social Services. The client should have received $84.00 twice a month instead of the double amount.

He now agrees to repay the money by equal deductions from his public assistance check over a period of 12 months. What will the amount of his next check be?

(A) $56
(B) $70
(C) $77
(D) $80

70. Suppose a study is being made of the composition of 3,550 families receiving public assistance. Of the first 1,050 families reviewed, 18% had four or more children. If, in the remaining number of families, the percentage with four or more children is half as high as the percentage in the group already reviewed, then the percentage of families with four or more children in the entire group of families is most nearly

(A) 12
(B) 14
(C) 16
(D) 27

71. Suppose that food prices have risen 13%, and an increase of the same amount has been granted in the food allotment given to people receiving public assistance. If a family has been receiving $406 a month, 35% of which is allotted for food, then the total amount of public assistance this family receives per month will be changed to

(A) $402.71
(B) $420.03
(C) $423.43
(D) $449.71

72. Assume that the food allowance is to be raised 5% in August but will be retroactive for four months to April, 1989. The retroactive allowance is to be divided into equal sections and added to the public assistance checks for August, September, October, November, and December 1989. A family which has been receiving $420 monthly, 40% of which was allotted for food, will receive what size check in August?

(A) $426.72
(B) $428.40
(C) $430.50
(D) $435.12

73. A client, who receives $105 public assistance twice a month, inherits 14 shares of stock worth $90 each. The client is required to sell the stock and spend his inheritance before receiving more monetary assistance. Using his public assistance allowance as a guide, how many *months* are his new assets expected to last?

(A) 6
(B) 7
(C) 8
(D) 12

74. The Department of Social Services has 16 service centers in Yodersville. These centers may be divided into those which are downtown (south of central street) and those which are uptown. Two of the centers are special service centers and are downtown, while the remainder of the centers are general service centers. There is a total of 7 service centers downtown. The percentage of the general service centers which are uptown is most nearly

(A) 56
(B) 64
(C) 69
(D) 79

75. On January 1, 1989, a family was receiving supplementary monthly public assistance of $56 for food, $48 for rent, and $28 for other necessities. In the spring their rent rose by 10%, and their rent allotment was adjusted accordingly. In the summer, due to the death of a family member, their allotments for food and other necessities were reduced by 1/7. Their monthly allowance check in the fall should be

(A) $124.80
(B) $128.80
(C) $132.80
(D) $136.80

76. Twice a month, a certain family receives a $170 general allowance for rent, food, and clothing expenses. In addition, the family receives a specific supplementary allotment for utilities of $192 a year, which is added to their semimonthly check. If the general allowance alone is reduced by 5%, what will be the total amount of their next semi-monthly check?

(A) $161.50
(B) $169.50
(C) $170.00
(D) $177.50

77. If each Eligibility Specialist in a certain unit sees an average of 9 clients in a 7-hour day and there are 15 Eligibility Specialists in the unit, approximately how many clients will be seen in a 35-hour week?

(A) 315
(B) 405
(C) 675
(D) 945

78. Under public assistance programs in many communities, allocations for payment of a client's rent and security deposits are given in check form directly to the welfare recipient, and not to the landlord. This practice is used mainly as an effort to

(A) increase the client's responsibility for his or her own affairs
(B) curb the rent overcharges made by most landlords
(C) control the number of welfare recipients housed in public housing projects
(D) limit the number of checks issued to each welfare family.

79. The crusade against environmental hazards in the United States is concentrated in urban areas mostly on the problems of

(A) air pollution, sewage treatment, and noise
(B) garbage collection
(C) automobile exhaust fumes and street cleanliness
(D) recycling, reconstitution, and open space.

Answer questions 80 through 83 solely on the basis of the information in the following passage.

City social work agencies and the police have been meeting at City Hall to coordinate efforts to defuse the tensions among teenage groups that they fear could flare into warfare once summer vacations begin. Police intelligence units, with the help of the District Attorneys' offices, are gathering information to identify gangs and their territories. A list of 3,000 gang members has already been assembled, and 110 gangs have been identified. Social workers from various agencies like the Department of Social Services, Neighborhood Youth Corps, and the Youth Board, are out every day developing liaisons with groups of juveniles through meetings at schools and recreation centers. Many street workers spend their days seeking to ease the intergang hostility, tracing potentially incendiary rumors, and trying to channel willing gang members into participation in established summer programs. The City's Youth Services Agency plans to spend a million dollars for special summer programs in ten main City areas where gang activity is most firmly entrenched. Five of the "gang neighborhoods" are clustered in an area forming most of the southeastern part of the borough of the Bronx, and it is here that most of the 110 identified gangs have formed. Special Youth Services programs will also be directed toward the Rockaway section of the borough of Queens, Chinatown and Washington Heights in the borough of Manhattan, and two neighborhoods in the northern part of the borough of Staten Island noted for a lot of motorcycle gang activity. Some of these programs will emphasize sports and recreation, others vocational guidance or neighborhood improvement, but each program will be aimed at benefiting all youngsters in the area. Although none of the money will be spent specifically on gang members, the Youth Services Agency is consulting gang leaders, along with other teenagers, on the projects they would like developed in their area.

80. The passage states that one of the steps taken by street workers in trying to defuse the tensions among teenage gangs is that of

    (A) conducting summer school sessions that will benefit all neighborhood youth
    (B) monitoring neighborhood sports competitions between rival gangs
    (C) developing liaisons with community school boards and parent associations
    (D) tracing rumors that could intensify intergang hostilities.

81. Based on the information given in this passage on gangs and gang members, it is correct to state that

    (A) there are no teenage gangs located in borough of Brooklyn
    (B) most of the gangs identified by the police are concentrated in one borough
    (C) there is a total of 110 gangs
    (D) only a small percentage of gangs in New York City is in the borough of Queens.

82. According to the passage, one important aspect of the program is that

    (A) youth gang leaders and other teenagers are involved in the planning
    (B) money will be given directly to gang members for use on their projects
    (C) only gang members will be allowed to participate in the programs
    (D) the parents of gang members will act as youth leaders.

83. Various City agencies are cooperating in the attempt to keep the City's youth "cool" during the summer school vacation period. The passage does not specifically indicate participation in this project by the city's

    (A) Police Department
    (B) District Attorneys' Office
    (C) Board of Education
    (D) Department of Social Services

Answer questions 84 through 86 solely on the basis of the information in the following passage.

It is important that interviewers understand to some degree the manner in which stereotyped thinking operates. Stereotypes are commonly held, but predominantly false, preconceptions about the appearance and traits of individuals of different racial, religious, ethnic, and subcultural groups. Distinct traits, physical and mental, are associated with each group, and membership in a particular group is enough, in the mind of a person holding the stereotype, to assure that these traits will be perceived in individuals who are members of that group. Conversely, possession of the particular stereotyped trait by an individual usually indicates to the holder of the stereotype that the individual is a group member. Linked to the formation of stereotypes is the fact that mental traits, either positive or negative, such as honesty, laziness, avariciousness, and other characteristics are associated with particular stereotypes. Either kind of stereotype, if held by an interviewer, can seriously damage the results of an interview. In general, stereotypes can be particularly dangerous when they are part of the belief patterns of administrators, interviewers, and supervisors, who are in a position to affect the lives of others and to stimulate or retard the development of human potential. The holding of a stereotype by an interviewer, for example, diverts his or her attention from significant essential facts and information upon which really valid assessments may be made. Unfortunately, it is the rare interviewer who is completely conscious of the real basis upon which he or she is making his or her evaluation of the people being interviewed. The specific reasons given by an interviewer for a negative evaluation, even though apparently logical and based upon what, in the mind of the interviewer, are very good reasons, may not be the truly motivating factors. This is why the careful selection and training of interviewers is such an important responsibility of an agency which is attempting to help a great diversity of human beings.

84. Of the following, the best title for the passage is

(A) Positive and Negative Effects of Stereotyped Thinking
(B) The Relationship of Stereotypes to Interviewing
(C) An Agency's Responsibility in Interviewing
(D) The Impact of Stereotyped Thinking on Professional Functions.

85. According to the passage, most interviewers

(A) compensate for stereotyped beliefs to avoid negatively affecting the results of their interviews
(B) are influenced by stereotypes they hold, but put greater stress on factual information developed during the interview
(C) are seldom aware of their real motives when evaluating interviewees
(D) give logical and good reasons for negative evaluations of interviewees.

86. According to the passage, which of the following is not a characteristic of stereotypes?

(A) Stereotypes influence estimates of personality traits of people.
(B) Positive stereotypes can damage the results of an interview.
(C) Physical traits associated with stereotypes seldom really exist.
(D) Stereotypes sometimes are a basis upon which valid personality assessments can be made.

Answer questions 87 through 91 solely on the basis of the information in the following passage.

The quality of the voice of Eligibility Specialists is an important factor in conveying to clients and co-workers their attitudes and, to some degree, their characters. The human voice, when not consciously disguised, may reflect a person's mood, temper, and personality. It has been shown in several experiments that certain character traits can be assessed with better than chance accuracy through listening to the voice of an unknown person who cannot be seen.

Since one of the objectives of Eligibility Specialists is to put clients at ease and to present an encouraging and comfortable atmosphere, a harsh, shrill, or loud voice could have a negative effect. A client who displays emotions of anger or resentment would probably be provoked even further by a caustic tone. In a face-to-face situation, an unpleasant voice may be compensated for to some degree by a concerned and kind facial expression. However, when one speaks on the telephone, the expression on one's face cannot be seen by the listener. Eligibility Specialists who wish to represent themselves effectively to clients should try to eliminate as many faults as possible in striving to develop desirable voice qualities.

87. If Eligibility Specialists use sarcastic tones while interviewing a resentful client, the client, according to the passage, would most likely

(A) avoid the face-to-face situation
(B) be ashamed of his or her behavior
(C) become more resentful
(D) be provoked to violence.

88. According to the passage, experiments comparing voice and character traits have demonstrated that

(A) prospects for improving an unpleasant voice through training are better than chance
(B) the voice can be altered to project many different psychological characteristics
(C) the quality of the human voice reveals more about the speaker than his or her words do
(D) the speaker's voice tells the hearer something about the speaker's personality.

89. Which of the following, according to the passage, is a person's voice most likely to reveal?

(A) His or her prejudices
(B) His or her intelligence
(C) His or her social awareness
(D) His or her temperament.

90. It may be most reasonably concluded from the passage that an interested and sympathetic expression on the face of an Eligibility Specialist

(A) may induce a client to feel certain he or she will receive welfare benefits
(B) will eliminate the need for pleasant vocal qualities in the interviewer
(C) may help to make up for an unpleasant voice in the interviewer
(D) is desirable as the interviewer speaks on the telephone to a client.

91. It may be concluded from the passage that the particular reason for an Eligibility Specialist to pay special attention to modulating his or her voice when talking on the phone to a client is that during a telephone conversation

(A) there is a necessity to compensate for the way in which a telephone distorts the voice
(B) the voice of the Eligibility Specialist is a reflection of his or her mood and character
(C) the client can react only on the basis of the voice and words he or she hears
(D) the client may have difficulty getting a clear understanding over the telephone

92. An applicant owns a three-family frame house, the income from which is barely adequate to meet taxes, interest, and mortgage amortization. He has no funds for

other maintenance. He is willing to permit your Bureau to place a lien on his property for aid extended. You would recommend that the agency

(A) deny aid on the assumption that property owners are not entitled to assistance
(B) grant aid taking lien on the property as agreed upon
(C) force the applicant to sell the property regardless of present market value and use the small balance left after all payments for his own needs
(D) take over management of the property to get better returns.

93. A client refuses to permit insurance adjustment, insisting he has kept his insurance because ethnic custom demands an elaborate funeral. The premium of the policy is being paid by a married daughter herself just able to manage. You would

(A) cut off aid, after persuasion has failed and the client still refuses to adjust the policy
(B) continue aid on basis of need
(C) persuade the daughter to drop the policy
(D) induce the insurance company to surrender cash value to the city to reimburse for aid granted.

94. An applicant for aid is the recipient of a pension from the firm in whose employ he had been for 30 years. This is inadequate for the needs of his family. You

(A) refuse aid because of income from this source
(B) grant supplemental aid
(C) induce the firm to increase the applicant's pension
(D) insist upon the applicant's securing work.

95. A wife complains that her husband spends most of his assistance check in drink, denying the family their needs. You would recommend that the agency

(A) discontinue aid because of the client's wastefulness
(B) arrest the husband for drunkenness
(C) arrange for the check to be given to the wife
(D) get the saloon keeper to refuse to sell him a drink.

96. A family consisting of a wife and three young children has been receiving aid for three years because of the husband's desertion. Persistent efforts have revealed no trace of the husband. You would

(A) continue assistance on the basis of continuing need
(B) force the wife to obtain a divorce on the grounds of desertion
(C) place the children in a foster home and force the wife to support herself
(D) make application for Aid to Dependent Children.

97. You find that an applicant for aid has a bank account. He explains that this is not his own money, but that the account has been placed in his name for safekeeping for an old friend who has returned to his native country for a temporary visit. He cannot give the exact whereabouts of his friend. You would

(A) accept this explanation and grant assistance
(B) deny aid on the assumption that story is implausible
(C) insist that he close the account and utilize the money
(D) interview neighbors to find out whether the applicant has such an old friend.

98. A complaint is received that a client and his wife neglect their two young children and beat them cruelly. Investigation bears out the truth of these statements. You would

(A) refer the matter to the agency responsible for the prevention of cruelty to children
(B) arrest the father and mother
(C) discontinue aid immediately
(D) continue aid on promise of parents to reform.

99. A formerly well-to-do family applies for aid. Their son is in his last year at law school, his tuition for the year having been paid. The last of their savings, a small amount, has been set aside for the son's maintenance at school for the balance of the year, rendering the parents immediately destitute. You would recommend

(A) the parents be required to use the money for their own needs
(B) insisting at once upon the son's leaving school and going to work
(C) giving aid on the assumption that when the son completes his education, he will be equipped to maintain himself and parents
(D) denying any aid on the basis that parents who are able to send their son to law school have other resources to draw on.

100. When a landlord complains to the Case Worker that a certain aid recipient has consistently neglected to pay his rent, present case work practice would indicate to the Case Worker that he or she should first

(A) arrange to discontinue aid payments until he or she can verify the reason for the nonpayment of rent
(B) tell the client to pay his rent within a certain period of time if he does not want his aid discontinued
(C) tell the client about the landlord's complaint and inform him that the Department of Social Services assumes that rent is an obligation the client is expected to settle directly with his landlord
(D) arrange for the landlord to collect his rent at the center in the future.

Correct Answers for Practice Examination IV

1. D	21. C	41. C	61. D	81. B
2. B	22. C	42. D	62. B	82. A
3. D	23. D	43. B	63. C	83. C
4. A	24. A	44. D	64. A	84. B
5. C	25. B	45. C	65. B	85. C
6. A	26. C	46. B	66. C	86. D
7. C	27. D	47. B	67. C	87. C
8. D	28. B	48. A	68. D	88. D
9. C	29. D	49. A	69. B	89. D
10. B	30. A	50. A	70. A	90. C
11. D	31. C	51. D	71. C	91. C
12. C	32. A	52. B	72. D	92. B
13. A	33. B	53. C	73. A	93. A
14. B	34. C	54. D	74. B	94. B
15. D	35. B	55. A	75. A	95. C
16. C	36. B	56. C	76. B	96. D
17. B	37. B	57. A	77. C	97. B
18. A	38. C	58. B	78. A	98. A
19. B	39. C	59. D	79. A	99. C
20. C	40. B	60. D	80. D	100. C

Explanations of Correct Answers for Practice Examination IV

1. **(D)** An Eligibility Specialist must understand the very natural reluctance of a new applicant for public assistance to show a stranger personal material and documents. This does *not* mean the material need not be seen, just that the worker must explain the need for such documents and must convince the client that such personal data will be examined only in connection with establishing eligibility.

2. **(B)** The good Eligibility Specialist knows that an unintelligible answer is best clarified at the time it is given. The best way to do this is to repeat the client's words and ask whether that is what is meant. Wrong Answer A may result in your having insufficient knowledge to proceed with the case. Wrong Answer C may confuse the client and still not produce an intelligible reply. Answer D may confuse and frighten the client and still produce no intelligible answer.

3. **(D)** A good interviewer knows that all of us, when faced with a question we find difficult to answer, will hesitate and think through our answer before replying. The worker should patiently wait for the response. If applicants don't understand the question, they will ask for an explanation.

4. **(A)** This is a basic rule in all public case work. All applicants and clients must be treated equally without regard to sex, ethnicity, or religion.

5. **(C)** A basic rule of good interviewing is that the applicant must clearly understand both the question asked and what information you are trying to elicit.

6. **(A)** Public assistance applicants and clients have certain responsibilities in establishing and maintaining eligibility, one of which should be filling out the applicant blank (see the chapter entitled "The Investigation Process.") Therefore, you should encourage the applicant to fill out the form as well as possible. Answers C and D are insufficient methods and may result in antagonism.

7. **(C)** A basic rule for all Eligibility Specialists in a public welfare agency is never to take the attitude that a client or applicant is purposefully lying. The best way to handle the situation where the response is obviously not true is to ask pertinent questions which should result in a correction of the response given.

8. **(D)** A basic rule in all social work interviewing is to begin by asking questions that can be easily answered. This will put the client at ease and help you to establish the rapport needed in order to elicit more difficult answers later on in the interview.

9. **(C)** An Eligibility Specialist must understand the nervousness of a new applicant and must try to calm the person so that the interview can proceed smoothly. Answers A and B may have the opposite effect. Never commit the mistake of assuring an applicant that eligibility for public assistance will be established since this may very well *not* be true (Answer D).

10. **(B)** Effective management requires that the agency have current, *accurate*, easily available information on the number of applications processed, approved, and disapproved so that fiscal, budgetary, and personnel adjustments can be made expeditiously. Errors on these reports will affect correct adjustments and, thus, hinder effective management.

11. **(D)** People give information in all the ways indicated in the four possible answers. Body language, however, can be the most difficult to interpret by a relatively untrained, inexperienced interviewer and can be most easily misinterpreted. Thus, for example, a person who constantly "speaks with his hands" during an interview may do so at all times, out of habit, which will give little clue to his personality or problems. The other possible answers serve as better indicators, although they too are subject to misinterpretation.

12. **(C)** Studies have shown that the best way to handle the situation described is given in the correct answer. Only if it proves unsuccessful should you consider terminating the interview.

13. **(A)** In the circumstances present, your best reply is indicated in the correct answer. There is no indication that the case has been pending for an unusually long period of time, but your assurance that the application is being checked and that a decision will be forthcoming as soon as possible should ease the client's worry. *Never* assure a client of probable case acceptance simply because it resembles so many other cases (Answer C). Each case is unique. *Never* promise to call back unless you intend to do so (Answer D). It is *not* good policy for a government worker in the situation described to suggest that a client write the worker's supervisor. It is *your* responsibility to follow up on the matter.

14. **(B)** Under the circumstances described, it would be best to test the reliability of the information received by rephrasing the original question later in the interview. *Remember*, you are *not* questioning the reliability of the response *nor* the overall veracity of the client. Note: Compare this question and explanation against the question and answer to Question 7 of this practice exam.

15. **(D)** As an Eligibility Specialist trying to establish eligibility for public assistance, your job is to accept the applicant's statement and continue with questions designed to determine such eligibility. The wrong answers are not pertinent to the establishment of eligibility.

16. **(C)** Wrong Answers A and B impede the determination of the client's usual occupation. Wrong Answer D does not give you information about the client's occupation. It just tells you the place of employment.

17. **(B)** Basic public social case work procedure requires that information about a client or applicant is never ordinarily divulged to any other persons without the client's permission. In this instance, the worker should remind the clerk of the agency's policy.

18. **(A)** In this situation, proper and most effective procedure would be to ask a question pertinent to the purpose of the interview. The wrong answers may annoy the applicant and disturb the relationship you are trying to establish.

19. **(B)** Good co-worker practice calls for you to simply show your peer the error so that the proper form will be used, but you will not give offense. It is not your function to teach your co-worker (Answer A) or to minimize the error (Answer C), and it is also bad for future relations with that worker and with the rest of the staff for you to report the worker to your superior (Answer D).

20. **(C)** The situation posed calls for you to be sensitive to the client's feelings and try to understand another's point of view. The client is angry, and reciting rules may not help him understand the rules (Answer A). You cannot and should not remain "uninvolved in a client's problems" (Answer D) since your function is to help to solve them.

21. **(C)** The tone of voice you use can be very helpful in making a client feel comfortable about discussing problems with you and listen and understand what you are trying to convey.

22. **(C)** A report of an interview with an applicant should include all information relevant to the establishment of eligibility. Only if the hostility shown by the applicant is useful in that respect or thought to be important in further interviews should it be included in the report.

23. **(D)** It is most necessary, in presenting recommendations in a report, that there are logical bases for the recommendations. There is no absolute rule whether recommendations should be placed after the evidence is given (Answer C) or before the evidence (Answer A), although the latter is generally preferable in long reports. In any event, the evidence *must* be in the report so that the recommendations are acceptable. Answer A may be a correct and fruitful idea in making recommendations in some reports but it is not of prime importance or called for in other reports.

24. **(A)** The three wrong answers are all useful points to remember in organizing a report. Personal beliefs should be kept to a minimum or omitted entirely in the type of report referred to in the question.

25. **(B)** The last sentence of the first paragraph of the passage clearly refers to irate landlords complaining about receiving late rent checks. The wrong answers are not expressed in the passage.

26. **(C)** The passage clearly states there would be one rent office for every three Social Service Centers in each of the five boroughs. $15 \div 3 = 5$.

27. **(D)** The second paragraph states that clients would receive monthly notification from the social service agency that rent had been paid.

28. **(B)** The third paragraph states that cases with rents from $151 to $250 would be placed in buff folders, while rents from $250 to $349 would be placed in blue folders. It also states the color of the folder should be changed if the rent changed into a new rental category.

29. **(D)** The first paragraph states that clients would continue to make direct contact on rental matters with their social service centers.

30. **(A)** There is nothing in the passage regarding the need for the floor number of a client's apartment *if there is an elevator in the building* where the client resides. All other data, as noted in the wrong answers, should be in the folder, according to the passage.

31. **(C)** The passage indicates the suggestion that an experimental project be set up on a small scale. The correct answer is the only answer in accord with that proposal.

32. **(A)** The fourth paragraph states the possible problem that clients would resist being unable to pay their own rent. It can be inferred that clients might feel a loss of independence from this statement. The other possible answers cannot be inferred from the passage.

33. **(B)** The passage (last sentence) clearly states the pilot program would determine what problems "may arise and how the program can be best implemented" by being started first as a pilot program.

34. **(C)** It is most important, especially in a public assistance agency serving thousands of persons daily, that the worker is certain of working on the correct case. This will avoid mistakes and save considerable time.

35. **(B)** When preparing a complex or lengthy report, a very useful device is to first write a list of all the points which have to be covered in the report. It is then a relatively easy task to compare the list with the finished report to make certain everything has been included. This is especially useful when several revisions and corrections have been found necessary.

36. **(B)** Visual aids can be very useful in explaining, emphasizing, and proving a point made in this report. With a table or chart in the main body of the text, the reader can understand that point more easily. If the chart is complex and might disturb the reader's ability to follow the arguments being given, it is more appropriate to include it in the appendix. If the reader is a very busy executive interested primarily in the "bottom line" (conclusions and recommendations), visual aids such as charts, results of experiments, etc., should be placed in the appendix. In sum, the purpose of the report and the visual aid must be considered in determining where to include the visual aids.

37. **(B)** Immediate information requested by a superior is best imparted by an oral report. The superior has not got the time to read a report if quick straightforward information or an answer to a simple question is needed in order to take immediate action. The wrong answers are situations where more detailed data is needed or where time is not of the essence and, therefore, written reports would be more suitable.

38. **(C)** While the wrong answers are also reasons why standardized forms are useful, the *most* important reason would have to be one which helps establish eligibility. Missing data, making such establishment impossible, is less likely to occur with the use of standardized forms.

39. **(C)** The wrong answers are all important considerations in determining the selection of which visual aids to use in a particular report. Each report is different, and visual aids useful in one report are useless in another. Thus, for example, a detailed statistical tabulation may be needed in an annual activity report going to management but is of no value in a report on a case closing which only your supervisor will read. Note: The question asks for the situation where there is *least* dependence on the selection of suitable visual aids.

Questions 40 through 49 require that you know the meaning of the italicized words, all of which are commonly used in determining eligibility and/or in writing public case work reports. Consult your dictionary if you have any difficulty with the correct answer or with the words given in the wrong answers.

40. **(B)**

41. **(C)**

42. **(D)**

43. **(B)**

44. **(D)**

45. **(C)**

46. **(B)**

47. **(B)**

48. **(A)**

49. **(A)**

50. **(A)** The paragraph tells you that the "cookie cutter" approach "assumes that all individuals in a culture turn out exactly alike." Note: The statements in the wrong answers frequently may be found in the reading but may *not* answer the question being asked. Thus, wrong Answer C could be thought to be the correct answer since the reading states that poverty is a subculture, but does *not* answer the question posed.

51. **(D)** The passage clearly states that every person "in an urban society" is a member of more than one subculture. While one or more of the statements *may* be correct statements, the reading passage does not include these statements. *Remember* that you must answer the questions "according to the passage" if you are so directed.

52. **(B)** The second paragraph of the passage clearly states that "within one culture...there are conflicts and contradictions." There is nothing in the passage to indicate that any of the wrong answers are correct.

53. **(C)** The last paragraph of the passage indicates that most individuals have a dual set of values and have to choose between "conflicting values." Note: It also states that "at any given moment," a person may have to choose between "conflicting values" within a culture or subculture, but it is the *values*, not the cultures (wrong Answer A) or subcultures (wrong Answer B) from which he has to choose.

54. **(D)** The passage indicates that of the 33 million poor people in the United States, 14.3 million are children. $33 \div 14.30 = 43.3\%$ children

55. **(A)** The passage states "these are the working poor . . . workers in seasonal industries."

56. **(C)** The passage states, "these are the nonworking poor . . . the disabled . . . mentally handicapped."

57. **(A)** The passage indicated that the "underemployed" include "those who would like full-time jobs but cannot find them." It can be inferred from the passage that such persons have part-time jobs.

58. **(B)** Number of children in Bergersville boarding homes

1985	1986	1987	1988	1989
12,389	13,271	14,012	14,558	4,759

Number of children in Bergersville in voluntary institutions

1985	1986	1987	1988	1989
7,187	7,277	7,087	6,717	6,777

Inspection of the two sets of figures shows that only in 1988 and 1989 were the number of children in boarding homes at least twice the number in voluntary institutions.

59. **(D) Bergersville**
Total number in voluntary institutions in 1989 = 6,777
Total number in voluntary institutions in 1988 = 6,717
6,777 − 6,717 = increase of 60 in Bergersville.
Upstate
Total number in voluntary institutions in 1989 = 3,024
Total number in voluntary institutions in 1988 = 2,987
3,024 − 2,986 = increase of 38 in upstate
Total increase in 1989 = 98 more
Total number in 1989 = 6,777 + 3,024 = 9,801
9,801 + 98 = 9,899

60. **(D)** Total number under care in Bergersville in 1985 = 22,510
22,510 ÷ 125% = 180.08 (one percent)
180.08 × 100% = 18,008 (answer)

61. **(D)** Step 1: Add all figures under column called "Total in Other" = 8,281
Step 2: Divide by 5 (number of years 1985 through 1989) 8,281 ÷ 5 = 1,656.2

62. **(B)** Step 1: Total number of children in foster family care in Johnston = 4,882
Step 2: Number 1 year of age or under in Johnston = 842
Step 3: $\dfrac{842}{4,882}$ = .1724 = 17%

63. **(C)** Step 1: All the children upstate who are in the wage work, or self-supporting category:
1985 = 90
1986 = 175
1987 = 64
1988 = 60
1989 = 55
Step 2: All the children upstate who are in the adoptive or free home category, ages 14–18:
2,902 × .01 = 29
2,943 × .01 = 29
3,261 × .01 = 33
3,445 × .01 = 34
3,606 × .01 = 36
Step 3: 1985 = 90 + 29 = 119 children in foster families
1986 = 175 + 29 = 204 children in foster families
1987 = 64 + 33 = 97 children in foster families
1988 = 60 + 34 = 94 children in foster families
1989 = 55 + 36 = 91 children in foster families
In three of the five years, the number of children ages 14–18 in foster families upstate exceeded 95.

64. **(A)** Number of two-year-olds in foster family care in all boroughs in 1989 = 4,361
4,361 ÷ 5 = 872.2

65. **(B)** Total number of children in foster family care in Kiley in 1989 = 3,443
Total number of children in foster family care in Richardson in 1989 = 1,224
3,443 − 1,224 = 2,219 more in Kiley

66. **(C)** Total number of one years of age or younger in Appleton in 1989 = 460
Total number 1 years of age or younger in Appleton in 1990 = 460 × 2 = 920
Total number two-year-olds in Appleton in 1989 = 555
Total number of two-year-olds in Appleton in 1990 = 555 × ⅘ = 444
920 + 444 = 1,364 children

67. **(C)** Just add the number of children over four years of age in all five boroughs of Bergersville. 445 + 484 + 361 + 305 + 112 = 1,707

68. **(D)** Family received $382.00 for two months (January and February) = $764.00
Family received $378.00 for five months (March through July) = $1,890.00
Family received $386.04 for five months (August through December) = $1,930.20
$764.00 + $1,890.00 + $1,930.00 = $4,584.20

69. **(B)** Received $168 a month extra for two months = $336. Over 12 months (24 checks) will pay back $14 per check ($336 ÷ 24 = $14). Semimonthly check = $84 − $14 = $70

70. **(A)** 1,050 × 18% = 189 families had 4+ children
3,550 − 1,050 = 2,500 × .9% = 225 more had 4+ children
189 + 225 = 414 of the 3,500 families had 4+ children
414 ÷ 3,500 = .118 (12%)

71. **(C)** $405 × .35 = $141.75 for food before increase
$141.75 × .13 = $18.43 more per month
$405 + $18.43 = $423.43 per month

72. **(D)** $420 × .40 = $168 per month for food before change
$168.00 × .05 = $8.40 more per check for food effective August 1
$8.40 for four months = $33.60 more is owed for months September through December
$33.60 ÷ 5 = $6.72 retroactive money each month
August check = $420 + $8.40 = 428.40 including old allowance and new amount for food but without retroactivity.
August check = $420 + $8.40 + $6.72 = $435.12

73. **(A)** $14 × 90 = $1,260 received from stock sale
$210 per month = monetary allowance
1260 ÷ 210 = 6 (month)

74. **(B)** 5 general service stations downtown (7 service stations − 2 special service centers = 5 general service stations)
9 general service stations are uptown (16 − 7 = 9)
14 general service stations of which 9 are uptown or 9 ÷ 4 = 64% uptown

75. **(A)** Allowance in January = $132 a month (56 + 48 + 28)
In Spring, $48 (rent) + .10 = $4.80 more per month for rent = $52.80
In Fall, $84 (56 + 28) was reduced by 1 ÷ 7 = $72
(84 × 6 × 7) for food and other necessities
$72 + $52.80 = $124.80 per month allowance in Fall

76. **(B)** $192 ÷ 24 = $8 semimonthly more for utilities
$170 ÷ .05 = $8.50 per check less because of general decrease
Therefore, $170 per check - .50 per check = $169.50 per check.

77. **(C)** 9 × 5 = 45 cases seen per worker per week
45 × 15 workers = 675 cases seen per week

78. **(A)** In accepting public assistance, a client also accepts certain responsibilities including maintenance of personal affairs as much as possible. The duty to pay rent is, in many cities, one of those responsibilities. (See chapter entitled, "The Investigative Process" in this book.)

79. **(A)** In most urban areas, the crusade against environmental hazards is currently focused on air pollution, sewage treatment, and noise. Garbage collection is emphasized as a major crusade only in those few cities where it has become a major environmental hazard.

80. **(D)** The paragraph clearly states that many street workers spend their days "tracing potentially incendiary rumors." It does not refer to the specific activities mentioned in the wrong answers.

81. **(B)** The passage mentions that five of the gang neighborhoods are in the southeastern part of the borough of the Bronx—"and it is here that most of the 110 gangs have formed."

82. **(A)** The last sentence in the passage states that the Youth Services Agency consults with gang leaders and other teenagers in the projects to be developed in their respective areas.

83. **(C)** There is *no* specific mention of the Board of Education anywhere in the passage. The roles of the agencies in the wrong answers *are* found in the passage.

84. **(B)** The main thrust of the passage is the effect stereotyped thinking can have on an interviewer. Wrong Answer A is not discussed in the passage, nor is wrong Answer B. The passage *does* discuss the impact of stereotyped thinking on "administrative interviewers and supervisors who are in a position to affect the lives of others and to stimulate or retard the development of human potential," but it is not concerned with the impact of such thinking on "professional functions" of persons *not* involved in concerns other than the development of human potential, so that Answer D is not correct as stated.

85. **(C)** The passage clearly notes that the specific reasons given by an interviewer for a negative evaluation of an interviewee "may not be the truly motivating factors." The correct answer can be inferred from that statement. The statements in the wrong answers cannot be found or inferred from the passage.

86. **(D)** You are asked to choose the statement which is *not* characteristic of stereotypes according to the passage. The entire reading emphasizes that stereotypes are *not* a basis for making valid personality assessments.

87. **(C)** The passage clearly states that a client "who displays . . . resentment would probably be further provoked by a caustic tone." That the client would "be provoked to violence" (Answer D) cannot be inferred from the passage.

88. **(D)** The passage states that the speaker's voice tells the listener something about the speaker's personality. While the "wrong" answers may or may not be true statements, they are not discussed or implied in the passage.

89. **(D)** A person's voice can, according to the passage, reveal temperament. The wrong answers are concerned with what the speaker *says*, not the tone or quality of his voice.

90. **(C)** The passage states that in a face-to-face interview, appropriate facial expressions can somewhat compensate for an unpleasant voice. The correct answer can be inferred from this statement. None of the other answers can be inferred from the passage.

91. **(C)** The passage clearly implies that the client on the phone can only react to the tone of the speaker's voice and to what the speaker is saying. While the other answers may be true, they cannot be concluded from the passage.

92. **(B)** In the situation described, the applicant has insufficient available funds to maintain himself. To force him to sell the property at less than its market value, and thus, stay off public assistance until the funds from the sales are exhausted, is counterproductive since the value of the land may increase and since he will ultimately have to go on public assistance and rent will then have to be paid for him. Answer D is contrary to public assistance policy. A welfare agency is not in the property management business. The best solution is to allow the applicant to keep the property, grant him public assistance, and place a lien on the property. If the property is ultimately sold, the agency will recoup part or all of the assistance moneys granted. (A lien is a legal claim on another person's property as security for a lawful debt.)

93. **(A)** Insurance adjustment means that the amount of the premium paid by or for the insured person is reduced. This affects the worth of the policy (amount paid) when it comes due. Public welfare policy would not permit the excessive premium rate which is indicated in this case because the extra money, if the policy is adjusted, could be used elsewhere.

94. **(B)** In this situation, the applicant receives money each month which is insufficient to meet all the family needs based on public assistance standards. Supplementary aid is, therefore, granted. The wrong answers are inappropriate under the circumstances presented (see the Glossary for definition of supplementary aid).

95. **(C)** In this situation, the best procedure would be for the wife to receive the check rather than the husband. The wrong answers are poor public assistance policy.

96. **(D)** The futility of the search mandates this action so that the children will not be neglected and proper assistance will be assured.

97. **(B)** Correct public assistance procedure mandates that the worker require verification of both the applicant's bank account and the utilization of money in that account under most circumstances. In this situation, the applicant's story about the account is highly implausible. It is the applicant's responsibility to prove the veracity of the story. Without such proof, financial aid should be denied.

98. **(A)** In this very serious situation, prompt contact with the municipal or private social agency responsible for handling matters involving child abuse should be made. Public assistance checks should not be discontinued pending disposition of the matter by the proper authorities.

99. **(C)** In the situation presented, the Case Worker/Eligibility Specialist should recommend that the family receive aid. Requiring that the small amount of money, previously set aside to maintain the son (Answer A), be utilized by the family, would keep the family off assistance for only a short time. Answer B may alienate the son and spoil his future. There is no basis in the facts given to justify wrong Answer D. Allowing the son to finish law school may very likely result in his ability to support the family completely or in large part so that, in the end, the agency will save money.

100. **(C)** It is the client's responsibility in this situation to pay the rent in a timely manner, and the worker's first responsibility to be sure the client understands the complaint and his own responsibility both to discuss the matter with the landlord and to pay his rent

in a timely manner. As noted in the explanations for previous questions, good social case work practice requires that a client be helped to maintain and develop as much control of daily life requirements as possible so that the landlord continues to be paid directly by the client in this situation. Only if the rent is continually not paid at all, and after the client has been spoken to by the worker, should the solutions given in the wrong answers be considered.

Answer Sheet for Practice Examination V

1. Ⓐ Ⓑ Ⓒ Ⓓ
2. Ⓐ Ⓑ Ⓒ Ⓓ
3. Ⓐ Ⓑ Ⓒ Ⓓ
4. Ⓐ Ⓑ Ⓒ Ⓓ
5. Ⓐ Ⓑ Ⓒ Ⓓ
6. Ⓐ Ⓑ Ⓒ Ⓓ
7. Ⓐ Ⓑ Ⓒ Ⓓ
8. Ⓐ Ⓑ Ⓒ Ⓓ
9. Ⓐ Ⓑ Ⓒ Ⓓ
10. Ⓐ Ⓑ Ⓒ Ⓓ
11. Ⓐ Ⓑ Ⓒ Ⓓ
12. Ⓐ Ⓑ Ⓒ Ⓓ
13. Ⓐ Ⓑ Ⓒ Ⓓ
14. Ⓐ Ⓑ Ⓒ Ⓓ
15. Ⓐ Ⓑ Ⓒ Ⓓ
16. Ⓐ Ⓑ Ⓒ Ⓓ
17. Ⓐ Ⓑ Ⓒ Ⓓ
18. Ⓐ Ⓑ Ⓒ Ⓓ

19. Ⓐ Ⓑ Ⓒ Ⓓ
20. Ⓐ Ⓑ Ⓒ Ⓓ
21. Ⓐ Ⓑ Ⓒ Ⓓ
22. Ⓐ Ⓑ Ⓒ Ⓓ
23. Ⓐ Ⓑ Ⓒ Ⓓ
24. Ⓐ Ⓑ Ⓒ Ⓓ
25. Ⓐ Ⓑ Ⓒ Ⓓ
26. Ⓐ Ⓑ Ⓒ Ⓓ
27. Ⓐ Ⓑ Ⓒ Ⓓ
28. Ⓐ Ⓑ Ⓒ Ⓓ
29. Ⓐ Ⓑ Ⓒ Ⓓ
30. Ⓐ Ⓑ Ⓒ Ⓓ
31. Ⓐ Ⓑ Ⓒ Ⓓ
32. Ⓐ Ⓑ Ⓒ Ⓓ
33. Ⓐ Ⓑ Ⓒ Ⓓ
34. Ⓐ Ⓑ Ⓒ Ⓓ
35. Ⓐ Ⓑ Ⓒ Ⓓ
36. Ⓐ Ⓑ Ⓒ Ⓓ

37. Ⓐ Ⓑ Ⓒ Ⓓ
38. Ⓐ Ⓑ Ⓒ Ⓓ
39. Ⓐ Ⓑ Ⓒ Ⓓ
40. Ⓐ Ⓑ Ⓒ Ⓓ
41. Ⓐ Ⓑ Ⓒ Ⓓ
42. Ⓐ Ⓑ Ⓒ Ⓓ
43. Ⓐ Ⓑ Ⓒ Ⓓ
44. Ⓐ Ⓑ Ⓒ Ⓓ
45. Ⓐ Ⓑ Ⓒ Ⓓ
46. Ⓐ Ⓑ Ⓒ Ⓓ
47. Ⓐ Ⓑ Ⓒ Ⓓ
48. Ⓐ Ⓑ Ⓒ Ⓓ
49. Ⓐ Ⓑ Ⓒ Ⓓ
50. Ⓐ Ⓑ Ⓒ Ⓓ
51. Ⓐ Ⓑ Ⓒ Ⓓ
52. Ⓐ Ⓑ Ⓒ Ⓓ
53. Ⓐ Ⓑ Ⓒ Ⓓ
54. Ⓐ Ⓑ Ⓒ Ⓓ

55. Ⓐ Ⓑ Ⓒ Ⓓ
56. Ⓐ Ⓑ Ⓒ Ⓓ
57. Ⓐ Ⓑ Ⓒ Ⓓ
58. Ⓐ Ⓑ Ⓒ Ⓓ
59. Ⓐ Ⓑ Ⓒ Ⓓ
60. Ⓐ Ⓑ Ⓒ Ⓓ
61. Ⓐ Ⓑ Ⓒ Ⓓ
62. Ⓐ Ⓑ Ⓒ Ⓓ
63. Ⓐ Ⓑ Ⓒ Ⓓ
64. Ⓐ Ⓑ Ⓒ Ⓓ
65. Ⓐ Ⓑ Ⓒ Ⓓ
66. Ⓐ Ⓑ Ⓒ Ⓓ
67. Ⓐ Ⓑ Ⓒ Ⓓ
68. Ⓐ Ⓑ Ⓒ Ⓓ
69. Ⓐ Ⓑ Ⓒ Ⓓ
70. Ⓐ Ⓑ Ⓒ Ⓓ
71. Ⓐ Ⓑ Ⓒ Ⓓ
72. Ⓐ Ⓑ Ⓒ Ⓓ

73. Ⓐ Ⓑ Ⓒ Ⓓ
74. Ⓐ Ⓑ Ⓒ Ⓓ
75. Ⓐ Ⓑ Ⓒ Ⓓ
76. Ⓐ Ⓑ Ⓒ Ⓓ
77. Ⓐ Ⓑ Ⓒ Ⓓ
78. Ⓐ Ⓑ Ⓒ Ⓓ
79. Ⓐ Ⓑ Ⓒ Ⓓ
80. Ⓐ Ⓑ Ⓒ Ⓓ
81. Ⓐ Ⓑ Ⓒ Ⓓ
82. Ⓐ Ⓑ Ⓒ Ⓓ
83. Ⓐ Ⓑ Ⓒ Ⓓ
84. Ⓐ Ⓑ Ⓒ Ⓓ
85. Ⓐ Ⓑ Ⓒ Ⓓ
86. Ⓐ Ⓑ Ⓒ Ⓓ
87. Ⓐ Ⓑ Ⓒ Ⓓ
88. Ⓐ Ⓑ Ⓒ Ⓓ
89. Ⓐ Ⓑ Ⓒ Ⓓ
90. Ⓐ Ⓑ Ⓒ Ⓓ

PRACTICE EXAMINATION V

Eligibility Specialist

DIRECTIONS: Each question has four suggested answers, lettered A,B,C, and D. Decide which one is the best answer and on the sample answer sheet locate the question number and with a soft pencil darken the area which corresponds to the answer that you have selected.

TIME ALLOWED FOR THE ENTIRE EXAMINATION: 3 HOURS

When answering questions on this test, assume that you are a Eligibility Specialist. Your duties and responsibilities are to determine and verify initial eligibility of applicants applying for public assistance and to determine and verify continuing eligibility of clients for social services whenever necessary.

If a question describes policy which differs from that followed by the social services agency in your locality the question should be answered on the basis of the policy described in the question.

1. Assume that an applicant, obviously under a great deal of stress, talks continuously and rambles, making it difficult for you to determine the exact problem and her need. In order to make the interview more successful, it would be best for you to

   (A) interrupt the applicant and ask her specific questions in order to get the information you need
   (B) tell the applicant that her rambling may be a basic cause of her problems
   (C) let the applicant continue talking as long as she wishes
   (D) ask the applicant to get to the point because other people are waiting for you.

2. An Eligibility Specialist must be able to interview clients all day and still be able to listen and maintain interest. Of the following, it is most important for you to show interest in the client because, if you appear interested,

   (A) the client is more likely to appreciate your professional status
   (B) the client is more likely to disclose a greater amount of information
   (C) the client is less likely to tell lies
   (D) you are more likely to gain your supervisor's approval.

3. The application process is overwhelming to applicant Marion King. She is very anxious and is fearful that she does not have all that she needs to be eligible for assistance. As a result, every time she is asked to produce a verifying document during the interview, she fumbles and drops all the other documents to the floor. Of the following, the most

effective method for you, the Eligibility Specialist, to use to complete the applicant process is to

(A) ask Ms. King not to be so nervous because you cannot get the work done if she fusses so much
(B) take the documents away from Ms. King and do it yourself
(C) suggest that Ms. King get a friend to come and help her with the papers
(D) try to calm Ms. King and tell her that you are willing to help her with the papers to get the information that you require.

4. An applicant for public assistance claims that her husband deserted the family and that she needs money immediately for food since her children have not eaten for two days. Under normal procedure, she has to wait several days before she can be given any money for this purpose. In accordance with departmental policy, no exception can be made in this case. Of the following, the best action for you to take is to

(A) tell her that, according to departmental policy, she cannot be given money immediately
(B) purchase some food for her, using your own funds, so that she can feed her children
(C) take up a collection among co-workers
(D) send her to another center.

5. Applicants for public assistance often complain about the length of the applicant form. They also claim that the questions are too personal, since all they want is money. It is true that the form is long, but the answers to all the questions on the form are needed so that the Department of Social Services can make a decision on eligibility. When applicants complain, which of the following would be the most appropriate action for you to take?

(A) Help such applicants understand that each question has a purpose which will help in the determination of eligibility
(B) Tell such applicants that you agree but that you must comply with regulations because it is your job
(C) Tell such applicants that they should stop complaining if they want you to help
(D) Refer such applicants to a supervisor who will explain agency policy.

6. Which one of the following statements best describes the primary goal of an Eligibility Specialist?

(A) Process as many clients in as short a time as possible
(B) Help clients
(C) Grow into a more understanding person
(D) Assert his or her authority.

7. Restating a question before the person being interviewed gives an answer to the original question is usually not good practice principally because

(A) the client will think you don't know your job
(B) it may confuse the client
(C) the interviewer should know exactly what to ask and how to put the question
(D) it reveals the interviewer's insecurity.

8. A white Eligibility Specialist can best improve his or her ability to work with black clients if he or she

(A) tries to forget that the clients are black
(B) tells the black clients that he or she has no prejudices
(C) becomes aware of the problems black clients face
(D) socializes with black workers in the agency.

9. A client warns that if he does not get what he wants he will report you, the Eligibility Specialist, to your supervisor and, if necessary, to the Mayor's Office. Of the following, the most appropriate response for you to make in this situation is to

(A) encourage the client to do as he threatens because you know that you are right
(B) call your supervisor in so that the client may confront him
(C) explain to the client how the decision will be made on his request
(D) try to understand the client's problem but tell him that he must not explode in the office because you will have to ask him to leave if he does.

10. Sometimes clients become silent during interviews. Of the following, the most probable reason for such silence is that the client is

(A) getting ready to tell a lie
(B) of low intelligence and does not know the answers to your questions
(C) thinking things over or has nothing more to say on the subject
(D) wishing he or she were not on welfare.

Questions 11 through 21 are to be answered solely on the basis of the following Schedule and Table and the given information and case situations. Questions 11 through 15 are based on Case Situation #1. Questions 16 through 21 are based on Case Situation #2.

SEMIMONTHLY FAMILY ALLOWANCE SCHEDULE (Based on Number of Persons In Household)

NUMBER OF PERSONS IN HOUSEHOLD						
One	Two	Three	Four	Five	Six	Each Additional Person
$47.00	$75.00	$100.00	$129.00	$159.00	$184.00	$25.00

CONVERSION TABLE—WEEKLY TO SEMIMONTHLY AMOUNTS

DOLLARS				CENTS			
Weekly Amount	Semi-Monthly Amount	Weekly Amount	Semi-Monthly Amount	Weekly Amount	Semi-Monthly Amount	Weekly Amount	Semi-Monthly Amount
$1.00	$2.17	$51.00	$110.50	$.01	$.02	$.51	$1.11
2.00	4.33	52.00	112.67	.02	.04	.52	1.13
3.00	6.50	53.00	114.83	.03	.07	.53	1.15
4.00	8.67	54.00	117.00	.04	.09	.54	1.17
5.00	10.83	55.00	119.17	.05	.11	.55	1.19
6.00	13.00	56.00	121.33	.06	.13	.56	1.21
7.00	15.17	57.00	123.50	.07	.15	.57	1.24
8.00	17.33	58.00	125.67	.08	.17	.58	1.26
9.00	19.50	59.00	127.83	.09	.20	.59	1.28
10.00	21.67	60.00	130.00	.10	.22	.60	1.30
11.00	23.83	61.00	132.17	.11	.24	.61	1.32
12.00	26.00	62.00	134.33	.12	.26	.62	1.34
13.00	28.17	63.00	136.50	.13	.28	.63	1.37
14.00	30.33	64.00	138.67	.14	.30	.64	1.39
15.00	32.50	65.00	140.83	.15	.33	.65	1.41
16.00	34.67	66.00	143.00	.16	.35	.66	1.43
17.00	36.83	67.00	145.17	.17	.37	.67	1.45
18.00	39.00	68.00	147.33	.18	.39	.68	1.47
19.00	41.17	69.00	149.50	.19	.41	.69	1.50
20.00	43.33	70.00	151.67	.20	.43	.70	1.52
21.00	45.50	71.00	153.83	.21	.46	.71	1.54
22.00	47.67	72.00	156.00	.22	.48	.72	1.56
23.00	49.83	73.00	158.17	.23	.50	.73	1.58
24.00	52.00	74.00	160.33	.24	.52	.74	1.60
25.00	54.17	75.00	162.50	.25	.54	.75	1.63
26.00	56.33	76.00	164.67	.26	.56	.76	1.65
27.00	58.50	77.00	166.83	.27	.59	.77	1.67
28.00	60.67	78.00	169.00	.28	.61	.78	1.69
29.00	62.83	79.00	171.17	.29	.63	.79	1.71
30.00	65.00	80.00	173.33	.30	.65	.80	1.73
31.00	67.17	81.00	175.50	.31	.67	.81	1.76
32.00	69.33	82.00	177.67	.32	.69	.82	1.78
33.00	71.50	83.00	179.83	.33	.72	.83	1.80
34.00	73.67	84.00	182.00	.34	.74	.84	1.82
35.00	75.83	85.00	184.17	.35	.76	.85	1.84
36.00	78.00	86.00	186.33	.36	.78	.86	1.86
37.00	80.17	87.00	188.50	.37	.80	.87	1.89
38.00	82.33	88.00	190.67	.38	.82	.88	1.91
39.00	84.50	89.00	192.83	.39	.85	.89	1.93
40.00	86.67	90.00	195.00	.40	.87	.90	1.95
41.00	88.83	91.00	197.17	.41	.89	.91	1.97
42.00	91.00	92.00	199.33	.42	.91	.92	1.99
43.00	93.17	93.00	201.50	.43	.93	.93	2.02
44.00	95.33	94.00	203.67	.44	.95	.94	2.04
45.00	97.50	95.00	205.83	.45	.98	.95	2.06
46.00	99.67	96.00	208.00	.46	1.00	.96	2.08
47.00	101.83	97.00	210.17	.47	1.02	.97	2.10
48.00	104.00	98.00	212.33	.48	1.04	.98	2.12
49.00	106.17	99.00	214.50	.49	1.06	.99	2.15
50.00	108.33	100.00	216.67	.50	1.08		

Public assistance grants are computed on a semimonthly basis. This means that all figures are first broken down into semimonthly amounts, and that when a client receives a check twice a month, each semimonthly check covers his or her requirements for a period of approximately 2-⅙ weeks. The grants are computed by means of the following procedures.

1. Determine the semimonthly allowance for the family from the SemiMonthly Family Allowance Schedule.
2. Determine total semimonthly income by deducting from the semimonthly gross earnings (the wages or salary before payroll deductions) all semimonthly expenses for federal, state, and city income taxes, Social Security payments, State Disability Insurance payments, union dues, cost of transportation, and $1.00 per work day for lunch.
3. Add the semimonthly allowance and the semimonthly rent (monthly rent must be divided in half).
4. Subtract the semimonthly income (if there is any income).
5. The formula for computing the semimonthly grant is:

$$
\begin{array}{ll}
\text{Family Allowance} + \text{Rent} & \text{(semimonthly)} \\
-\text{Total Income} & \text{(semimonthly)} \\
\hline
=\text{Amount of Grant} & \text{(semimonthly)}
\end{array}
$$

6. Refer to the Conversion Table in order to convert weekly amount into semimonthly amounts.

Case Situation #1

The Smiths receive public assistance. The family includes John Smith, his wife Barbara, and their four children. They occupy a five-room apartment for which the rent is $105.00 per month. Mr. Smith is employed as a porter and his gross wages are $100 per week. He is employed five days a week and spends $.70 a day carfare. He buys his lunches. The following weekly deductions are made from his salary:

Social Security	$6.00
Disability Benefits	.38
Federal Income Tax	4.30
State Income Tax	2.80
City Income Tax	1.00

Case Situation #2

The Jones family receives public assistance. The family includes Steven and Diane Jones and their two children. They occupy a four-room apartment for which the rental is $85.00 a month. Mr. Jones is employed as a handyman, and his gross wages are $90 per week. He is employed 4 days a week and spends $.70 a day carfare. He buys his lunches. He has the following weekly deductions made from his salary:

Social Security	$4.00
Disability Benefits	.27
Federal Income Tax	3.89
State Income Tax	2.05
City Income Tax	.62

When answering questions 11 through 15, refer to Case Situation #1.

11. The weekly amount that Mr. Smith contributes towards Social Security, Disability Benefits, and Income Taxes is

(A) $31.37
(B) $23.14
(C) $14.48
(D) $10.58

12. The semimonthly family allowance for the Smith family is

(A) $129.00
(B) $159.00
(C) $184.00
(D) $184.50

13. What is the total of semimonthly expenses related to Mr. Smith's employment which will be deducted from semimonthly gross earnings to compute semimonthly income?

(A) $49.78
(B) $42.20
(C) $38.95
(D) $22.98

14. Which of the following amounts is the total semimonthly income for the Smith family?

(A) $216.67
(B) $200.00
(C) $166.89
(D) $22.98

15. The semimonthly amount of the grant which the Smith family is entitled to receive is

(A) $236.50
(B) $184.00
(C) $139.22
(D) $69.61

When answering questions 16 through 21, refer to Case Situation #2.

16. The weekly amount that Mr. Jones contributes towards Social Security, Disability Benefits, and Income Taxes is

(A) $10.83
(B) $17.63
(C) $23.43
(D) $23.74

17. The semimonthly allowance for the Jones family is

(A) $75.00
(B) $100.00
(C) $122.00
(D) $129.00

18. The total of semimonthly expenses related to Mr. Jones' employment which will be deducted from semimonthly gross earnings is

(A) $17.23
(B) $18.93
(C) $38.20
(D) $40.72

19. Which of the following amounts is the total semimonthly income for the Jones family?

(A) $128.20
(B) $155.32
(C) $156.80
(D) $212.23

20. The grant which the Jones family will receive is

(A) $14.70
(B) $29.40
(C) 129.00
(D) $171.50

21. If Mr. Jones' monthly rent were $105, what would the amount of the grant be?

(A) $24.70
(B) $49.40
(C) $77.20
(D) $182.20

Each of questions 22 through 26 consists of information given in outline form and four sentences labelled, A,B,C, and D. For each question choose the one sentence which correctly expresses the information given in outline form and which also displays proper English usage.

22. Client's Name—Joanna Jones   Client's Income—None
Number of Children—3   Client's Marital Status—Single

(A) Joanna Jones is an unmarried client with three children who have no income.
(B) Joanna Jones, who is single and has no income, a client she has three children.
(C) Joanna Jones, whose three children are clients, is single and has no income.
(D) Joanna Jones, who has three children, is an unmarried client with no income.

23. Client's Name—Bertha Smith   Client's Rent—$105 per month
Number of Children—2   Number of Rooms—4

(A) Bertha Smith, a client, pays $105 per month for her four rooms.
(B) Client Bertha Smith has two children and pays $105 per month for four rooms.
(C) Client Bertha Smith is paying $105 per month for two children with four rooms.
(D) For four rooms and two children client Bertha Smith pays $105 per month.

24. Name of Employee—Cynthia Dawes
Number of Cases Assigned—9
Date Cases Were Assigned—12/16/89
Number of Assigned Cases Completed—8

(A) On December 16, 1989, employee Cynthia Dawes was assigned nine cases; she has completed eight of these cases.
(B) Cynthia Dawes, employee on December 16, 1989, assigned nine cases, she completed eight.
(C) Being employed on December 16, 1989, Cynthia Dawes completed eight of nine assigned cases.
(D) Employee Cynthia Dawes, she was assigned nine cases and completed eight, on December 16, 1989.

25. Place of Audit—Broadway Center
Names of Auditors—Paul Cahn, Raymond Perez

Date of Audit—11/20/89
Number of Cases Audited—41

(A) On November 20, 1989 at the Broadway Center 41 cases was audited by auditors Paul Cahn and Raymond Perez.

(B) Auditors Raymond Perez and Paul Cahn has audited 41 cases at the Broadway Center, on November 20, 1989.

(C) At the Broadway Center, on November 20, 1989, auditors Paul Cahn and Raymond Perez audited 41 cases.

(D) Auditors Paul Cahn and Raymond Perez at the Broadway Center, on November 20, 1989, is auditing 41 cases.

26. Name of Client—Barbra Levine   Client's Monthly Expenses—$452
Client's Monthly Income—$210

(A) Barbra Levine is a client, her monthly income is $210 and her monthly expenses is $452.

(B) Barbra Levine's monthly income is $210 and she is a client, with whose monthly expenses are $452.

(C) Barbra Levine is a client whose monthly income is $210 and whose monthly expenses are $452.

(D) Barbara Levine, a client, is with a monthly income which is $210 and monthly expenses which are $452.

Answer questions 27 through 31 solely on the basis of the information contained in the following passage.

Any person who is living in New York City and is otherwise eligible may be granted public assistance whether or not he or she has New York State residence. However, since New York City does not contribute to the cost of assistance granted to persons who are without State residence, the cases of all recipients must be formally identified as to whether or not each member of the household has State residence.

To acquire State residence, a person must have resided in New York State continuously for one year. Such residence is not lost unless the person is out of the State continuously for a period of one year or longer. Continuous residence does not include any period during which the individual is a patient in a hospital, an inmate of a public institution or of an incorporated private institution, a resident on a military reservation, or a minor residing in a boarding home while under the care of an authorized agency. Receipt of public assistance does not prevent a person from acquiring State residence. State residence, once acquired, is not lost because of absence from the State while a person is serving in the U.S. Armed Forces or the Merchant Marine; nor does a member of the family of such a person lose State residence while living with or near that person in these circumstances.

Each person, regardless of age, acquires or loses State residence as an individual. There is no derivative State residence except for an infant at the time of birth. He or she is deemed to have State residence if he or she is in the custody of both parents and either one of them has State residence, or if the parent having custody of him or her has State residence.

27. According to the passage, an infant is deemed to have New York State residence at the time of birth if

(A) he or she is born in New York State but neither of the parents is a resident

(B) he or she is in the custody of only one parent, who is not a resident, but his or her other parent is a resident

(C) his or her brother and sister are residents

(D) he or she is in the custody of both parents but only one of them is a resident.

28. The Jones family consists of five members. Jack and Mary Jones have lived in New York State continuously for the past eighteen months after having lived in Ohio since they were born. Of their three children, one was born ten months ago and has been in the custody of his parents since birth. Their second child lived in Ohio until six months ago and then moved in with his parents. Their third child had never lived in New York until he moved with his parents to New York eighteen months ago. However, he entered the Armed Forces one month later and has not lived in New York since that time. Based on the passage, how many members of the Jones family are New York State residents?

   (A) 2
   (B) 3
   (C) 4
   (D) 5

29. Assuming that each of the following individuals has lived continuously in New York State for the past year, and has never previously lived in the State, which one of them is a New York State resident?

   (A) Jack Salinas, who has been an inmate in a State correctional facility for six months of the year.
   (B) Fran Johnson, who has lived on an Army base for the entire year.
   (C) Arlene Snyder, who married a nonresident during the past year.
   (D) Gary Phillips, who was a patient in a Veterans Administration hospital for the entire year.

30. The passage implies that the reason for determining whether or not a recipient of public assistance is a State resident is that

   (A) the cost of assistance for nonresidents is not a New York City responsibility
   (B) nonresidents living in New York City are not eligible for public assistance
   (C) recipients of public assistance are barred from acquiring State residence
   (D) New York City is responsible for the full cost of assistance to recipients who are residents.

31. Assume that the Rollins household in New York City consists of six members at the present time—Anne Rollins, her three children, her aunt, and her uncle. Anne Rollins and one of her children moved to New York City seven months ago. Neither of them had previously lived in New York State. Her other two children have lived in New York City continuously for the past two years, as has her aunt. Anne Rollins' uncle had lived in New York City continuously for many years until two years ago. He then entered the Armed Forces and has returned to New York City within the past month. Based on the passage, how many members of the Rollins' household are New York State residents?

   (A) 2
   (B) 3
   (C) 4
   (D) 6

32. You are interviewing a client to determine whether financial assistance should be continued and you find that what he is telling you does not agree exactly with your records. Of the following, the best way to handle this situation is to

   (A) recommend that his public assistance payments be stopped, since you have caught him lying to you
   (B) tell the client about the points of disagreement and ask him if he can clear them up
   (C) give the client the benefit of the doubt and recommend continuation of his payments
   (D) show the client the records and warn him that he must either tell the truth or lose his benefits.

33. An applicant for public assistance gets angry at some of the questions you must ask her. Of the following, the best way to handle this situation is to
    (A) assume that she is trying to hide something and end the interview
    (B) skip the questions that bother her and come back to them at the end of the interview
    (C) tell her that she must either answer the questions or leave
    (D) explain to her that you are required to get answers to all the questions in order to be able to help her.

34. At the end of an interview to determine whether financial assistance should be continued, the client offers to take you to lunch. Of the following, the best response to such an invitation is to
    (A) tell the client that you do not take bribes and report the matter to your supervisor
    (B) accept the invitation if you have the time, but do not let it influence your recommendation as to his eligibility for continuing public assistance
    (C) politely refuse the invitation, and do not let it influence your recommendation as to his continuing public assistance
    (D) point out to the client that his budget does not include money for entertaining.

Answer questions 35 through 39 solely on the basis of the information, the assumptions, and the table on the following page.

Each question describes an applicant family. You are to determine into which of the four categories (A,B,C, or D) each of the applicant families should be placed. In order to do this, you must match the description of the applicant family with the factors determining eligibility for each of the four categories. Each applicant family must meet all of the criteria for the category.

Assumptions for all questions

1. The information in the following table does not necessarily reflect actual practice in a municipal Department of Social Services.
2. The date of application is January 25, 1984.
3. Each applicant family that cannot be placed in categories A,B, or C must be placed in category D.
4. A "dependent child" is a child who is less than 18 years of age, or less than 21 years of age if attending school full time, who depends upon its parents for support.
5. A mother in a family with one or more dependent children is not expected to work and her work status is not to be considered in establishing the category of the family.

CATEGORY OF APPLICANT FAMILY	FACTORS DETERMINING ELIGIBILITY
A	(1) There is at least one dependent child in the home. (2) Children are deprived of parental support because father is (a) Deceased (b) Absent from the home (c) Incapacitated due to medically verified illness (d) Over age 65 (e) Not fully employed because of verified ill health. (3) 1 or more parent or guardian reside in the same home as the children. (4) Applicant family must have resided in New York State for a period of one year or more.
B	(1) There is at least one dependent child in the home. (2) Both parents are in the home and are not incapacitated. (3) Both parents are the children's natural parents. (4) Father unemployed or works less than 70 hours per month. (5) Father has recent work history. (6) Father not currently receiving Unemployment Insurance Benefits. (7) Father available and willing to work. (8) Applicant family must have resided in New York State for a period of one year or more.
C	(1) There is a veteran of the Vietnam War in the home. (2) Applicant families do not meet the criteria for Categories A or B.
D	Applicant families do not meet the criteria for Categories A, B, or C.

35. Woman, age 52, with child 6 years old whom she states was left in her home at the age of 2. Woman states child is her niece, and she has no knowledge of whereabouts of parents or any other relatives. Both woman and child have resided in New York State since June 15, 1983.

36. Married couple with 2 dependent children at home. Family has resided in New York State for the last 5 years. Wife cannot work. Husband, veteran of Korean War, can work only 15 hours a week due to kidney ailment (verified).

37. Married couple, both age 35, with 3 dependent children at home, 1 of whom is 17 years of age. Wife available for work and presently working 2 days a week, 7 hours each day. Husband, who was laid off two weeks ago, is not eligible for Unemployment Insurance Benefits. Family has resided in New York State since January 1, 1983.

38. Married couple with 1 dependent child at home. They have resided in New York State since January 25, 1982. Wife must remain home to take care of child. Husband veteran of World War II. Husband is available for work on a limited basis because of heart

condition which has been verified. A second child, a married 17-year-old son, lives in California.

39. Married couple with 2 children, ages 6 and 12, at home. Family has resided in New York State since June 12, 1970. Wife not available for work. Husband, who served in the Vietnam War, was laid off three weeks ago and is receiving Unemployment Insurance Benefits of $50.00 weekly.

40. Of the following, the most important reason for referring public assistance clients for employment or training is to
    (A) give them self-confidence
    (B) make them self-supporting
    (C) have them learn a new trade
    (D) take them off the streets.

41. The applicant you are interviewing is a man in his late forties who has recently lost his job and has a family of eight to support. He is very upset and tells you he does not know where he will get the money to purchase food for the family and pay the rent. He does not know what he will do if he is found not eligible for public assistance. He asks you whether you think he will be eligible. You feel the applicant has a good chance and you think he should receive financial assistance, but you are not completely certain that he is eligible for public assistance under departmental policy. Of the following, the best action for you to take is to
    (A) reassure the applicant and tell him you are sure everything will be all right, because there is no sense in worrying him before you know for certain that he is not eligible
    (B) tell the applicant that as far as you are concerned he should receive public assistance but that you are not certain the department will go along with your recommendation
    (C) tell the applicant that you are not sure that he will be found eligible for public assistance
    (D) adopt a cool manner, and tell the applicant that he must behave like an adult and not allow himself to become emotional about the situation.

42. When conducting an interview with a client receiving public assistance, it would be least important for you to try to
    (A) understand the reasons for the client's statements
    (B) conduct the interview on the client's intellectual level
    (C) imitate the client's speech as much as possible
    (D) impress the client with the agency's concern for his or her welfare.

Answer questions 43 through 46 on the basis of the case history of the Foster family which follows on page 163.

THE FOSTER CASE HISTORY

Form W-341-C
Rev. 3/1/82
600M-804077-S-200 (73)-245

Date: Jan 25, 1989
Case Name: Foster
Case #: ADC-3415968

Family Composition:
Ann Foster,	b. 7.23.52
Gerry	b. 1.7.77
Susan	b. 4.1.79
John	b. 5.3.82
Joan	b. 10.14.85

Mrs. Foster was widowed in June 1986 when her husband was killed in a car accident. Since that time the family has received public assistance. Mrs. Foster has been referred for housekeeping service by the Social Service Department of Lincoln Hospital where she is being treated in the neurology clinic. Her primary diagnosis is multiple sclerosis. The hospital reports that she is going through a period of deterioration characterized by an unsteady gait, and weakness and tremor in the limbs. At this time her capacity to manage a household and four children is severely limited. She feels quite overwhelmed and is unable to function adequately in taking care of her home.

In addition to the medical reasons, it is advisable that a housekeeper be placed in the home as part of a total plan to avoid further family breakdown and deterioration. This deterioration is reflected by all family members. Mrs. Foster is severely depressed and is unable to meet the needs of her children, who have a variety of problems. Joan, the youngest, is not speaking, is hyperactive, and in general is not developing normally for a child her age. John is showing learning problems in school and has poor articulation. Susan was not promoted last year and is a behavior problem at home. Gerry, the oldest, is deformed due to a fire at age two. It is clear that Mrs. Foster cannot control or properly discipline her children, but even more important is the fact that she is unable to offer them the encouragement and guidance they require.

It is hoped that providing housekeeping service will relieve Mrs. Foster of the basic household chores so that she will be less frustrated and better able to provide the love and guidance needed by her children.

43. The age of the child who is described as not developing normally, hyperactive, and not speaking is
(A) 4
(B) 7
(C) 10
(D) 13

44. Which of the following cannot be verified on the basis of the Foster case history?
(A) William Foster was Ann Foster's husband
(B) Mrs. Foster has been seen in the neurology clinic at Lincoln Hospital.
(C) John Foster has trouble with his speech.
(D) The Foster family has received public assistance since June 1986.

45. The form on which the information about the Foster family is presented is known as
(A) Family Composition Form
(B) Form Rev. 3.1/82
(C) Form W-341-C
(D) ADC-3415968

46. According to the preceding case history, housekeeping service is being requested primarily because
(A) no one in the family can perform the household chores
(B) Mrs. Foster suffers from multiple sclerosis and requires assistance with the household chores
(C) the children are exhibiting behavior problems resulting from the mother's illness
(D) the children have no father.

47. You notice that an applicant whom you rejected for public assistance is back at the Center the following morning and is waiting to be interviewed by another Eligibility Specialist in your group. Of the following, the best approach for you to take is to

(A) inform the Eligibility Specialist, before she interviews the applicant, that you had interviewed and rejected him the previous day
(B) not inform the Eligibility Specialist about the situation and let her make her own decision
(C) approach the applicant and tell him he was rejected for good reason and will have to leave the Center immediately
(D) ask the Specialist Officer at the Center to remove the applicant.

48. You have just finished interviewing an applicant who has a violent temper and has displayed a great amount of hostility toward you during the interview. You find he is ineligible for public assistance. Departmental policy is that all applicants are notified by mail in a day or so of their acceptance or rejection for public assistance. However, you also have the option, if you think it is desirable, of notifying the applicant at the interview. Of the following, the best action for you to take in this case is to

(A) tell the applicant of his rejection during the interview
(B) have the applicant notified of the results of the interview by mail only
(C) ask your supervisor to inform the applicant of his rejection
(D) inform the applicant of the results of the interview, with a Special Patrolman at your side.

49. You are interviewing a client who speaks English poorly and whose native language is Spanish. Your knowledge of Spanish is very limited. Of the following, the first action it would be best for you to take is to

(A) try to locate an Eligibility Specialist at the Center who speaks Spanish
(B) write out your questions, because it is easier for people to understand
(C) do the best you can, using hand gestures to make yourself understood
(D) tell the client to return with a friend or relative who speaks English.

50. During an interview with a client of another race, she accuses you of racial prejudice and asks for an interviewer of her own race. Of the following, which is the best way to handle the situation?

(A) In a friendly manner, tell the client that eligibility is based on regulations and the facts, not on prejudice, and ask her to continue with the interview.
(B) Explain to your supervisor that you cannot deal with someone who accuses you of prejudice, and ask your supervisor to assign the client someone of her own race.
(C) Assure the client that you will lean over backwards to treat her application favorably.
(D) Tell the client that some of your friends are of her race and that you could therefore not possibly be prejudiced.

In order to answer questions 51 through 55, assume that you, as a Eligibility Specialist, have been asked to write a short report on the basis of the information contained in the following passage about the granting of emergency funds to the Smith family.

Mr. and Mrs. Smith, who have been receiving public assistance for the last six months, arrive at the Center the morning of August 2, 1983 totally upset and anxious because they and their family have been burned out of their apartment the night before. The fire seems to have been of suspicious origin because at the time it broke out witnesses spotted two neighborhood teenagers running away from the scene. The police officers, who arrived on the scene shortly after the firefighters, took down the pertinent information about the alleged arsonists.

The Smiths have spent the night with friends but now request emergency housing and emergency funds for themselves and their four children to purchase food and to replace the clothing which was destroyed by the fire. The burned-out apartment had consisted of five rooms and a bath, and the Smiths are now worried that they will be forced to accept smaller accommodations. Furthermore, since Mrs. Smith suffers from a heart murmur, she is worried that their new living quarters will necessitate her climbing too many stairs. Her previous apartment was a one-flight walk-up which was acceptable.

As an Eligibility Specialist you have studied the case, determined the amount of the emergency grant, made temporary arrangements for the Smiths to stay at a hotel, and reassured Mrs. Smith that everything possible will be done to find them an apartment which will meet with their approval.

51. Which of the following would it be best to include in the report as the reason for the emergency grant?

(A) "The police have decided that the fire is of suspicious origin."
(B) "Two neighborhood teenagers were seen leaving the scene of the fire."
(C) "The apartment of the Smith family has been destroyed by fire."
(D) "Mrs. Smith suffers from a heart murmur and cannot climb stairs."

52. Which of the following would it be best to accept as verification of the fire?

(A) A letter from the friend with whom the Smiths stayed the previous night.
(B) A photograph of the fire.
(C) A dated newspaper clipping describing the fire.
(D) A note from the Smiths' neighbors.

53. A report of the Smith family's need for a new apartment must be sent to the Center's Housing Specialist. Which of the following recommendations for housing would be most appropriate?

(A) two bedrooms, first floor walk-up
(B) five rooms, ground floor
(C) two-room suite, hotel with elevator
(D) three rooms, building with elevator

54. For which of the following are the Smiths requesting emergency funds?

(A) Furniture
(B) Food
(C) A hotel room
(D) Repairs in their apartment.

55. Which of the following statements provides the best summary of the action taken by you, the Eligibility Specialist, on the Smith case and is most important for inclusion in your report?

(A) Mr. and Mrs. Smith arrived upset and anxious and were reassured.
(B) It was verified that there was a fire.
(C) Temporary living arrangements were made and the amount of the emergency grant was determined.
(D) The case was studied and a new apartment was found for the Smiths which met with their approval.

56. It is important that you remember what has happened between you and a client during an interview so that you may deliver appropriate services. However, the one of the following which is the most likely reason that taking notes during the interview may not always be a good practice is that

(A) you may lose the notes and have to go back and see the client again
(B) some clients may believe that you are not interested in what they are saying
(C) you are the only one who is likely to read the notes
(D) some clients may believe that you are not smart enough to remember what happened in the interview.

57. Before an applicant seeking public assistance can be interviewed, he or she must fill out a complex applicant form which consists of eleven pages of questions requesting very detailed information. Of the following, the best time for the Eligibility Specialist to review the information on the application form is

(A) before beginning to interview the applicant
(B) after asking the applicant a few questions to put him or her at ease
(C) towards the end of the interview to have a chance to think about the information received during the interview
(D) after the interview has been completed.

In questions 58 through 60, choose the letter word which means most nearly the same as the underlined word in the sentences.

58. "He needed monetary assistance because he was incapacitated." The word incapacitated means, most nearly,

(A) uneducated
(B) disabled
(C) uncooperative
(D) discharged.

59. The Case Worker explained to the client that signing the document was compulsory." The word compulsory means, most nearly,

(A) temporary
(B) required
(C) different
(D) discharged.

60. The woman's actions did not jeopardize her eligibility for benefits. The word jeopardize means, most nearly,

(A) delay
(B) reinforce
(C) determine
(D) endanger.

Answer questions 61 through 64 solely on the basis of the information given in the Fact Situation and Sample form below and on page 167.

FACT SITUATION

On October 7, 1983, John Smith (case # ADC-U 1467912) applied and was accepted for public assistance for himself and his family. His family consists of his wife, Helen, and their children: William, age 9; John Jr., age 6; and Mary, age 2. The family has lived in a five-room apartment located at 142 Wales Street, Midvale City, since July 18, 1977. Mr. Smith signed a 2-year lease for this apartment on July 18, 1983, at a rent of $250 per month. The maximum rental allowance for a family of this size is $210 a month. Utilities are included in this rent-controlled multiple dwelling.

Since the cost of renting this apartment is in excess of the allowable amount, the Eligibility Specialist is required to fill out a "Request for Approval of Exception to Policy for Shelter Allowance/Rehousing Expenses." A sample of a section of this form follows.

SAMPLE FORM

REQUEST FOR APPROVAL OF EXCEPTION TO POLICY FOR SHELTER ALLOWANCE/REHOUSING EXPENSES

Case Name	Case Number or Pending	Acceptance Date	Group No.
Present Address Zip	Apt. No. or Location	No. of Rooms	Rent per Mo. $	Occupancy Date

HOUSEHOLD COMPOSITION *(List all persons living in the household)* Column 1		Column 2	Col. 3	Column 4 Relation to	Column 5 Marital	Column 6 P.A.
Surname	First	Birthdate	Sex	Case Head	Status	Status

61. Based on the information given in the Fact Situation, which one of the following should be entered in the space for "Occupancy Date"?

(A) October 7, 1983
(B) July 18, 1983
(C) July 18, 1977
(D) Unknown

62. What amount should be entered in the space labeled "Rent per Mo."?

(A) $250
(B) $210
(C) $150
(D) $40

63. Based on the information given in the Fact Situation, it is impossible to fill in which one of the following blanks?

(A) "Case Number or Pending"
(B) "Acceptable Date"
(C) "Apt. No. or Location"
(D) "No. of Rooms"

64. Which of the following should be entered in Column 4 for Helen Smith?

(A) wife
(B) head
(C) mother
(D) unknown

In questions 65 through 73, perform the computations indicated and choose the correct answer from the four choices given.

65. Add $4.34, $3.50, $6.00, $101.76, $90.67. From the result subtract $60.54 and $10.56.

(A) $76.17
(B) $156.37
(C) $166.17
(D) $300.37

66. Add 2,200; 2,600; 252; and 47.96. From the result subtract 202.70; 1,200; 2,150; and 434.43.

(A) 1,112.83
(B) 1,213.46
(C) 1,341.51
(D) 1,348.91

67. Multiply 1850 by .05 and multiply 3300 by .08 and then add both results.

(A) 242.50
(B) 264.00
(C) 333.25
(D) 356.50

68. Multiply 312.77 by .04. Round off the result to the nearest hundredth.

(A) 12.52
(B) 12.511
(C) 12.518
(D) 12.51

69. Add 362.05, 91.13, 347.81, and 17.46 and then divide the result by 6. The answer, rounded off to the nearest hundredth, is

(A) 138.409
(B) 137.409
(C) 136.41
(D) 136.40

70. Add 66.25 and 15.06 and then multiply the result by 2 1/6. The answer is most nearly

(A) 176.18
(B) 176.17
(C) 162.66
(D) 162.62

71. Each of the following options contains three decimals. In which case do all three decimals have the same value?

(A) .3; .30; .03
(B) .25; .250; .2500
(C) 1.9; 1.90; 1.09
(D) 3.5; .350; .035

72. Add 1/2 the sum of (539.84 and 479.26) to 1/3 the sum of (1,461.93 and 927.27). Round off the result to the nearest whole number.

(A) 3,408
(B) 2,899
(C) 1,816
(D) 1,306

73. Multiply $5,906.09 by 15% and then divide the result by 1/3.

    (A) $295.30
    (B) $885.91
    (C) $8,859.14
    (D) $29,530.45

Answer questions 74 through 78 solely on the basis of the information provided in the following passage.

The ideal relationship for the interview is one of mutual confidence. To try to pretend, to put on a front of cordiality and friendship, is extremely unwise for the interviewer because he or she will almost certainly convey, by subtle means, his or her real feelings. It is the interviewer's responsibility to take the lead in establishing a relationship of mutual confidence.

As the interviewer, you should help the interviewee to feel at ease and ready to talk. One of the best ways to do this is to be at ease yourself. If you are, it will probably be evident; if you are not, it will almost certainly be apparent to the interviewee.

Begin the interview with topics for discussion which are easy to talk about and nonmenacing. This interchange can be like the conversation of people when they are waiting for a bus, at the ball game, or discussing the weather. However, do not prolong this warm-up too long, since the interviewee knows as well as you do that these are not the things he or she came to discuss. Delaying too long in getting down to business may suggest to him or her that you are reluctant to deal with the topic.

Once you get onto the main topics, do all you can to get the interviewee to talk freely with as little prodding from you as possible. This will probably require that you give him or her some idea of the area, and of ways of looking at it. Avoid, however, prejudicing or coloring the interviewee's remarks by what you say; especially, do not in any way indicate that there are certain things you want to hear, others which you do not want to hear. It is essential that the interviewee feel free to express his or her own ideas unhampered by your ideas, your values, and preconceptions.

Do not appear to dominate the interview, nor have even the suggestion of a patronizing attitude. Ask some questions which will enable the interviewee to take pride in his or her knowledge. Take the attitude that the interviewee sincerely wants the interview to achieve its purpose. This creates a warm, permissive atmosphere that is most important in all interviews.

74. Of the following, the best title for the above passage is

    (A) Permissiveness in Interviewing
    (B) Interviewing Techniques
    (C) The Factor of Pretense in the Interview
    (D) The Cordial Interview.

75. Which of the following recommendations on the conduct of an interview is made by the above passage?

    (A) Conduct the interview as if it were an interchange between people discussing the weather.
    (B) The interview should be conducted in a highly impersonal manner.
    (C) Allow enough time for the interview, so that the interviewee does not feel rushed.
    (D) Start the interview with topics which are noncontroversial and not threatening to the interviewee.

76. The passage indicated that the interviewer should

    (A) feel free to express his or her opinions
    (B) patronize the interviewee and display a permissive attitude
    (C) permit the interviewee to give the needed information in his or her own fashion
    (D) provide for privacy when conducting the interview.

77. The meaning of the word "unhampered" as it is used in the last sentence of the fourth paragraph of the preceding passage is most nearly

    (A) unheeded
    (B) unobstructed
    (C) hindered
    (D) aided.

78. It can be inferred from the passage that

    (A) interviewers, while generally mature, lack confidence
    (B) certain methods of interviewing are more successful than others in obtaining information
    (C) there is usually a reluctance on the part of interviewers to deal with unpleasant topics
    (D) it is best for the interviewer not to waiver from the use of hard and fast rules when dealing with clients.

79. The applicant whom you are interviewing is not talking rationally, and he admits that he is under the influence of alcohol. Which of the following is the best way of handling this situation?

    (A) Call a security guard and have the applicant removed.
    (B) Tell the applicant that unless he gets control of himself, he will not receive financial assistance.
    (C) Send out for a cup of black coffee for the applicant.
    (D) End the interview and plan to schedule another appointment.

80. During an interview, an applicant who has submitted an application for assistance breaks down and cries. Of the following, the best way of handling this situation is to

    (A) end the interview and schedule a new appointment
    (B) be patient and sympathetic, and encourage the applicant to continue the interview
    (C) tell the applicant sternly that crying will not help matters
    (D) tell the applicant that you will do everthing you can do to get the application approved.

81. The family budget is a device used by many social service agencies to

    (A) determine changes in the cost-of-living index
    (B) estimate the needs of families and the amount of assistance necessary to meet these needs
    (C) evaluate its financial condition
    (D) estimate probable expenditures during a given period.

Answer questions 82 through 84 solely on the basis of information contained in the following passage on page 171.

A city's policy might well tackle the problem of homelessness by having the following two goals:

1. Prevent both individuals and families from becoming homeless.

   If we are to halt the growth of homelessness, we must help both single persons and families attain or maintain self-sufficiency. We must not only continue but expand existing governmental programs which directly and indirectly help those who are potentially or actually threatened with eviction so that they will not be forced to abandon their place of residence.

2. Increase the number of permanent homes which are affordable and available to both the homeless and to those who are potentially homeless.

Both of these goals are based on the belief that aside from certain individual cases, people are better off if they live outside of municipal shelters. Although there is no doubt that the conditions under which many people live today are horrifying and include terrible and/or unstable housing and family situations, utilization of the shelter system on a long-term basis will solve neither these housing nor these familial problems. A municipal shelter cannot provide the physical space, privacy, or amenities an individual or family needs if they are to lead normal lives. It affords them no real chance to live in a viable community. Above all, long-term residence in a municipal shelter almost inevitably results in a disincentive to independence.

82. Assume a family has been living in a municipal shelter set up for the temporary housing of the homeless for almost a year. Based on the passage above and on good social case work practice, you, the social Case Worker at the shelter, should

(A) take steps immediately to have the family leave the shelter, since law and public policy do not permit long-term residence at a shelter

(B) bring the matter of their long-term residence at the shelter to the immediate attention of those persons in charge of finding suitable housing outside the shelter for the family for possible priority consideration

(C) allow the family to remain at the shelter since they have apparently adjusted well to that type of living arrangement

(D) inquire of the family whether they desire to remain in the shelter or would prefer housing elsewhere and take action based on their response.

83. According to the passage, of the following, the most important reason for not allowing a family or an individual to remain in a shelter for an extended period of time is that

(A) it has been determined that it is more expensive to provide shelter care in a city-run shelter than in a privately owned hotel

(B) allowing an individual or family to remain in the city-owned shelter for a long time prevents placement of another newly homeless person or family in the facility, and there are only a limited number of accommodations available in the facility

(C) long-term reliance on housing in a public facility is detrimental to an individual's or family's ability or interest in retaining independence and interest in becoming self-supporting.

(D) shelters are not usually attractive or well-managed and are very crowded so that long-term residence at a municipal shelter causes depression.

84. Assume the landlord of a family on public assistance has stated that he is going to raise the family's rent above the amount currently being paid. Of the following, based on the passage, you, the family's social Case Worker, should

(A) refuse to allow the family to pay the increase even if they are going to be evicted because it is exorbitant
(B) threaten to bring the landlord to court for extortion
(C) remove the family from the apartment and send them to a municipal shelter since it will be less expensive for the agency than paying the increased rent
(D) recommend that the rental increase be allowed if it is still within the agency's maximum rental allowance.

Answer questions 85 through 87 based solely on the information contained in the following passage.

Over the past few years there has been increasing concern over the many thousands of children forced to reside with their parents or guardians in welfare shelters or in hotels catering to the welfare population. At the same time, it has been found that many of these children are not attending school and are not living under the normal family conditions thought to be proper for youngsters in these United States. Neighbors and other residents of the hotels in which these families are forced to reside often complain of the mischief and vandalism allegedly perpetrated by the youngsters.

There has also been increasing fear, however, that, even if a family is ultimately placed in an apartment owned by the municipality, such dwelling is often substandard and in a dangerous environment. These apartments have been specifically rehabilitated and are rented at a lower cost primarily to homeless people. Although these dwellings may be an improvement over these families' prior housing accommodations and are in better condition than other houses in the neighborhood, nevertheless, it is *not* good economic, social, or humanitarian practice to *re-develop* housing which, when completed, is still substandard. Many of the houses rehabilitated by a municipal agency soon become dilapidated and in need of significant repair. Recent studies have shown that, contrary to the belief of many neighbors, very often it is not the poor personal habits of the new tenants that cause deterioration, but rather the substandard nature of the rehabilitation work done on the accommodations that is the basis of the rapid decline of the building.

85. According to the passage, the neighbors of the formerly homeless families who have been accommodated in the municipally-owned apartments frequently

(A) believe their own rents should be lowered since the buildings in which they live are similiar or in worse condition than the ones occupied by the formerly homeless familics
(B) believe that the presence of poor families in their neighborhood decreases the value of their own homes or apartment houses
(C) frequently are of the opinion that the deterioration of the municipally-owned building is primarily the fault of the formerly homeless people who have been moved into them
(D) suspect that the children in these families have not been properly cared for or controlled by their parents.

86. According to the passage, it is poor economic practice to

    (A) house the homeless in municipal shelters which are more costly than placing them in apartments or dwellings

    (B) place the homeless in city-owned dwellings because such people rapidly spoil the dwelling and diminish its worth

    (C) move people into substandard dwelling rather than into hotels which are less costly

    (D) rehabilitate a city-owned building in such a substandard manner that it quickly deteriorates.

87. Assume that a homeless AFDC family with two children, ages 9 and 12, has been moved into a single-room-occupancy (SRO) hotel six weeks previously. You, the social Case Worker, are visiting the dwelling for the first time. Based solely on the passage, it would be good case work practice to

    (A) arrange that the rent be paid by your agency directly to the hotel management to avoid possible thefts of same

    (B) ascertain from the hotel management if the homeless family has actually paid the rent

    (C) inquire whether the children have been registered in and are attending school

    (D) discuss with the family your plans to move them into a municipal shelter since living in a SRO hotel is not healthy for children

Answer questions 88 through 90 based solely on the information contained in the following paragraph.

All scientific evidence indicates that AIDS is *not* spread through casual contact with persons having AIDS. It has been determined, for example, that a person cannot get AIDS by any of the following activities:

1. donating blood at the Red Cross
2. being in a classroom with a person with AIDS
3. sharing a room with a person having AIDS
4. kissing a person who has AIDS on the cheeks
5. using the same towel as a person who has AIDS
6. eating food prepared by a person who has AIDS
7. using a toilet seat used by a person with AIDS
8. being sneezed upon by a person with AIDS
9. shaking hands with a person with AIDS

HIV, the virus causing AIDS, is *not* transmitted through the air as are illness such as colds or measles. Neither is it transmitted to humans through bites or through contact with insects or animals as is malaria or rabies. You cannot contract AIDS by drinking contaminated food or water or by contact with inanimate objects like doorknobs or tissues or by touching the normal skin of a person with the disease. In sum, while the dangers of AIDS transmission are real and devastating, unwarranted fear about exposure in an individual's home and in public places, including schools, can be alleviated by knowledge and by prudent actions based on such knowledge.

88. The mother of an AFDC family that is temporarily living in a hotel comes to the welfare center in great distress. She tells you, her Case Worker, that the family must share the toilet with an AIDS victim and is afraid her family will contract the disease. Based on the passage and on good case work practice, you should

(A) arrange for immediate housing elsewhere
(B) arrange for immediate notification of the proper authorities about the AIDS victim
(C) explain that other housing is not easily available and that a great deal of trouble had been taken to find suitable housing for the family, so that nothing can be done about the matter.
(D) calmly explain that AIDS cannot be contracted by use of the same toilet facility, so that the family's health is not in danger.

89. Assume that you, the Case Worker in the case, are visiting an AFDC family on a Wednesday morning and find the two children, ages 9 and 12, at home. Upon inquiry, you learn the mother is keeping the children at home because her children state there are children in their classrooms who are AIDS victims. Based on the passage, of the following, you should

(A) notify the school immediately of the need to remove the children with AIDS from the classrooms
(B) warn the mother that she has no proof that the children supposedly with AIDS actually have the disease and that the school authorities will be sending a truant officer to inquire about the AFDC children's failure to be in school
(C) personally inquire at the school regarding their handling of the matter since the presence of AIDS children in classroom is a danger to all the other children
(D) inform the mother that AIDS is not contracted by casual contact with schoolmates and direct her to send the children to school.

90. It can be inferred from the passage that

(A) while AIDS is a devastating illness, it is sufficiently rare that normal behavior will prevent exposure to it
(B) science has made significant strides in determining the causes and cures for AIDS
(C) knowledge and the prudent use of same can lessen the dangers of the spread of AIDS
(D) if an individual is knowledgeable about the facts given in the passage, his or her chances of contracting AIDS will be greatly reduced.

Correct Answers for Practice Examination V

1. A		19. C		37. B		55. C		73. A
2. B		20. A		38. A		56. B		74. B
3. D		21. A		39. C		57. A		75. D
4. A		22. D		40. B		58. B		76. C
5. A		23. B		41. C		59. B		77. B
6. B		24. A		42. C		60. D		78. B
7. B		25. C		43. A		61. C		79. D
8. C		26. C		44. A		62. A		80. B
9. C		27. D		45. C		63. C		81. B
10. C		28. B		46. B		64. A		82. B
11. C		29. C		47. A		65. C		83. C
12. C		30. A		48. B		66. A		84. D
13. A		31. C		49. A		67. D		85. C
14. C		32. B		50. A		68. D		86. D
15. D		33. D		51. C		69. C		87. C
16. A		34. C		52. C		70. B		88. D
17. D		35. D		53. B		71. B		89. D
18. C		36. A		54. B		72. D		90. C

Explanations of Correct Answers for Practice Examination V

1. **(A)** The best way to make the interview successful and retain the applicant's confidence is to tactfully interrupt her rambling by asking specific questions directly related to establishing eligibility or to problems she is having. The wrong answers will make her hostile and will not be helpful in expediting the interview. Remember that you will have to see many applicants and clients each day and cannot afford the luxury of listening to aimless rambling.

2. **(B)** Of the possible answers, the most important reason to show interest in the client is that it will help you to obtain the information you need in order to deal with the specific problems or issues concerning that client.

3. **(D)** The situation described is a familiar one. Although the applicant is responsible for producing the verifying documents, it would be most productive to calm her agitation and help her find them.

4. **(A)** Department policy in this instance requires that in no instance can you obtain money for the client immediately. You must tell her this fact. Public agency and good social case work policy is that you should never give or lend her your own or co-worker's money or buy food for her. You can also discuss possible government or private agencies to help her meet immediate needs.

5. **(A)** In this instance, *all* the data on the form must be completed to determine eligibility including the items thought by the applicant to be personal in nature. It is your responsibility to make certain that the applicant understands and accepts this fact, cooperates, but still remains confident of your support. To do the latter, you must assure the client

that the responses to the personal questions will not be used in any way except to determine eligibility.

6. **(B)** Your primary role is to help the client, and all your work activities should be undertaken with that in mind.

7. **(B)** To restate the question *before* receiving an answer will only confuse the person being interviewed. Correct interviewing procedure allows interviewees time to answer the question that is being asked.

8. **(C)** An Eligibility Specialist will be concerned with many applicants and clients of different races, religions, sex, etc., and must be aware of the problems peculiar to that group of individuals so that they can be dealt with objectively. The special problems facing black clients are real ones, and a white Eligibility Specialist will be able to work best with them only if those problems are understood.

9. **(C)** As an Eligibility Specialist, you may expect that at some time in your career you will be confronted by this situation. The best response you can make is to try to make the client understand how the decision on the request will be made. To follow any of the other proposed responses may disturb your future relationship with the client and lessen your authority in the client's eyes. Use your supervisor's help only if *your* attempts to handle the situation are fruitless.

10. **(C)** Experienced interviewers know that when a client becomes silent during an interview, that client is probably either trying to frame an answer or question correctly, thinking over what has been said, or has no more to say on the subject.

11. **(C)** Just add up the weekly figures given for social security, disability benefits, and income taxes in case situation #1. $6.00 + $.38 + $4.30 + $2.80 + $1.00 = $14.48

12. **(C)** The Smiths' semimonthly allowance is $184 because they are a family of six (see chart on page 153).

13. **(A)** The expenses related to Mr. Smith's employment include the figures given in question 11 above concerning his semimonthly costs *plus* his semimonthly lunch expenses *plus* his semimonthly travel expenses.
Taxes etc. = $14.48 weekly = $31.37 semimonthly
Lunch = $5.00 weekly = $10.83 semimonthly
Travel = $3.50 weekly = $7.58 semimonthly
Total = $49.78 semimonthly

14. **(C)** Income = $100 a week = $216.67 semimonthly
Expenses (see question 13 above) = $49.78
Total = $166.89

15. **(D)** Family allowance + rent − total income = grant $184.00 semimonthly allowance + $52.50 semimonthly rent = $236.50 − $166.89 (total semimonthly income) = $69.61

16. **(A)** Just add the weekly deductions listed in case situation #2. $4.00 + $.27 + $3.89 + $2.05 + $.62 = $10.83

17. **(D)** There are four persons in the Smith family. Family allowance (semimonthly) per table on page 154 = $129

18. **(C)** Deductions = $10.83 weekly = $21.67 + $1.80 = $23.47 semimonthly.
Travel = $2.80 weekly = $4.33 + $1.73 = $6.06 semimonthly
Lunch = $4.00 weekly = $8.67 semimonthly
$23.47 + $6.06 + $8.67 = $38.20

19. **(C)** Total semimonthly income = gross semimonthly income − taxes − lunch − travel. $195.00 − $38.20 = $156.80

20. **(A)** Family allowance and rent (semimonthly) − total income (semimonthly) = amount of grant (semimonthly). So, $129.00 + $42.50 = $171.50
$171.50 − $156.80 = $14.70

21. **(A)** If rent was $105.00, semimonthly rent = $52.50. So, $129.00 + $52.50 = $181.50
$181.50 − $156.80 = $24.70

22. **(D)** The correct answer is written in clear, grammatically correct English, and states all the pertinent facts. Answer A says the children have no income, not that both Mrs. Jones and the children have no income. Answer B uses incorrect English and makes no sense. While Answer C says the three children *are* clients, it incorrectly states that Mrs. Jones has no income.

23. **(B)** The correct answer is clear, accurate, shows proper English usage, and states all the pertinent facts. Answer A makes no reference to the two children in the case. Answer C in the case states Ms. Smith is paying $105 a month for two children who have four rooms! Answer D states Ms. Smith pays $105 a month for four rooms and two children.

24. **(A)** The correct answer is written in clear, grammatically acceptable English, correctly punctuated, and states all the pertinent facts. Answer B states Ms. Dawes was employed on December 16, 1989, not that she was assigned nine cases that day. It also places a verb (*was*) before the word *assigned*. Instead of placing the comma before the word *she*, there should be either the word *and* or a semicolon for proper English usage. Answer C does *not* tell you that the cases were assigned on December 16, 1989. It implies that the cases were assigned because she was employed on that date. It also implies that the cases were completed on that date which is not a fact given to you. Answer D also implies that the cases were assigned and completed on December 16, 1989. The word *she* is improperly used and is not necessary in the sentence.

25. **(C)** The correct answer states *all* the pertinent facts clearly and shows proper English usage and grammar. Answer A demonstrates incorrect use of the singular verb *was*. It should be *were*. The subject is plural (41 cases). Therefore, the plural verb *were* is needed. In Answer B, the correct verb *is audited* or *had audited* is required, not *has audited*. In Answer D, the verb should be in the past tense, i.e., *audited* not *is auditing*. The sentence is confusing. Using proper English, the sentence would read as follows: Auditors . . . audited 41 cases at Broadway Center on November 20, 1989.

26. **(C)** The correct answer uses proper English and grammar and contains all the facts. In Answer A, the plural word *expenses* requires the use of a plural verb, *are* not *is*. In addition, the sentence is really two sentences. The comma after the word *client* should be a period, and the word *her* should be capitalized. Answer B exhibits very bad English usage and is extremely unclear. Answer D demonstrates bad English usage. *Is with* should be *has*, *which is* should be *of*, and *which are* should be *of*.

27. **(D)** The paragraph clearly states the facts given. The correct answer is found in the last sentence of the passage.

28. **(B)** Jack and Mary Jones have state residence, having lived in the state continuously for 18 months. The infant born 10 months previously has residence, having been born to and in the custody of parents who have state residence. The second and third children do *not* have state residence according to the passage. Residence is not derivative for them because the second child has been in the state only six months and the third child was not a resident when he entered the armed services.

29. **(C)** According to the passage, residence is not lost for the reason stated in the correct

answer but is *not* gained if the individual previously lived in the state for only one year of which six months were spent in prison, or totally on an army base or public institution.

30. **(A)** The passage clearly states that the city does *not* contribute to the cost of assistance of nonstate residents. Other parts of the passage are *not* stated in the passage.

31. **(C)** Anne Rollins and the four children who moved to the state seven months ago do *not* have residence. The two children and the aunt with whom they lived have residence since they lived in the state for two years. The uncle also has residence having lived in the state continuously. Residence was not lost by entrance into the armed forces. Thus, four persons have state residence.

32. **(B)** In this situation, your best approach is to tell the client about the points of disagreement and ask for an explanation. To follow the approaches given in Answer A may lose rapport and is contrary to the general social case work principle that you should assume truthfulness on the part of clients. To follow suggestion C is bad public welfare procedure. You are accountable for disbursement of public funds and must be sure that they are given only to those entitled to them.

33. **(D)** It is the applicant's responsibility to assist you in establishing her eligibility for public assistance by providing you with the correct answers to your questions and the documentation you need. The best way to handle the situation is to calmly explain the need for your questions and how her responses will help her to obtain assistance.

34. **(C)** It is *not* good public or social welfare policy to allow acceptance of gifts or social invitations from clients, and many public jurisdictions have rules to this effect. You should presume the client has no ulterior motives for extending the invitation and not let it influence the decision regarding continuation of eligibility.

35. **(D)** The case does *not* fit the criteria for categories A, B, or C. It does not fit category A since the woman may not be the child's guardian, and they have not lived in the state for one year. It does not fit category B because both parents are not in the home. It does not fit category C since there is no Vietnam War veteran in the home.

36. **(A)** The case fits all the factors for determining eligibility listed in category A.

37. **(B)** The case does *not* fit category A because the children are not deprived of parental support. It does fit category B since factors B 1-8 are all present.

38. **(A)** The case fits all the factors for determining eligibility in category A, i.e., factors A 1, 2e, 3, and 4.

39. **(C)** The case does not fit category A (no child deprived of parental support because of factors 2a through e). It does not fit category B because the father *is* receiving unemployment insurance. It does fit category C since the father is a Vietnam War veteran.

40. **(B)** One of the primary responsibilities of the worker is to make certain that clients are given all the services needed to help them return to a condition of self-support.

41. **(C)** In this situation, your best reply is a truthful one, i.e., you are not sure. Answer A may cause the client further anguish and anger him if he is ultimately found not to be eligible. Answer B leaves the client confused about agency policy and may result in leaving you in an awkward position with him if he is not found eligible. Answer D may only further upset the client and hinder further relations with him.

42. **(C)** *Never* try to imitate the client's speech pattern. It may well appear that you are making fun of the speech pattern. The wrong answers are *good* interviewing techniques which you should know and follow.

43. **(A)** The Foster case history shows the date of the history to be January 25, 1989. It also states that Joan is hyperactive and not developing normally and that she was born on October 14, 1985 and is therefore four years old.

44. **(A)** The Foster case history gives all the data in the wrong Answers B, C, and D.

45. **(C)** Answer A is wrong since the form is not *just* about the family composition but is rather about the Foster case history. Answer B is wrong since it just indicates the date the form was revised. Wrong Answer D tells you the family's case type and number (Aid to Dependent Children—345968). The correct answer is the form number, i.e., Form W-341-C.

46. **(B)** The case history clearly states that the housekeeper's service will relieve Mrs. Foster of basic housekeeping chores since she has multiple sclerosis and her capacity to manage both a household and four children is "severely limited."

47. **(A)** *Everyone* has a right to apply for public assistance even if recently denied. Eligibility Specialists are very busy individuals, however, and it is good policy, in this instance, to inform the co-worker of the facts you had learned and the reasons for the very recent rejection of the case, in order to prevent needless duplication of effort.

48. **(B)** Good procedure, in this situation, would be to take advantage of the option of mailing a denial letter to the client. This may avoid or lessen the chance of provoking a possible disruptive scene at the welfare center. Having the supervisor tell the man of his ineligibility may not prevent an altercation and may even exacerbate it. Nor will the presence of a special patrolman necessarily prevent a commotion disrupting other workers or clients. The applicant may still return to the center after receiving the denial in the mail, but the chances are better that he will have calmed down by the time he does so and a worrisome or even dangerous scene may be avoided.

49. **(A)** In areas of the United States where there is a relatively large number or percentage of Spanish-speaking people, there are usually at least a few Eligibility Specialists who can converse with applicants or clients who speak only Spanish or are very limited in their ability to speak English. The *first* action you should take, in these instances, is to try to find a Spanish-speaking Eligibility Specialist to assist you. Answer D would be appropriate only if there is no co-worker able to assist you.

50. **(A)** The situation is a familiar one to workers in the public assistance occupation and you must be prepared to deal with it. As an Eligibility Specialist, you are bound to consider only the facts of the case and the rules concerning the initial granting and the continuation of public assistance. You must relay this to the client in a manner that will convince her that you are treating her in the same manner, under the same rules and regulations, as every other Eligibility Specialist or Case Worker in the agency would and ask her to continue the interview.

51. **(C)** The only possible answer which will give the reason for the emergency grant is that the family has no place to live. Wrong Answers A and B are irrelevant, and wrong Answer D refers only to the type of dwelling which may be needed, not to the reason for the grant.

52. **(C)** Written communication from a friend or relative is not good verification of the fire, nor is a photograph which could be of another building or of a prior time, or show only prior destruction. The best verification, of the choices given, is a dated newspaper which describes the extent of the fire.

53. **(B)** You know that there are two adults and four children in the family so that a five-room apartment would be the most suitable one. You also know Mrs. Smith has a heart murmur, so a ground-floor apartment would be most appropriate. Note: Answer A is

not appropriate because, although there might be a room suitable to be used for a third bedroom, Mrs. Smith would have to walk up a flight of stairs.

54. **(B)** The data given tells you the Smiths are requesting emergency money for food and clothing.

55. **(C)** The best summary of your actions is the one that indicates the solutions you effectuated in response to the requests made. In this instance, these would be the temporary housing arrangement you made and the amount of the emergency grant you requested and for which you obtained approval.

56. **(B)** As noted in previous explanations on this issue, the amount of note-taking during an interview depends on the situation, on your own ability to remember facts, and on the client's reactions to note-taking. There are occasions when your interview with a client requires you to concentrate on what is being said, other instances where note-taking may frighten the applicant or client, and still other occasions when you must show the client that you are truly interested in what he or she is saying. Note-taking, other than the bare minimum in the latter instance, may cause clients to believe you aren't really interested in or concerned with what they are saying. Note-taking must not result in losing rapport with the client.

57. **(A)** It is most important that the Eligibility Specialist be aware of the situation and the problems in a case *before* interviewing the applicant so that the interview can focus on these problems. In addition, the worker can spot confusing contradictions and points needing further clarification that must be handled in order to establish eligibility.

Questions 58 through 60 test your knowledge of the meaning of certain words which are frequently used in connection with the work of an Eligibility Specialist.

58. **(B)**

59. **(B)**

60. **(D)**

61. **(C)** The Fact Situation tells you that the Smith family has lived in the apartment since July 18, 1977, which is the occupancy date. Note: The Fact Situation also alerts you to a two-year lease on July 18, 1983, but that is *not* the information called for in the box "Occupancy Date" on the sample form.

62. **(A)** The form is a request for approval of exception to policy for shelter allowance. Therefore, the amount to be put in the box "Rent per Month" is $250 which is the desired rent.

63. **(C)** The form has space to indicate "Apartment No. or Location," but this information is not given to you in the Fact Situation.

64. **(A)** The Fact Situation tells you that Mr. Smith is the case head since he applied for "self and family." Helen Smith is the *wife* in the Smith case, and the word wife should be indicated in column 4, "Relationship to Case Head."

Questions 65 through 73 entail the ability to do simple arithmetic calculations, an important part of an Eligibility Specialist's job. Follow the directions given in each question carefully. Note: Be sure to find out whether you may use a hand calculator at the civil service exam.

65. **(C)** 1. Add the first five numbers = 237.27
2. Add 60.54 and 10.56 = 71.10
3. 237.27 − 71.10 = 166.17

66. **(A)** 1. Add the first four numbers = 5099.96
    2. Add the second set of four numbers = 3987.13
    3. 5099.96 − 3987.13 = 1112.83

67. **(D)** 1. Multiply 1850 × .05 = 92.50
    2. Multiply 3300 × .08 = 264.00
    3. 92.50 + 264.00 = 356.50

68. **(D)** 1. Multiply 312.77 × .04 = 12.5108
    2. Rule in rounding off numbers to the nearest hundredths (two places after the decimal point): If the third number after the decimal point is 5 or more, change the second number after the decimal point to the next higher number. If the third number is less than 5, disregard it.
    3. 12.5108 = 12.51

69. **(C)** 1. 362.05 + 91.13 + 347.81 + 17.46 = 818.45
    2. 818.45 ÷ 6 = 136.408
    3. 136.408 = 136.41

70. **(B)** 1. 66.25 + 15.06 = 81.31
    2. $81.31 \times 2\frac{1}{6} =$

    $$81.31 \times \frac{13}{6} = \frac{1057.03}{6} = 176.17$$

71. **(B)** Correct Answer B $= \frac{1}{4}\left(\frac{25}{100}\right); \frac{1}{4}\left(\frac{250}{1000}\right); \frac{1}{4}\left(\frac{2500}{1000}\right)$

A zero added at the end of a decimal number does not change the value of the number.

72. **(D)** 1. 539.84 + 479.26 = 1019.10 ÷ 2 = 509.55
    2. 1461.93 + 927.27 = 2389.20 ÷ 3 = 796.40
    3. 509.55 + 796.40 = 1305.95
    4. To round off a decimal to the nearest whole number: If the numbers after the decimal point are .5 or more, add 1 to the number just before the decimal point, e.g., 1305.95 = 1306.

73. **(A)** 1. $5906.09 × .15 = $885.90
    2. $885.90 ÷ 3 = $295.30

74. **(B)** The passage covers various techniques involved in good interviewing procedures. The title should therefore indicate the overall nature of the passage, and the correct answer indicates this generalized nature of same. The wrong answers give only individual techniques.

75. **(D)** The passage clearly indicates that the interviewer should begin with a discussion about matters that are "easy to talk about and nonmenacing." The passage does not convey the advice given in any of the wrong answers.

76. **(C)** The passage clearly states that the interviewer should "get the interviewee to talk freely with as little prodding . . . as possible." This is exactly what the correct answer states. The statements in the wrong answers cannot be found in or inferred from the passage.

77. **(B)** The word *unhampered* in the last sentence of the fourth paragraph of the passage can be replaced by the word *unobstructed*.

78. **(B)** None of the statements in the wrong answers can be inferred from the passage. The statement that some interview methods are better than others for obtaining information

(correct Answer B) *can* be inferred because the entire passage really is giving you what the author considers are the best methods of obtaining information.

79. **(D)** An Eligibility Specialist must interview many people during the day. Spending time trying to understand a nonrational, intoxicated person is generally counterproductive since you cannot trust the information given, *if* you can even comprehend it. Further, trying to deal with him while he is intoxicated may encourage him to appear at subsequent interviews in the same state. The best solution is to end the interview and schedule another appointment.

80. **(B)** An applicant for public assistance is very frequently, and understandably, distressed and the situation presented is not uncommon. The worker should try to calm the applicant, express an awareness of and sympathy toward all problems, and after a reminder that the worker's primary function is to help, continue the interview. There is no guarantee that the applicant will find the courage to come for another interview if this one is terminated with no progress having been made towards solving the client's problems and determining eligibility. REMEMBER: Never tell a client the case will be approved and *never* say that you will try to get it approved before you know the facts in the matter.

81. **(B)** A budget is a plan in dollars and cents, and in this case it is a plan expressed in money to assure that the basic needs of a family during a given time are met.

82. **(B)** The passage emphasizes that long-time residence in a shelter is detrimental to a family's well-being. Immediate steps should be taken to find more suitable permanent housing for the family. In the situation presented, the shelter is designed only as temporary housing and does not allow for permanent residence.

83. **(C)** The passage emphasizes that one tends to lose his or her ability to take independent action after being housed in a municipal shelter for a long period of time.

84. **(D)** Based on the facts presented in the preamble of the question and the reasoning contained in the passage, it would be good social work practice to allow the rent increase to be paid by the municipality.

85. **(C)** The passage indicates that this is a common belief. The information in the other choices may or may not be true. However, they cannot be given serious consideration because they are not contained in the passage.

86. **(D)** Refer to the final sentence of the passage.

87. **(C)** Remember that you are to stick to the information contained in the passage. The problem of children not attending school regularly is a fact stated in the passage. The other choices contain information and facts which are not referred to in the passage.

88. **(D)** This fact is stated in the passage, and the Case Worker should make every effort to convince the mother of it.

89. **(D)** Not only is this solid case work practice, the information in this choice is stated in the passage which should be your guide to answering this and other questions.

90. **(C)** The passage only lists some of the major ways AIDS is not contracted. However, it fails to indicate the ways it is passed on from one person to another. The statement contained in this choice may be inferred from the passage.

Part Three

Background Material and Examination Questions Classified by Subject Matter

THE INVESTIGATION PROCESS

General Principles Relating to the Initial Investigation or Reinvestigation

The initial investigation and the reinvestigation consists of the collection, verification, analysis, and appraisal of pertinent and precise information by which a determination of eligibility or ineligibility for financial assistance and service is made. The principles and techniques given below, except where indicated, primarily refer to establishing eligibility for financial assistance (including the programs of Aid to Families with Dependent Children (AFDC) and financial assistance to needy individuals and families not eligible for the special programs of AFDC or the Supplementary Security Income (SSI) programs administered by the federal government. These same principles and techniques are generally applicable also to establishing eligibility for other programs providing assistance to the poor, including the Food Stamp and Medicaid programs and the various assistance programs under SSI (Aid to the Disabled, Aid to the Blind, and Old Age Assistance). You will learn the more specialized requirements for the programs for which your agency is responsible once you are on the job, but will find that the process given here is generally applicable to them all.

Cities or states differ in specifying which public employees are responsible for various aspects in determining eligibility for financial assistance. Thus, is some jurisdictions, a Case Worker is responsible for both establishing eligibility and also for providing services to clients, while in other jurisdictions, a worker may be responsible only for establishing financial need, while a Case Worker has the duty of providing ancillary services. Thus, for example, in the City of New York, workers in the title Eligibility Specialist are responsible for establishing eligibility, while Case Workers' duties are involved with providing individualized programmatic services such as handling foster care cases, placement in nursing homes, etc. Careful reading of the examination announcement will show you just what the responsibilities of the job entail. In any event, the material in the following pages is useful and should be understood by everyone in the public welfare field, including those who are not directly responsible for granting or denying assistance, be it financial aid, medicaid, or food stamps.

Note that for purposes of consistency, we are calling the person responsible for establishing eligibility an Investigator.

The investigation is a businesslike and individualized process which inquires into the past and current maintenance, employment, resources, and employability of the applicant or client. The essential information and documentation which are necessary will vary in each case depending upon the individual factors presented by each applicant or client and the type of assistance for which eligibility is being investigated or reinvestigated. Note especially that in most jurisdictions, and especially with reference to programs which are administered and/or funded or partially funded by the federal government, no applicant or client may be discriminated against because of religion, race, color, or national origin. Applicants or clients must be informed of their right to protest against alleged discrimination and be given information, if desired, regarding procedures for filing a discrimination complaint.

The applicant or client, as well as the Investigator, has definite, specific responsibilities in establishing eligibility or ineligibility for assistance and care. It is the applicant's or client's obligation not only to give factual information about the situation but also to submit proof of initial and continuing financial need. The applicant or client has a responsibility, from the time the application is presented until contact with the Agency is terminated, to submit full information regarding eligibility and any changes in the situation which affect initial or continued eligibility for assistance, as well as to cooperate in the verification of these factors. In every instance, the burden of proof rests with the applicant or client except when the applicant or client is mentally or physically incapable of producing such proof. Therefore, it is important for the applicant or client to understand the eligibility requirements in order to be able to: (a) give the necessary information; (b) help verify it; (c) report promptly any change in the situation affecting initial or continuing eligibility for assistance.

The Investigator must determine eligibility for assistance and care at the time of the application and must constantly re-examine his or her entire caseload in order to certify its validity.

The Investigator is responsible for seeing that no needy person eligible for assistance is denied assistance and that no ineligible person receives assistance. Part of the Investigator's function is to recognize that the denial or withdrawal of assistance is as constructive a factor as the granting of assistance, both to the client and the community.

The investigation process begins with the intake interview and continues in the field investigation through interviews in the home and with collateral references. The applicant's or client's contact with the Department both during the period the application is being investigated and while the client is receiving assistance should be channeled through the Investigator. However, consultant services related to employment, resources, housing, health, and management may be available to the Investigator and to the applicant or client, if referred for consultation service by the Investigator. Through the use of these consultants, particularly those concerned with employment or with utilization of client resources, a decision may quickly be reached that assistance is unnecessary or that assistance can be withdrawn. Also, through the use of these consultant services, the Investigator gains increased knowledge in the management of the caseload and receives assistance in formulating plans to meet specific problems through the agency or appropriate outside source.

Responsibilities of the Investigator

The responsibilities of the Investigator and of all the other members of the social service staff are:

a. To determine eligibility (i.e., financial need plus the other qualifying considerations applicable by law to the type of assistance applied for) or lack of eligibility in any respect and to recommend promptly acceptance or nonacceptance for assistance or continuance or discontinuance of assistance, as the finding warrants.

b. To verify and evaluate both actual and potential resources, and to make sure that all available resources are utilized which will reduce or eliminate the condition of need.

c. To issue assistance in eligible cases in strict compliance with the policies and the established budget schedules of the agency. No budget items should be included in the grant routinely.

d. To issue emergency assistance only when absolutely necessary to meet an acute need and only for those items which are essential until the investigation is complete.

e. To render such services which would reduce or eliminate the condition of need and which would make for a return to self-maintenance. Where other service not provided by the department is needed, to refer promptly to such public or private agencies as may appropriately render the required service.

f. To establish clearly in the written record the initial or continuing eligibility, or ineligibility for public assistance. The record should show precisely and clearly why assistance is given, denied, or withdrawn, and, if given, the amounts and kinds of assistance, and such other material as is related to eligibility to receive assistance, and only such other information as is pertinent to the functions of the agency.

g. To organize and execute work on a planned basis and with the most effective use of time.

h. To perform these functions in such a way as to enable the applicant or client to retain self-respect and his or her capacity for self-direction.

Intake

In some large jurisdictions, an initial interview of all applicants for assistance and/or care is conducted by an Appointment Interviewer, then an Intake Interviewer or Investigator. In other smaller jurisdictions, a receptionist may merely refer applicants to an Interviewer, or to the Investigator ultimately responsible for the case, for this initial interview as well as for the follow-up steps and discussions needed to establish eligibility. Regardless of who actually conducts this initial interview, certain specific preliminary information must be learned and decisions made.

All applicants must be interviewed. Any person who wishes to apply for assistance may do so. However, assistance may not be granted until eligibility to receive assistance has been established, except in emergency situations.

In most instances, applications for assistance are made in person. In some situations of advanced age, ill health, or other special problems, applications may be received by mail or telephone from the applicant or an agency or individual interested in his or her welfare. Applications must be cleared with the agency master file to determine that the applicant has not already requested or is receiving assistance, that the applicant registered with the Social Service Exchange if such is maintained in the jurisdiction; and that appropriate arrangements have been made for either an interview in the office or a visit to the home, if that is necessary.

Initial determinations must be made. It must be determined that the person is applying for assistance and care administered by the agency; that he or she resides within the jurisdiction of the welfare center; that the applicant and the members of his or her family have State residence; and that the applicant and the members of his or her family are not eligible for veteran certification if the jurisdiction has provision for such special certification forms required by agency procedure. The worker interviews the applicant, or a representative for the applicant, and, if the above conditions are met, determines the type of assistance for which the applicant and each member of the family is presumed eligible, prepares and has signed all additional forms required by current procedure, issues the appropriate pamphlet describing eligibility requirements for each type of assistance for which there is presumptive eligibility, and if an appointment for the applicant with another worker is being scheduled issues a separate application blank for the applicant and for each member of the family who is presumptively eligible for another type of assistance, or who is presumptively eligible for the same type of assistance if separate cases are required.

The application blank is the applicant's own statement and declaration of his or her need. It is essential, therefore, that the applicant understand that it must contain full and accurate information. The applicant may fill it out alone, or may request the help of the Investigator or Interviewer if he or she needs or desires assistance in filling it out. Each member of the household 18 years of age and over who is included in the application for assistance shall sign the application blank for the type of assistance for which he or she is presumptively eligible.

Intake Interview

After the completion of these basic steps, the Intake Interviewer or Investigator is ready to conduct the actual interview and to carry out the following functions:

a. Determining the applicant's presumptive eligibility for assistance on the basis of need.

b. Determining the type or types of assistance being requested, and the type or types of assistance for which there is presumptive eligibility.

c. Obtaining information regarding the residence status of each member of the family.

d. Reviewing previous available records of the family making reapplication for assistance in order to determine why assistance was not given or was discontinued and to relate the past records to the current information in order to help determine present eligibility.

e. Advising the applicant of his or her rights under the law.

f. Making sure that the applicant has received the appropriate eligibility pamphlet for the type of assistance for which he or she is making application.

g. Rejecting at intake those applicants who are ineligible for assistance and explaining the reasons for the decision verbally and in writing.

h. Referring to other agencies or other units of this agency those persons who are ineligible for public assistance but whose needs may be met through the services provided by such other agencies or units (i.e., Medicaid, food stamps, etc.).

i. Determining those situations where the applicant's financial need could be fully met by a referral to special employment or resource units if they exist in the agency and making the necessary referrals to those units.

j. Deferring decisions when necessary and advisable to give the applicant an opportunity to clarify his or her eligibility or to explore further his or her own resources.

k. Referring the request for assistance for further investigation if presumptive need is established, or conducting such further investigation, if both Intake and Investigation is handled by one person.

l. Interpreting Agency policies for the applicant so that he or she will understand the investigation process.

m. Recognizing emergency situations, giving such situations prompt and effective attention, and arranging for immediate financial assistance where there is *substantial* evidence that *emergency assistance is essential*.

It should be noted that the nature and direction of the interview conducted at the time of the initial interview will be determined primarily by the applicant's statement of the reasons for his or her need for public assistance, including why the applicant is unable to meet his or her own maintenance problem in whole or in part. In order to understand the basis for dependency at the point of application, the Investigator or Interviewer must know how the applicant has maintained himself or herself prior to the application, why he or she is no longer able to manage without assistance, and what efforts he or she has made to utilize actual or potential resources which may be available directly or through relatives or other sources. Obtaining such information from the applicant often proves to be a difficult job. There are many techniques that can be used depending on the client's personality and the situation. When reading the application filled out by the applicant such things should be considered as:

1. consistency in the facts presented—evidence of unexplained apparent contradictions
2. long periods of time not accounted for by the applicant
3. applicant's life style: it cannot be expected, for example, that an applicant with an arrest record will give as clear an explanation of his past maintenance (outside of prison) as the applicant with a consistent work record.

The statement of the applicant, augmented by the application blank, the Social Service Exchange report, previous records, and any other documents which the applicant presents, are the basis upon which the Investigator or Interviewer makes a decision to have the case investigated or to reject the application at this point.

Specific Instructions Regarding the Initial Investigation or Reinvestigation

After the initial intake interview and the preparation of the application and the initial determinations referred to above are completed, the actual investigation commences. Again, the steps in the process may be the responsibility of the initial Interviewer or it may be the Investigator or Case Worker, regardless of who performs the investigatory role.

Actual initial investigation begins with a study of the content of the intake interview, the application blank, the Social Service Exchange report, and in cases of reapplication, a review of the previous record. The Investigator's job in a reinvestigation, i.e., where the applicant has asked for and/or been reviewed or been referred for financial aid in the past, begins with a review of the case record and other pertinent records.

Through the use of this available material, the Investigator determines:

a. What facts are already known.
b. What additional facts are needed.
c. What sources of information are available for securing these facts.

If one of the sources of available information for the Investigator is a previous record, this should be studied in order to gain a greater understanding of the present situation both to help in determining current eligibility and to prevent repetition for both the applicant and the agency.

Home and Office Visits

Many jurisdictions mandate that field investigations be made to applicants' homes prior to determining eligibility in order to obtain whatever additional data are necessary from the applicant and the family, to observe the living conditions, and to interpret agency policy procedure further to the family.

Since the applicant or client and all other adult members of the family are primary sources of information regarding the factors in their own situations relating to eligibility for public assistance, the Investigator should always interview these individuals in the home or in the office and the family setup shall be verified as part of the initial investigation or reinvestigation.

In addition to the sources of information which are available before the home visit or office interview, other leads will become apparent during the interviews with members of the family.

Collateral Contact

Collateral contacts refer to contacts with individuals outside the immediate family group. These contacts may be with relatives, employers, landlords, physicians, hospitals, government departments, social agencies, fraternal and religious organizations, unions, the clergy, friends, and any others who can give pertinent information concerning the family's need for public assistance.

Collateral contacts assist the applicant or client as well as the agency in determining eligibility for assistance and care, in securing complete or partial support for relatives, and in clarifying employment possibilities and developing resources useful to the applicant or client.

When collateral contacts are discussed with the applicant or client, it is not for the purpose of gaining permission to make such visits but to give an explanation of the procedure regarding collateral visits and the necessity for making them. If the applicant or client refuses to have a necessary collateral visit made and another reference cannot be reasonably substituted, the Investigator must explain to him or her the agency's inability, under these circumstances, to continue with the investigation or to grant or continue assistance.

In making collateral contacts, the Investigator should reveal no more than the minimum information necessary to accomplish his or her purpose and should limit the discussion to relevant material. The Investigator should utilize the opportunity to interpret agency policies with respect to the particular point in question since such interpretation may enlist a more active cooperation with the person interviewed.

The method employed by the Investigator in making these collateral contacts is selected with regard to the nature of agency policy and purpose of the contact. It may be by personal visit, telephone call, or correspondence. Generally, correspondence is suitable for contacts with large organizations. Whenever possible, a personal interview should be arranged if the contact is with an individual who has a personal relationship with the applicant or client, such as a relative or friend, or an employer who has had direct or close contact with the applicant or client.

Information Relating to Eligibility

Any or all of the following items (the list below is not all-inclusive) as well as any other items which have a bearing on eligibility should be investigated in relation to the determination of eligibility. All available or potential resources should be completely explored and frankly discussed.

I. *Past Maintenance*—In an initial investigation, information shall be obtained regarding maintenance prior to application for assistance. This information should establish clearly the exact way in which the present situation differs from the past, why public assistance is now necessary, and what resources are still available. In a reinvestigation, information regarding past maintenance and verification thereof, if pertinent to the determination of continuing eligibility, and information regarding management while in receipt of assistance, shall be obtained. This information shall be of such a nature as to establish present and continuing need and to insure that the public assistance grant meets the purpose for which it is issued.

II. *Employment*—The Investigator shall be responsible for determining if the applicant or client or any member of the family is employed.

    A. The following information shall be secured and verified for each member of the family of employable age:

        1. Names and addresses of employers

2. Earnings; length of employment
3. Reason for termination of jobs
4. The type of work he or she is qualified to do
5. The job prospects in his or her field
6. The efforts and results he or she has made to secure employment
7. The efforts he or she has made and is making to secure employment outside his or her field
8. Registration with the state's Employment Service and eligibility for Unemployment Insurance Benefits
9. Union affiliations
10. Odd Jobs—For those workers who have had what are called "odd jobs" or workers who have not had the trade training and who have gone from job to job as the opportunity presented itself, a careful analysis of why such contacts are no longer available is important. Determination should be made regarding:
    a) Present availability of odd jobs
    b) The source the applicant or client has used to secure these jobs
    c) Whether these jobs have been in his or her trade or outside of the trade
    d) Earnings—It is important that addresses, periods of such employment, and earnings for each job be secured, since this is an aid in understanding the applicant's or client's past and present management as well as resources for future management.
11. Seasonal Employment—Those workers who have been engaged in industries which have seasonal slack periods would normally be expected to plan through their own resources for these recurring slack periods. Therefore, the following must be explored in each situation:
    a) What resources has the applicant or client used to manage previously during slack periods?
    a) Why are these resources not now available?
    b) Is the present slack period longer than usual?
    c) When does the season begin?
    d) Has he or she any borrowing capacity?
    e) Is he or she eligible for Unemployment Insurance Benefits?
12. Educational or trade training as it relates to employment or re-employment possibility

B. The following information, as well as the pertinent information listed above, should be obtained and verified from each employed applicant or client or any member of the family whose earnings are not sufficient to enable the applicant to maintain himself or herself or family without public assistance supplementation:
   1. What are the wages paid, the work schedule, and the nature of the duties performed by the employed person?
   2. Is he or she employed at maximum capacity?
   3. Does his or her work schedule permit securing additional employment?
   4. Could he or she increase wage-earning capacity by a program of retraining?
   (e) Does his or her field of employment have slack periods? If so, what has been This person's plan for self-maintenance during such periods?
   (f) What opportunities does the family have for supplementing income through its own resources?

C. If the applicant or client is unable to continue working because of own ill health, the Investigator should ascertain:
   1. The nature of the health problem
   2. What medical care is being received
   3. Specific data as to the probable duration of the illness and incapacity

4. Whether any wages or disability allowance is being received from any sources during his or her illness

5. Whether this person's old job is being held for him or her

6. Whether there is an ability to work part-time during the illness

7. *Whether the client is fully or partially employable at an occupation other than his or her regular trade*—Verification of all statements is important and careful control of such cases in terms of time is essential. When a collateral visit is made to or with an employer, its purpose is not only to verify the employment status and to determine the possibility for re-employment, but also to obtain information regarding other possible openings in the industry, its seasons of greatest activity, its wage scale, and its method of employing. This enables the Investigator to discuss employment possibilities intelligently with the applicant or client and to stimulate interest in seeking employment in his or her trade at a time when work is available. If any of the applicants or clients are employed or employable, current procedure with respect to payroll clearances with the state's Division of Placement and Unemployment Insurance shall be followed.

III. *Relatives*—Relatives of applicants or clients constitute an invaluable resource to the applicant or client and to the agency. The relative can often supply necessary and pertinent information regarding the eligibility of the client, his or her past maintenance, and present need. Relatives are frequently an important employment resource as they can often suggest employment opportunities which would be available.

A careful and individualized consideration of the ability of relatives to support is essential to determine eligibility and degree of need. For this purpose, all legally responsible relatives must be contacted, as well as those socially responsible relatives from whom there is a possibility of assistance. Every effort should be made to obtain full support from the relatives. If it is established that the relatives' resources are insufficient for them to provide full or partial maintenance for the applicant or client, effort should then be directed toward obtaining their assistance in supplying such special needs as clothing, medical care, surgical appliances, care of children during employment of the applicant or client, or help with housekeeping during illness. Such assistance from relatives is important for its monetary value and in maintaining and strengthening family ties.

In situations where there is a deserting husband, or a putative or adjudicated father, who is not contributing to the support of the family, child, or children, it is the primary responsibility of the applicant or client to make every effort to find or assist in finding the missing husband or father, and to obtain support. When it appears that relatives who are legally responsible for the support of the applicant or client are able but unwilling to provide such support in full or in part in accordance with the relatives' circumstances, it is the responsibility of the applicant or client to seek support through appropriate court action. When court action is indicated or necessary, failure on the part of the applicant or client to institute or cooperate with the agency in the necessary legal proceedings may result in ineligibility for assistance.

IV. *Friends*—When friends have assisted in the past it is important to know the names, addresses, the extent of their assistance, and under what circumstances the assistance was given. Their present willingness and ability to assist should be explored. Are any other friends possible resources at the present time? Information obtained from friends should be carefully evaluated as to its objectivity.

V. *Landlords*—Present landlords should be contacted with reference to the following: What is the rent? Is the rent paid to date? Does the applicant or client pay his or her rent regularly? What amount has he or she paid? By whom has the rent been paid? Is the applicant or client a janitor; if so, what is his or her compensation for this service? Can the landlord give any information regarding boarders or lodgers? Has rent been established in accordance with legal controls, or is rent not subject to control? The legal rent must be verified with appropriate agencies exercising control.

In some instances it may be advisable for the Investigator also to contact the previous landlord for pertinent information concerning the applicant's or client's eligibility for assistance.

VI. *Resources*—The Investigator is responsible for determining the total available resources of each applicant or client and each member of the family.

    A. *Insurance*—What insurance policies are carried by each member of the family? Have they been reviewed by the expert consultant or resource in your sgency? Has any cash or benefits been realized from the selling of policies or from death benefits, loans, disability or accident insurance? Is sickness or disability insurance carried now? How is the family paying the insurance premiums?

    B. *Banks*—In the initial investigation, there shall be an inquiry and a determination regarding present or past bank accounts and safe deposit boxes. Whenever there has been or is an indication of a bank account, this should be cleared in accordance with current procedure. The Investigator should see the bank book or bank statement to correlate withdrawals and deposits with the story of past management and assets. A review of the amount of the withdrawals is important since cancellation of an account in one bank does not necessarily mean there is no account in another bank.

    C. *U.S. Savings Bonds*—United States Savings Bonds have cash value and must be considered a liquid asset. The Investigator must ascertain location and total current value of any bonds held by the applicant.

    D. *Property*—There must be a discussion with each applicant regarding what real or personal property he or she has had in the past or now has, and such property must be evaluated with the expert consultant on resources in your agency in order that complete information may be obtained to determine how it can be utilized for the applicant's present maintenance. In a reinvestigation, it is essential to determine whether adequate information has been obtained concerning real or personal property the client has had or now has. When necessary, clearances or reclearances shall be initiated.

    E. *Compensation*

        1. Has the applicant or client or any member of the family had an industrial accident? Is Workers' Compensation possible? Is a claim pending? Has the applicant or client ever received an award?

        2. Is the applicant or client or any member of the family receiving disability insurance or allowance?

    F. *Pending Civil Suits*

        1. Are there any pending civil suits?

        2. Can damages for personal injuries (accidents) be collected?

        3. Can outstanding loans be collected?

    G. *Pensions and Benefits*

        Is any member of the family eligible for:

        1. Pension for service in a public department, such as police, fire, education, or other

        2. Pensions or benefits from private industry; for example, from railroads or for personal service over an extended period

        3. Unemployment insurance benefits

        4. Veteran's bonus, pensions, benefits, and other allowances

    H. *Allowances*

        1. Is applicant or client or any member of the family receiving an allowance through your state or county's Family Court, Supreme Court, or Court of Special Sessions, or other legal process?

2. How often are these payments made? What is the amount?
3. Should applicant or client be referred to one of these sources?

I.   *Trust Funds and Estates*—Can moneys be obtained from these resources at this time?

J.   Other resources which family may have, such as

1. Janitorship—Is the compensation free rent, utilities, etc.?
2. Lodgers or boarders—Is there any present income from this source? Was this ever a source of income to the family? Is it a feasible plan at this time?
3. Lodges and Unions—Does the family belong to any organization granting benefits? Under what circumstances are they paid? Does any member of the family have union affiliations? Are current dues paid? Date of last payment, amount, and how met? What are the possibilities for re-employment through this source? How often does each employable member contact this union?

VII. *Debts*—Amounts and dates should be secured in relation to past management. To whom owed, and under what circumstances borrowed? Has any part of the debt been repaid? What arrangements have been made for payment? Does applicant have further borrowing facilities? If money has been borrowed, were there co-makers to the loan? If so, who were they? Have they been contacted?

VIII. *Residence*—Although state residence may not be required for eligibility for financial assistance in many jurisdictions or for participation in the Medicaid or Food Stamps programs, information must always be available as to the residence status of each person included in the application. It should be included in the application for financial assistance or included in the grant unless the previous case record contains acceptable documentary evidence for each individual and their residence has not changed since that time. The Investigator shall give the applicant or client such assistance as he or she may require in obtaining of proof of residence. Every case record must contain proof of the applicant's or client's living arrangements, be it a hotel, subsidized housing project, apartment, living arrangement with nonwelfare relatives, friends, etc.

IX.   *Eligibility for Aid to Families with Dependent Children (AFDC)*—All applicants and cases must be investigated to determine whether the applicants or clients are eligible or presumptively eligible for this type of assistance. If so, all legal requirements regarding their eligibility must be investigated and documented. These requirements include such factors as relationship of the adult to the minor child or children, actual presence of the child or children in the home, school attendance, presence or absence of one or more parents, reasons for inability of parents or guardians to support the child or children, etc. All of these factors must be verified, documented, and evaluated in order for AFDC to be granted. If eligibility for AFDC has been established but all documentary evidence has not been secured, assistance may be given only through the pre-investigation grant procedure.

X.   *Eligibility for Supplemental Security Income (SSI)*—Programs giving financial assistance to individuals who are aged, disabled, or blind are administered by the federal government through the Social Security Administration. Applicants must meet most, or all, of the requirements referred to above and also meet the specific requirements of the assistance program for which they are applying. Note that a family cannot receive both SSI payments and AFDC payments, but must choose the program that best fits their needs.

Methods and Sources of Proof

I.   *General Considerations*—It is the responsibility of the Investigator to obtain proof of the financial and social data upon which eligibility for public assistance is based. The principle of client participation is applicable in this, as in other phases of the investigation process. The applicant should be given an opportunity to produce proof and to exercise some choice, if possible, in the manner or method of obtaining this. The Investigator should offer suggestions, if necessary. For example, an applicant for SSI may be able to produce a birth certificate to establish an age of 65 or older. If no proof is readily at hand, he or she may prefer to apply for a birth certificate copy, or, if ill or otherwise not able to assume this responsibility, it may be necessary for the Investigator to obtain this verification for the applicant. The reliability of the proof obtained needs to be carefully evaluated by the Investigator since records vary in accuracy, and statements offered by individuals, such as employers, relatives or landlords, may be prejudiced for or against the family. It is therefore important to determine the validity of records and testimonial evidence. The following criteria may be helpful: If the information for the record was supplied by the applicant, when was it given and under what circumstances would it have been to his or her interest to falsify? If the information is given by other persons, when and under what circumstances did the other person acquire such information? What is the nature of his or her attitude towards or interest in the applicant? Is there any reason why he or she might have motivation for misrepresenting or withholding information?

When a record is in conflict with the applicant's statements or other evidence, the conflicting data should be compared. If possible, more conclusive proof should be obtained. If conclusive proof is not available, the Investigator must select the most reliable source as the basis for determining the fact to be established and explain this in the case record.

II. *Sources of Proof*

A. *As to Age*—The following may be accepted as proof of age:

Birth Certificate—Original, transcript, or a written notification from the municipal or state Bureau of Vital Statistics.

Baptismal Certificate—Original or transcript from the church, duly certified by the custodian of such records.

If the above records cannot be produced, proof of age may be obtained by secondary evidence such as the sources listed below. (It should be noted that this listing is alphabetical for easier reference. The reliability of these sources may vary.)

1. Affidavits of reliable and disinterested persons
2. Bank and postal saving records
3. Bible or family records
4. Birth certificates of children
5. Birth or baptismal certificates (when based upon information filed at a later date)
6. Census records, state and federal
7. Church records
8. Court records
9. Hospital and clinic records
10. Immigration records
11. Insurance policies
12. Naturalization records
13. Passports
14. Physicians' records
15. Records of public or private social agencies
16. School records
17. Social Security records
18. Vaccination records

When the possibilities of securing proof of the exact age—that is, day, month, and year of birth—have been exhausted, an approximate birthdate is acceptable by many jurisdictions. This method is used only in extreme situations, such as cases involving foundlings, children placed for adoption, and persons who were born in communities in which such registration was not a legal requirement or, when a requirement was not enforced. Such persons might have no way of ascertaining their exact birthdate and yet would be permanently denied the right to receive SSI benefits or AFDC benefits unless this modification is permitted.

A signed statement of medical findings by a physician where the age of an individual is not unreasonably close to the minimum prescribed by law, may be accepted in support of the information.

B. *As to Residence*
1. Automobile registration
2. Bank records (deposit slips and records at time of opening account)
3. Bills, such as utilities, telephone, or tax
4. Birth certificates of children born in the jurisdiction where financial assistance is being sought
5. Census records
6. Citizenship papers
7. Civil Service records
8. Employment registration cards of United States and the jurisdiction's services
9. Hospital and clinic records
10. Installment purchase books
11. Insurance payment books
12. Library cards
13. Licenses such as barber's, chauffeur's, driver's, marriage, or peddler's
14. Rent receipts, records of landlord or landlord's representatives, leases, dispossession and eviction notices
15. School records
16. Social agencies' records
17. Social Security registration
18. Statements and receipts of service from utility companies
19. Voting records

Many of these sources need to be carefully evaluated in regard to reliability. Postmarked envelopes are poor evidence since letters may be sent to mailing addresses while the addressee lives elsewhere. A statement from an individual or organization is not always sufficient proof of residence and it may be necessary to interview the writer. A statement regarding residence does not have increased value by being notarized.

Sufficient proof of residence should be secured to cover the total period being used as the basis for establishing the residence status of the individual.

C. *As to Death*
1. Cemetery, hospital, insurance, physician's, and undertaker's records
2. Diaries or letters written near time of death
3. Family Bibles
4. Newspaper items
5. Registration of death—Bureau of Vital Statistics
6. Signed statements of responsible individuals who have knowledge of the fact

D. *As to Military Service*
1. Certificates of eligibility for allotments, disability pensions, educational benefits, etc.
2. Certification of veteran status by an approved veteran organization
3. Discharge papers or photostatic copy thereof

E. *As to Imprisonment*
1. Court record
2. Penal institution

F. *As to Marriage*
   1. Civil or Ceremonial
      a) Marriage certificate
      b) Records of marriage in the jurisdiction's or the state's Bureau of Vital Statistics
         Where records have been destroyed, verification may be through church records, citizenship papers, deeds, insurance policies, mortgages, and passports. Also, statements as to time and place of marriage by persons who performed the ceremony, by persons who were present or who knew of the marriage, are satisfactory verification.
   2. *Common-law*—A common-law marriage is one in which a man and woman under no legal disability, and willing to contract, do, by consent to live together presently as husband and wife, promise in each other's presence to become husband and wife and thereafter live as husband and wife. The validity of common-law marriage varies in each jurisdiction and sometimes depends on the year such marriage was contracted and the state in which it was contracted.

Action Taken as Result of Investigation

Upon completion of the investigation or reinvestigation and the budget computation, it is the Investigator's responsibility to recommend that an application be accepted or not accepted or that assistance be continued or withdrawn. This recommendation should be based on complete, factual, verified information clearly stated so that there is no doubt as to eligibility or ineligibility of the applicant or client. Generally, the supervisor has the responsibility for approving or disapproving the Investigator's recommendation.

If, after the investigation or reinvestigation, it is determined that the applicant or client is not eligible for public assistance, the basis for the nonacceptance of the application or the closing of the case must generally be given to the applicant or client and confirmed in writing in accordance with current procedure. If the rejected applicant or client whose case is being closed has problems or needs which may be met through services available from some other public or private agency, it is usually the responsibility of the Investigator to inform the applicant or client of this, to explain the services or facilities available and to make suitable referral if the applicant or client so desires.

If the Investigator has determined that the applicant is eligible for public assistance, the family should be informed of the amount of public assistance which it will receive and the manner in which the grant will be issued. There should also be an explanation of the specific items which will be included in the regular grant. The client should be informed of the services available through the agency, such as medical care or dental care, and should be asked to discuss his or her needs for such services with the Investigator if they should arise. A written copy of the budget should be given to the client.

The same principles as outlined in the above paragraph apply to under-care cases and should be followed whenever a case is reinvestigated and reauthorized, when there is a change in grant, or when there is need for a special allowance or special service. In every instance, when there is a change of grant, a written copy of the new budget should usually be given to the client.

If the client has additional financial or other needs which cannot be met by the agency but for which there are other community facilities, the Investigator is responsible for the interpretation of these to the family and for making the referral to the appropriate source. For example, an ill person may require referral to a clinic or hospital; an employed or employable mother may need referral to a day care center for the proper supervision of her children during her working hours.

It is important that the Investigator explain fully, clearly, and emphatically the client's responsibility for making continuing efforts toward self-maintenance and legal responsibility to inform the agency of any change in his or her financial or social situation affecting eligibility. A review with the family of the basis on which present eligibility is established will help to define more sharply the factors which are subject to change and which may affect the continued eligibility for assistance or the amount of the grant.

Granting of initial assistance—It is important that the family's minimum financial needs, if they cannot otherwise be met, be provided in accordance with the agency's budget allowance, but it is equally important that all items *should not* be granted routinely.

Assistance is usually granted on any of the following bases:

- Full assistance

- Supplementary assistance

- Short-term assistance

- Emergency assistance

Full assistance is the budget allowance granted by the agency when there are no other resources available and shall be granted *only* after eligibility has been determined.

Supplementary assistance is partial assistance which supplements the family's financial resources. This should be given in accordance with the agency's budgetary policy and shall be granted *only* after eligibility has been determined.

Short-term assistance is full or supplementary assistance given to meet a critical, immediate, and isolated situation, such as illness, after which the client can manage for himself or herself. The inability of the applicant or client to meet his or her needs during this short period shall be fully documented in the case record. A clear notation regarding the probable duration of the need for short-term public assistance should be made in the case record, and there shall be immediate and continued follow-up to insure the prompt withdrawal of assistance when the period of temporary need terminates. Short-term assistance is usually granted *only* after eligibility has been determined. Recurring allowances for certain items of the budget such as clothing, household equipment, and supplies, and recurring allowances for items required only during certain seasons, such as fuel for heating and school expenses, are not routinely included in the grant in short-term cases.

Emergency assistance—Assistance to meet an acute need until investigation is completed is sometimes necessary in individual situations. The amount and kind of assistance depend upon the circumstances. This involves a careful consideration of all the facts to ascertain if there is any other way that this emergency can be met. Telephone verification and, wherever possible, a home visit, must be made prior to the granting of emergency assistance.

Responsibility of the Investigator for Total Under-Care Caseload

I. *General Considerations*—It is the Investigator's responsibility to be certain:
   A. That there is continued eligibility for the assistance granted to his or her under-care cases
   B. That there has not been heretofore any employment that has not been disclosed

to the agency; that there has not been any change in the financial status of the family (income, earnings, and other resources) since the last contact with the client

C. That his or her under-care cases are given such services as may restore the family to self-support

D. That his or her under-care cases are given such services as are the function of the agency.

The frequency and purpose of further contacts with the client are based upon discharging the functions of the agency efficiently and appropriately and rendering adequate service to the client. In larger jurisdictions, these contacts are usually made at the public assistance center rather than through visits to the home.

Mandatory contacts must be made in accordance with the specific laws or rules of the agency. Cases in which eligibility has been fully established and in which there is little likelihood of change need not be contacted more frequently than the statutory requirements. More frequent contact than the minimum required should be maintained in cases:

E. Where there is likelihood of any changes affecting eligibility status

F. Where the family is in need of specific services in meeting essential needs or in being helped to return to self-support.

II. *Study of the Records*—It is only by a frequent rereading of the cases that the Investigator avoids repetition in interviewing and recording and is able to plan purposeful contacts.

III. *Continued Purposeful Contacts with Clients*—These are not for the purpose of repeating factual information already obtained but should be related to the following:

A. Employment

1. Complete current information regarding every employable member. Is there any employment not previously reported?
2. What efforts are employable members making to secure employment?
3. Has this information been verified?
4. Has every employable member been interviewed both by the Investigator and an Employment Interviewer if the agency provides for same?
5. Has every employable member registered with the State's Employment Services?
6. What employment possibilities can the Investigator suggest to the client?
7. Has the health situation changed so that a member of the family is not employable?
8. Have any of the children reached working age?

B. *Odd Jobs*—It is of the utmost importance that this possibility be discussed frankly and regularly. The Investigator should know the addresses, the periods of employment, and the earnings in each job, so that any earnings can be correlated with budgetary needs and changes in the amount of assistance granted. Suggested topics for discussion with client:

1. What is the present availability of odd jobs?
2. What sources has the client used to obtain these jobs?
3. Have these jobs been in his or her regular trade or outside of that trade?
4. What have been the earnings?
5. How have these earnings been budgeted?

C. *Seasonal Employment*

1. When does the season begin?
2. Is the present slack period longer than usual?
3. How has he or she met similar situations in the past?

D. *Unions*—When any member of the family has union affiliation:

1. Are current dues paid?
2. Date of last payment—amount and how met?

      3. What are the possibilities for employment through this source?

      4. How often does each employable member contact this union?

      5. Has the Investigator contacted the union?

E. *Family Composition*

      1. Have there been any changes which are not noted in the record?

        a) Births?

        b) Deaths?

        c) Marriages?

      2. Have any relatives moved in or out of the household? What are the reasons for this?

      3. Has the budget been adjusted in accordance with these changes?

      4. Have any other family units been established?

F. *Resources*—Resources must be reviewed periodically.

      1. Insurance

        a) Has it become adjustable since last analyzed?

        b) Has any cash been realized through sources other than adjustment by the Department?

        c) Are death benefits available?

        d) Is the family paying insurance premiums?

        e) Is there any health insurance?

        f) If adjustment is pending, has the Investigator discussed with the family the plan for the use of any money which may be made available through this adjustment, in accordance with agency regulations?

      2. Pensions or Benefits

        a) Has any member of the family become eligible for a benefit or a form of public assistance other than that administered by the agency such as SSI?

        b) Is any member of the family eligible for a pension through service in a public department?

        c) Is there a possibility of a pension or benefit through private industry?

        d) Is any member of the family eligible for a veteran's pension?

      3. Lodges and Unions

        a) Does the family belong to any organization granting benefits?

        b) Under what circumstances are they paid?

      4. Property

        a) Has there been a recent review of property assets?

        b) Is the income the same as previously recorded?

        c) Is the income budgeted in accordance with policy?

        d) Has there been a property search?

      5. Bank Accounts

        a) Have any deposits been made since the family began receiving public assistance?

      6. Boarders and Lodgers

        a) Is there any present income from this source?

        b) Is the income budgeted in accordance with policy?

        c) Was this ever a source of income for the family?

        d) Is it a feasible plan at this time?

      7. Civil Suits

        a) Has an attempt been made to collect outstanding debts in this way?

        b) Is referral to Legal Aid Society indicated?

      8. Support Fixed by Order of the Court

        a) Are allowances paid through the court received regularly?

        b) Are these included in the budget?

        c) Is the assistance of a court worker needed to obtain current information from the court?

d) Is further court action indicated?

9. Trust Funds

a) Can moneys from trust funds be obtained at this time?

b) Is referral to the resource specialists in the agency needed?

10. Frozen Assets

a) Can they be liquidated at this time?

11. *Relatives*—Assistance from relatives is subject to greater change than any other type of resource; therefore, it should always be considered a subject for discussion between the client and the Investigator.

a) Has the financial situation of legally responsible relatives changed?

b) Are they or other relatives now making any contributions?

c) Is there a possibility that they could assume responsibility for part of the budget?

d) Are they called upon to meet emergencies or special needs or services?

e) Have any legally responsible relatives left the home?

G. *Health*—The agency has a responsibility for health problems.

1. They can be funded by the medical assistance which the agency gives in addition to Medicaid and as the medical problems affect the assistance granted by the agency:

a) Has the family requested frequent care and nursing services not provided by Medicaid?

b) Are all requests for such medical care essential, or is this service used indiscriminately by the family?

c) Have allowances been granted, such as those for special diet, or clinic carfare, due to health conditions?

d) Has there been adequate follow-up to ascertain if these are still necessary?

2. They can affect employability:

a) Is the employable member receiving treatment?

b) If he or she is not receiving treatment, should he or she be referred?

c) Has follow-up been made in order to ascertain how his or her health condition affects present and future employability?

d) If physical condition makes former employment impossible, has he or she been considered for other types of employment or has he or she been referred to an agency for vocational training?

3. Health problems may involve a referral to another agency for treatment which is not provided by the agency, e.g., tuberculosis:

a) Is continued financial assistance necessary or will the other agency assume complete responsibility?

4. Health problems may involve potential resources which may be available:

a) Does the family carry health insurance?

b) Is Workers' Compensation a possibility?

c) Is consultation with the State's Department of Labor, After-Care Service of the Workers' Compensation Division indicated?

d) In case of accident, was insurance collected?

e) Is litigation pending?

f) Are there any benefits from lodges, etc.?

g) Is nursing service provided by insurance companies?

H. *Management on Public Assistance*—It is the responsibility of the Investigator to relate the assistance grant to the current needs.

1. Is full assistance being granted when only partial assistance is now necessary?

2. Does the client require aid in planning expenditures in order that he or she may derive the maximum benefits from the assistance given?

3. Should the Agency's Home Economist be consulted for aid in advising the client?

4. Is a restricted grant advisable?

I. *Further Continued Purposeful Contact with Collateral Sources*—Although contact with collateral sources may have been made during the initial investigation, further visits are necessary. This applies to those references previously seen, as well as to others from whom assistance or significant information may be obtained at this time.

1. *With Employers*—It is important to consider recontacting employers who have already been contacts. These may be necessary because:

   a) The investigator knows the client is employed and it is necessary to have current information regarding exact earnings

   b) The employer previously indicated the possibility of re-employment at a future date

   c) In certain seasonal industries, it is necessary to revisit the employer in order to determine the present possibilities for re-employment

   d) Conditions in certain industries are changing and there may be a greater possibility of re-employment than at the time the visit was originally made

   e) With some employers it is possible to keep alive an interest in rehiring former employees who are now receiving assistance.

2. *With Relatives*—Contact with certain relatives and others may be indicated. During continued contact with the family, the Investigator may become aware of relatives hitherto not mentioned to whom a visit or contact with may be advisable. The Investigator should always bear in mind that certain relatives are legally responsible and that he or she has an obligation to secure current knowledge of their ability to assist in whole or in part.

3. *With Others*—The Investigator's discussion with the client may reveal the need for interviews with other collateral sources or for appropriate clearances or reclearances. He or she should be alert to and follow up any leads hitherto unknown.

J. *Use of Other Agencies*—If the client has problems or needs which may be met through services not provided by the agency but available from some other public or private agency, it is the responsibility of the Investigator to inform the client of the availability of such services or facilities and to make suitable referral, if the client so desires. Referral to units within the agency for Medicaid and Food Stamps is especially important, and it should be checked that clients are receiving such aid. If necessary, consent of the agency for the referral should be secured prior to making the referral.

K. *Withdrawing of Assistance*—Assistance is generally withdrawn when:

1. There is no further need

2. There is lack of proof of need

3. There is income from any source which covers the budget

4. There are available assets or resources, such as trust funds, bank accounts, or insurance from which the client can be maintained

5. The client refuses to allow the Investigator to verify his or her financial need

6. There is a job refusal

7. There is refusal to comply with agency policies

8. The client has been admitted to an institution or hospital making continued assistance unnecessary

9. The client dies

10. The client's whereabouts are unknown

11. The client has moved permanently out of the state. When a case is closed due to resources which the client had while in receipt of public assistance, appropriate refund or recovery action shall be initiated.

CASE WORKER GLOSSARY

Abandoned Child

A child under the age of 16 years who is abandoned or deserted in any place by both parents, or by the parent having its custody, or by any other person or persons lawfully charged with its care or custody, and left (a) in destitute circumstances, or (b) without proper food, shelter or clothing, or (c) without being visited or having payments made toward his or her support, for a period of at least one year, by his or her parent, guardian or lawful custodian without good reason.

Active Case

A case receiving public assistance.

Adoption

A legal proceeding in which an adult person takes another adult or a minor into the relationship of child and thereby acquires the rights and incurs the responsibilities of parent in respect to the adopted person. The adoption process is controlled by laws which have as their purpose the protection of the child, the natural parents, and the adoptive parents. Two types of adoption are recognized in the law: voluntary adoption and adoption through an authorized agency.

Applicant

A person who is applying for public assistance and care, either directly or through a representative.

Application Form

A form required by the local and/or state and federal agencies responsible for providing public assistance to be filled in by applicants for such assistance. It is the applicant's statement of pertinent facts and is used in helping to determine his or her potential eligibility for financial assistance.

Application Rejected

A statistical definition used by many public assistance agencies denoting that an application for public assistance has been rejected at the time of the initial interview without further investigation.

Assignment

A transfer to another of any property, real or personal, in possession or in action; or of any estate or right therein.

Authorization Form (Regular)

Used to authorize assistance for two or more issues of a recurring allowance, to a maximum of six monthly issues, for all types of assistance.

Authorized Agency

Any agency, corporation, institution, or other organization which is incorporated or organized under the laws of the state with corporate power or empowered by law to care for, to place out, or to board out children, and which actually has its place of business in this state and is approved, visited, inspected, and supervised by the State Board of Social Welfare or which submits and consents to the approval, visitation, inspection and supervision of the Board as to any and all acts in relation to the welfare of children.

Basic Case Name and Number

The name and case number of the eligible payee designated as the responsible head in either a single case or a composite case.

Basic Case Record

The case folder maintained either for a case consisting of one eligible payee (single case) or for a case consisting of two or more eligible payees (composite case) where members of the household are budgeted together as a family unit.

Boarder

A person who receives and pays for meals in a client's home but does not reside with the client or pay rent.

Boarder-Lodger

A person who lives in the home of a client and receives meals there and pays for rent and board.

Board Out

To arrange for the care of a child in a family other than that of a relative within the second degree of the parents of such child where payment is made or agreed to be made for care and maintenance.

Budget Deficit

The difference between those items in the budget which are required by individuals or families and the income or other resources in cash or in kind available to such individuals or families to meet these needs. The amount of the regular recurring grant is the budget deficit.

Case Closed

A statistical definition denoting that public assistance has been terminated.

Caseload

The total number of cases assigned to one Investigator.

Case Number

The serial number assigned to a public assistance case. The case number includes a prefix, the abbreviation of the type of assistance; and the suffix, the abbreviation of the form of charge; e.g., AB 100001 LC; OAA 214032 PSC.

Case Record

A folder containing application form, face sheet, verification sheet when applicable, recorded material, and other pertinent material including required forms and correspondence. (Sometimes called "case folder".)

Client (Recipient)

A person in receipt of public assistance and care.

Collateral Visits

Visits to relatives, friends, former employers, landlords, etc., for the purpose of verifying information given by the applicant or client for establishing initial or continuing eligibility for public assistance.

Composite Case

The case of a family group in which there is more than one eligible payee.

Cooperative Cases

Cases that are jointly carried by the Department and private agencies.

Correctional Institution

A prison or other institution for the confinement of persons legally committed because of violation of the penal law.

Cross Reference Case and Number

The name and case number of a basic case whose record contains pertinent information and documentation concerning individuals included in another basic case.

Delinquent Child

A child over 7 and under 16 years of age who violates any law or municipal ordinance; or who commits any act which, if committed by an adult would be a crime, except a child of 15 years of age who commits an act which if committed by an adult would be punishable by death or life imprisonment unless an order removing the action to the Children's Court has been made and filed; who is incorrigible or ungovernable or habitually disobedient and beyond the control of its parent or guardian, custodian or other lawful authority; who is habitually truant; who repeatedly deserts his home without just cause or the consent of his parent or guardian; who engages in an illegal occupation; who associates with immoral or vicious persons; or who frequents any place the existence of which is in violation of the law; or who habitually uses obscene or profane language; who begs or solicits alms or money in public places under any pretense; or who so deports himself willfully as to injure or endanger the morals or health of himself or others.

Dependent Child

A child who is in the custody of, or wholly or partly maintained by, an authorized agency, institution, or other organization of charitable, eleemosynary, or correctional, or reformatory character.

Destitute Child

A child under the age of 6 years who, through no neglect on the part of its parent, guardian or custodian, is destitute or homeless, or in a state of want or suffering due to lack of sufficient food, clothing, or shelter, or medical or surgical care.

Direct Grant

An allowance given directly to a client either by cash or check.

Eligible Payee

The person designated to receive a public assistance check.

Fair Hearing

If requested by the applicant or client and considered necessary by the State Department, that Department will conduct a fair hearing.

The Commissioner of Social Welfare designates a referee to conduct the hearing, who is empowered to subpoena witnesses, administer oaths, take testimony and compel the production of all records relevant to the hearing. Hearings are private and open only to interested parties, witnesses, counsel and representatives of the State Department of Social Welfare and the Department of Welfare. The proceedings and testimony are recorded. The referee transmits his or her findings to the Commissioner of Social Welfare, who renders the decision on the case. This decision is binding upon the Department of Welfare and must be complied with by the public welfare officials involved.

Family Home (For Adults)

Home of a relative or close friend in which a client resides and where the arrangement for board and care is not a commercial one. Ordinarily, payment would not exceed cost of food and shelter; i.e. there would be no charge for service and no element of profit.

Federal Participation

That part of the total grant on which the federal government reimburses the state.

Forms of Charge

LC-Local Charge
PCS-Presumptive State Charge

Foster Care

Care of a destitute, neglected or delinquent child in an institution or foster home by an agency.

Foundling

A deserted infant whose parents are unknown.

Geographic Caseload

A caseload having fixed territorial boundaries.

Guardian

One who legally has the care and management of the person, or the estate, or both, of a child during its minority.

Indirect Grant

An allowance made payable to a third party for goods or services provided to a client.

LIAB

An abbreviation for the Life Insurance Adjustment Bureau, which is a service organized by the Metropolitan, Prudential, and John Hancock Life Insurance Companies for the purpose of (1) advising all public and private social agencies in the United States in adjusting, serving, and liquidating insurance policies; (2) assisting in securing benefits from policies carried by clients.

Lien

A legal claim on property as security for a debt or charge.

Lodger

A person who occupies a room in a client's home and pays rent but prepares meals or eats elsewhere.

Master File

The 5″ × 8″ card system maintained in welfare centers and other public assistance granting divisions, where the names of applicants and clients with whom the particular welfare center or division has had any contact are recorded. Its purpose is the proper identification of applicants and clients, and prevention of duplication of public assistance.

Mortgage

A pledge or security of particular property for the payment of a debt or the performance of some other obligation.

Neglected Child

A child under the age of 16 years who is without proper guardianship; or whose parent, guardian, or person with whom the child lives, by reason of cruelty, mental incapacity, immorality or depravity is unfit to care properly for such child; or who is under unlawful or improper supervision, care, custody or restraint by any person, corporation, agency, or other organization; or who wanders about without lawful occupation or restraint; or who is unlawfully kept out of school, or whose parent, guardian or custodian neglects or refuses, when able to do so, to provide necessary medical, surgical, institutional or hospital care for such child; or who is found in any place the existence of which is in violation of the law; or who is in such condition of want or suffering, or is under such improper guardianship or control, as to injure or endanger the morals or health of the child or other.

Non-Geographic Caseload

A caseload without territorial boundaries within the territory covered by the case unit (partially non-geographic caseload); or within the territory covered by the welfare center (totally non-geographic caseload).

Non-Recurring Expenditures or Grant (Special Grant)

A special allowance granted, when necessary, to meet a specific need as it arises.

Non-Reimbursable

Used for any item for which the City of New York bears the total cost and does not receive reimbursement from the State Department of Social Welfare.

Not Accepted

A statistical definition denoting that, after field investigation of an application for public assistance, a determination has been made that the applicant is ineligible.

Other Eligible Payee (Only in Composite Case)

Eligible payee(s) other than the responsible head.

Pending Case

A statistical definition denoting that an application for public assistance is under field investigation but no decision to accept or reject has yet been reached.

Petitioner

A complainant in a legal action.

Physically Handicapped Child

A person under 21 years of age who, by reason of physical defect or infirmity, whether congenital or acquired by accident, injury or disease, is or may be expected to be totally to partially incapacitated for education or for renumerative occupation.

"Physically handicapped child" does not include the deaf and the blind.

Private Home for the Aged

A non-profit-making institution caring for the aged which is incorporated and is approved and inspected by the State Department of Social Welfare.

Private Nursing Home

A home which is privately owned and operated for profit and which offers board, room and bedside care for compensation to persons 16 years of age and over. All private nursing homes are inspected and licensed and, if approved, a certificate is issued stating the maximum bed capacity, such certification being valid for only one year.

Proration

The method used to calculate the amount of the recurring grant if it is to be issued for a period other than the regular payment period.

Public Assistance Roll

Used by the Disbursing Section of the Division of Accounting to record the public assistance checks prepared in accordance with the authorization of the welfare center or division.

Readjustment (Of Cases)

The reallocation of cases of individual caseloads within a case unit, where caseloads are maintained on a non-geographic basis, with no resultant change in the total number of caseloads in the case unit.

Realignment

A general reallocation of the cases of an office resulting in an increase or decrease in the total number of caseloads or case units. The change may involve all of the territory administered (total) or a portion thereof (partial).

Reapplicant

An applicant who has previously applied to the Department for public assistance.

Reassignment (Of Cases)

The temporary allocation of cases of an uncovered caseload, without statistical transfer, to other caseloads in the same unit in order to provide coverage for all cases administered. A caseload is considered uncovered when no Investigator has been assigned to it, or when the Investigator formerly assigned has been absent from the assignment for any reason for any period in excess of thirty days.

Rebudgeting

Recomputation of each item of the budget as required when there is a change in the family situation involving needs or income; or whenever the budget schedules of the Department are revised.

Reclassification

The action taken when an active case receiving one type of assistance is found eligible for another type of public assistance, or when it is necessary to change the form of charge, or a combination of the two. Portions of one case may be reclassified from one type of assistance to one or more types of public assistance. Pending cases may be reclassified, when necessary, at the point of acceptance.

Redelivery

The action taken when a public assistance check returned undelivered by the United States Postal Service is delivered to the client personally either in the welfare center or in his or her home.

Redistribution

The reallocation of cases of individual caseloads within a case unit, where the caseloads and case unit are maintained on a geographic basis, resulting in changes in the caseload boundaries but with no change in the total number of caseloads in the case unit.

Reimbursable

Used for any expenditure for which part or all of the amount is repaid to the city by the state or by the federal government through the state, or both.

Residence Club and Residence Center

Congregate living arrangements providing private rooms and common dining room facilities for persons needing protective care and desiring social contacts.

Respondent

A person in a legal proceeding who occupies the position of a defendant.

Responsible Head

In a single case, the responsible head is the eligible payee. When both the husband and the wife are designated as eligible payees, the husband is the responsible head.

In a composite case, the responsible head is the eligible payee who takes primary responsibility for the family group.

Restricted Payment

A payment made to a third party for goods or service provided to a client or a grant or allowance given to a client with instructions that it be used for a specific purpose.

Service Interview

An interview with a client in the service section of the intake unit regarding information submitted by the client, requests for assistance or services, complaints or inquiries.

Single Case

The case of an individual or family group in which there is only one eligible payee.

Single Issue Authorization Form

Form used to authorize assistance for only one issue, for any and all items included in the budget or any single item not part of the regular budget, for a new or reopened case; for any single item which is in addition to the items included in the previous authorization; or for the replacement of a lost, stolen, or destroyed public assistance check or the proceeds thereof; or when the duplication of an allowance is necessary; or for any or all items included in the budget for under-care cases when the current Department policy prohibits the authorization of an allowance for two or more issues.

SSE

An abbreviation for Social Service Exchange. The Social Service Exchange is operated by the Welfare Council of New York and serves as a central registration and clearance agency for public and private social agencies. Member agencies register their cases and agree to furnish information from their records to other member agencies.

This system provides for exchange of information between agencies and reduces the possibility of duplication of assistance and services by different agencies. Member agencies pay for each clearance and registration.

Status

Statistical classification of a case; i.e., pending, active, closed.

Stop Authorization Form

Form used to stop the issuance of public assistance for a particular case as of the date indicated on the form.

Supplementation (Supplementary Assistance)

Term used when the Department contributes only part of the total needs if there is outside income or contribution from relatives or other persons or agencies.

Temporary Care

Care of a destitute or neglected child in an institution for a period less than three months.

SOCIAL WORK QUIZZER

Social Work Vocabulary

This selection of questions is particularly important and relevant in preparing you for the exam. The answer key to these test questions will be found at the end of the test.

1. "Clinics are now seeing many people who complain of seriously disturbed feelings and other symptoms relating to <u>traumatic</u> war experiences."In the preceding sentence the underlined word means most nearly

   (A) recent
   (B) worldwide
   (C) prodigious
   (D) shocking.

2. "There should be no <u>opprobrium</u> attached to the term 'second-hand housing' since every house is second-hand after the first occupancy." The underlined word in the preceding sentence means most nearly

   (A) stigma
   (B) honor
   (C) rank
   (D) credit.

3. To say that the Community Chest movement seems to have been <u>indigenous</u> to the North American continent describes this movement, in terms of the underlined word in this sentence, most nearly as

   (A) important
   (B) essential
   (C) native
   (D) homogeneous.

4. The pair of terms most similar in meaning is

   (A) feebleminded and mentally deficient
   (B) illiterate and unintelligent
   (C) client investigator
   (D) rehabilitation and remuneration.

5. The legal proceedings by which a municipality may take private property for public use is known as

   (A) search and seizure
   (B) elective franchise
   (C) habeas corpus
   (D) condemnation proceedings.

6. "The Alcoholics Anonymous Program, which in essence amounts to a <u>therapeutic</u> procedure, is codified into twelve steps." The underlined word in the preceding sentence means most nearly

   (A) compensatory
   (B) curative
   (C) sequential
   (D) volitional.

7. When people <u>vicariously</u> live out their own problems in novels and plays, they are engaging in an experience that is, in terms of the underlined word in this sentence,

   (A) dynamic
   (B) monastic
   (C) substituted
   (D) dignified.

8. "Local responsibility for the relief of economic need long having been recognized as inadequate, the state and federal governments have established plans of <u>categorical</u> assistance and social insurance." In the preceding sentence the underlined word means most nearly

   (A) conditional
   (B) economic
   (C) pecuniary
   (D) classified.

9. If the interests of a social welfare agency are concerned with bringing opportunities for self-help to underprivileged <u>ethnic</u> groups, its activities involve most nearly, in terms of the underlined word in this sentence,

(A) racial factors
(B) minority units
(C) religious affiliation
(D) economic conditions.

10. "Increased facilities for medical care (though interrupted to some extent by the <u>exigencies</u> of wartime) will safeguard the health of many children who in previous generations would have been doomed to an early death or to physical disability." In the foregoing sentence the most nearly correct equivalent of the underlined word is

(A) obstacles
(B) occurrences
(C) extenuations
(D) exactions.

11. The written authority for one person to act for another in legal matters is called

(A) a deposition
(B) a power of attorney
(C) an endorsement
(D) legal tender.

Each of the following numbered words or phrases is followed by four suggested words or phrases. In each item, one of the suggested words or phrases has a meaning which is almost the same as the meaning of the numbered word or phrase. Circle the letter preceding the word or phrase which has most nearly the same meaning as the numbered word or phrase.

12. postulate

(A) protest
(B) expostulation
(C) hypothesis
(D) prognathism

13. domination

(A) denomination
(B) denial
(C) manifesto
(D) control

14. reprisal

(A) reward
(B) retaliation
(C) embezzlement
(D) reappraisal

15. parity

(A) similarity
(B) equivalence
(C) supremacy
(D) agreement

16. hegemony

(A) dictatorship
(B) homogeneity
(C) leadership
(D) inheritance

17. amortization

(A) liquidation
(B) improvement
(C) interest
(D) principal

18. rapport

(A) mutual service
(B) controversial issue
(C) emotional dependency
(D) harmonious relationship

19. prognosis

(A) progenitor
(B) prediction
(C) causal relationship
(D) prophetic vision

20. sibling

(A) relative by marriage
(B) relative by adoption
(C) blood relative
(D) legally responsible relative

21. congenital

(A) a trait always transmitted in the germ plasm
(B) a condition dating from birth
(C) a characteristic acquired in adolsence
(D) an inherited physical characteristic

22. psychosis

(A) mental disease
(B) compulsive neurosis
(C) mental deficiency
(D) psychometrics

23. coercion

(A) immersion
(B) restraint
(C) persuasion
(D) inclusion

24. adoption

    (A) legal custody of a child
    (B) legal guardianship of a child
    (C) power of attorney of a child
    (D) provision of foster parents

25. occupational therapy

    (A) curative handicraft
    (B) job analysis
    (C) diatherm treatment
    (D) vocational guidance

26. "The nature of the <u>pathology</u> underlying the compulsion is obscure." In the preceding sentence, the underlined word means most nearly

    (A) drive
    (B) disease
    (C) deterioration
    (D) development.

27. Group work in the field of social work applies most properly to

    (A) the classification of various groups eligible for certain types of relief such as old age pension, mothers' assistance, etc.
    (B) all recreational activities
    (C) the theory and practice of managing clubs, teams and similar activities in neighborhood houses
    (D) insurance of employees in groups.

28. The case of Mary Smith, who ordered her husband out of the house and then begged his pardon before he could leave, if accepted as characteristic behavior on the part of this woman, is best considered as an illustration of

    (A) ambivalence
    (B) compensation
    (C) retrogression
    (D) frustration

ANSWER KEY

1. D	7. C	13. D	19. B	25. A
2. A	8. D	14. B	20. C	26. B
3. C	9. A	15. B	21. B	27. C
4. A	10. B	16. C	22. A	28. A
5. D	11. B	17. A	23. B	
6. B	12. C	18. D	24. A	

II. Eligibility for Assistance

1. In attempting to discover whether an applicant for aid to dependent children has had any previous experience as an aid recipient through other social service agencies in the community, the Case Worker should

    (A) check the application for such aid with the social service exchange
    (B) send the fingerprints of the applicant to the Police Department
    (C) consult the latest records of the Department of Social Services
    (D) ask the applicant to submit a notarized statement to the effect that such aid has not been received from any other source.

Select the letter preceding the best reason for asking clients the questions listed below. For example, if you believe that identification is the best reason for obtaining information about the maiden name of wife, write (A) next to question 2. If you believe that eligibility is the best reason for asking this question, write (B) next to question 2. This example is intended to help you understand the method you are to use in answering these questions; it is not intended to tell you the answer to any question. You are to decide for yourself the correct answer in each item.

Reasons

    (A) identification
    (B) Eligibility aside from income
    (C) Income or financial resources
    (D) Debts and obligations

2. Maiden name of wife.

3. Address and name of landlord.

4. Equity in the home.

5. Army, navy, or marine service.

6. Mortgages on home.

7. Duration of previous employment.

8. Amounts of premiums on insurance.

9. Adult children employed away from home.

10. Prior occupation.

11. Apartment number and floor.

12. Official information with regard to the naturalization of a client is most properly obtained from the

    (A) Department of Commerce
    (B) U.S. Department of Labor
    (C) State Department of Labor
    (D) U.S. Department of Justice.

13. The most generally accepted reason for emphasizing the techniques of interviewing in training personnel is that the interview is

    (A) a means through which the Case Worker acquires knowledge of the clients' problems
    (B) the best method for determining whether or not a person is telling the truth
    (C) a main tool of the agency for publicizing its services
    (D) a means of developing the Case Worker's objectivity.

14. The essential value of the case record to a Case Worker newly assigned to a case is that it helps the Case Worker to improve the quality of service to the client by

    (A) reading about the client and his or her situation as expressed in the record
    (B) reviewing with the client all data and recommendations found in the record
    (C) giving the Case Worker more security with the client by learning from the record the personal reactions of the previous social investigator
    (D) interpreting to the client the prejudice of the community as expressed in the record.

15. Of the following, the least reliable form of proof showing continuous residence is

    (A) rent receipts
    (B) leases
    (C) school records
    (D) dispossess and eviction notices.

16. Mr. Ritter asks the Department of Social Services to place his son, age five, in a foster home. In a subsequent interview Mr. Ritter refuses to divulge what sources of income are at his disposal. As the Case Worker trying to obtain this

information, you should explain to Mr. Ritter that

(A) you want to know whether he is seeking placement for his son because he does not want to provide for him financially

(B) part of the placement procedure involves determining the extent of financial responsibility parents can continue to assume

(C) if he makes no payment, his parental rights will be affected

(D) the frequency of his visits will depend on the amount of support he continues to furnish.

17. Accurate information regarding the employment history of a client will most probably be yielded by

(A) personally interviewing persons for whom the client has worked

(B) asking the client to fill out a questionnaire

(C) writing to persons for whom the client says he or she has worked

(D) writing to relatives of the client.

18. In making social investigations, a least desirable procedure is

(A) gaining the confidence of the family

(B) evaluating the employment potentialities of members of the family

(C) telling the clients any misrepresentations on their part will result in an arrest

(D) helping the family to get needed medical and dental care.

19. A least desirable procedure in making social investigations is

(A) calculating the minimum needs of the family according to a budget

(B) telling the family they will have to adjust to a minimum budget whether they like it or not and that the family must remember that they are a charity case

(C) obtaining from other agencies with whom clients have had contact, some knowledge of their work with those clients

(D) acquainting the family with the purpose of the assistance program planned for them.

20. The following are practices involved in making social investigations of persons applying for aid. The one which is of the greatest immediate importance is

(A) discovering the recreational habits of the family

(B) discovering any evidence of criminality

(C) searching property records to find the exact status of property which the family may have owned in the past

(D) discussing economic needs frankly.

21. The chief purpose of social investigation is to

(A) gather statistical data

(B) understand the causes of distress and maladjustment so that suitable legislation may be devised and enacted

(C) understand the situation of the client so as to discover causes and possible treatment of the particular case

(D) determine whether the client had ever before been a beneficiary of public aid.

22. Suppose an applicant for assistance objects to answering a question regarding his recent employment and asks "What business is it of yours?" As the Case Worker conducting the interview, the most constructive course of action for you to take under the circumstances would be to

(A) tell the applicant you have no intention of prying into his personal affairs and go on to the next question

(B) refer the applicant to your supervisor

(C) rephrase the question so that only a "yes" or "no" answer is required

(D) explain why the question is being asked.

23. Inasmuch as periodic visits to clients at home are required by the Department, according to good case work practice it is most desirable for the investigator to

(A) visit without appointment as this gives him or her a chance to see the person and the house "as they really are" and forestalls changing things to create a different impression

(B) write giving an appointment time as this saves the investigator from visiting when people are not at home and helps in planning work more efficiently

(C) write suggesting an appointment time so that the client may be prepared for the interview and the investigator may use his or her time economically

(D) advise all applicants during their first interview that they will be visited periodically but will not be given definite appointments.

24. Under the law it is always necessary to establish eligibility for public assistance. While the facts that must be established are clearly defined by law and by policy, the Case Worker has a good deal of freedom in choice of method. Of the methods given below for obtaining desired information from applicants for assistance, the one considered the best interviewing method in social work practice, and therefore recommended, is to

(A) work from an outline, asking the questions in the order in which they appear and requiring the applicant to give specific answers

(B) let the applicant tell what he has to say in his own way first, the interviewer then taking responsibility for asking questions on points not covered

(C) tell the applicant all the facts that it is necessary to have, then letting him give the information in any way he chooses

(D) verify all such facts as birthdate, income, and past employment before seeing the applicant, then asking the applicant to fill in the remaining gaps when he is interviewed.

ANSWER KEY

1. A	6. D	11. A	16. B	21. A
2. A	7. D	12. D	17. A	22. D
3. D	8. C or D	13. A	18. C	23. C
4. C	9. A	14. A	19. B	24. B
5. B or C	10. D	15. D	20. D	

III. Eligibility for Assistance

1. A woman applying for supplementation of her earnings explains that she earns $150 weekly but that the doctor has advised her to work only four days a week in order to safeguard her health. Under the reduced schedule, her earnings would drop to $100 a week and she would be unable to continue supporting her 62-year-old mother. Assuming that this information has been duly verified, the woman's request for supplementary aid should be

   (A) granted because she supports her elderly mother
   (B) not granted because she can still manage to work a full week
   (C) granted because the reduction of work is necessary to preserve her health
   (D) not granted because her mother can get old age assistance.

2. The best of the following reasons for closing a case which is active with the agency is that

   (A) the attitude of the client is defiant
   (B) the client complains about the worker to the head of the agency
   (C) the client fails to call for his relief check or to make further requests
   (D) the client is flighty or irresponsible.

3. Continued contact with assistance recipients is maintained by Eligibility Specialists employed by the Department mainly because

   (A) changes in aid need to be made in accordance with financial changes in the family situation
   (B) many people do not report changes in income promptly
   (C) most people do not understand that reports of their earnings are required
   (D) the department wishes to see that the aid given is properly used.

4. Mrs. Rose complains to the Case Worker about the inadequacy of her allowance although she is being granted the maximum amount for a person in her situation. It is acknowledged by the Department of Social Services that the amount of the grant is not based on current prices. Under these circumstances, the most

considerate reply to make to this complainant is that

   (A) the grant is based on a scientific calculation of needs for subsistence and is only a small percentage short of what is actually needed
   (B) the investigator knows that it is difficult to manage since the cost of living is steadily rising, but that the amount granted was all the Department of Social Services schedule allows at the present time
   (C) Mrs. Rose would be worse off if there were no public assistance
   (D) many people in other countries do not have even the small grant allowed Mrs. Rose.

5. Mr. Russell complains to his Case Worker that he is too feeble to cook his own food and needs more money in order to eat in restaurants. If investigation of the request proves that Mr. Russell's condition is as indicated, the Case Worker should

   (A) explain why no provision can be made for this additional expense
   (B) suggest that Mr. Russell get a neighbor to help with the cooking
   (C) recommend that the allowance be increased
   (D) explain that aid recipients should not eat in restaurants.

6. It is most important for a client to understand what assistance eligibility is

   (A) so that he will be able to help others in need of aid
   (B) because his family may be suffering
   (C) so that he can immediately assume his share of responsibility by giving the necessary information and helping in the verification of it
   (D) because the law requires it.

7. Definitions of need by which to determine eligibility for aid vary. The condition which most

nearly approximates the definition of need according to current practice, is

(A) applicant has no income to meet the minimum standards of the Department, no liquid resources, and no relatives able to contribute to his or her support

(B) applicant has insufficient income to meet the minimum standards set by the Department, no insurance, and no relatives able to contribute to his or her support

(C) applicant has insufficient income to meet the minimum standards set by the Department, no employed relatives, and no more than $2000 worth of insurance

(D) applicant has insufficient income to meet the minimum standards set by the Department, no relatives able to contribute to his or her support, and no liquid resources.

8. Although the establishment of eligibility for aid must usually be a cooperative process, the ultimate burden of proof rests on

(A) the investigator, because it is his or her sole responsibility to verify eligibility

(B) the client, because it is his or her responsibility to provide data concerning eligibility

(C) the supervisor, because he or she authorizes giving of aid

(D) the resource consultant, because he or she is responsible for preventing "chiseling."

9. The Carter family is applying for aid for the first time because of unemployment. They are a young couple with one child. All are in good health. Mr. Carter is a skilled laborer in a seasonal trade. The intake interviewer, in order to recommend emergency aid, must know if Mr. Carter

(A) feels that his needs are emergent

(B) has siblings who are legally responsible for his support

(C) is receiving any union benefits or unemployment insurance

(D) has a $2,000 life insurance policy.

10. The Brown family, applicants for aid, live in a fine apartment in a high rent district. The landlord, a prominent businessman, has carried the family for some time without payment of rent. The family is unaccustomed to privation. Of the following the best procedure for the

Worker to follow in making a first visit to the family is to

(A) explain to the family that the rules of the agency do not permit a budget large enough to continue that scale of living

(B) tell the family that no aid can be given them until they get out of this apartment

(C) tell the family to move out without telling the landlord of their plans to do so

(D) explain to the family that the landlord will have to be allowed to worry about the rent while the family meets other obligations.

11. Mrs. Mary Wooster, who has been caring for her 10-year-old orphaned niece, applies for aid to dependent children when her husband's income is reduced. If you are the one assigned to this case, you should tell Mrs. Wooster that her application

(A) cannot be accepted for investigation because her niece must be removed from her home and placed out by the state

(B) can be accepted for investigation because she falls within the group of relatives who are eligible to receive aid to dependent children

(C) cannot be accepted for investigation because relatives other than parents are never granted help through aid to dependent children

(D) can be accepted for investigation because her niece is her legal responsibility.

12. The primary purpose in discussing with an applicant the steps in determining his or her eligibility and the kind of verification of facts which the agency will need is to

(A) enable the applicant to understand the basis of eligibility and participate in determining it

(B) protect the position of the agency so that there will be no comeback if aid is not granted

(C) give the applicant an opportunity to modify any statement he or she may have made previously

(D) promote public relations for the agency, since the applicant will tell others how the agency is operating.

13. One of the following disclosures is made regarding an applicant for old age assistance and he is accordingly disqualified to receive the grant requested. In the recommendation sub-

mitted by the Case Worker, the applicant would be found ineligible because he

(A) is not a citizen
(B) has $100 in a bank account which he is saving for burial purposes
(C) has three married children and could probably live with one of them
(D) refuses to give information concerning a bank account of $5,000 which had been in his name until four months prior to his application.

14. When he applies for public assistance, a man gives a complete and straightforward account of his past employment and earnings, of the inability of his relatives to help, and of his attempts to find work. The way the family has managed in the past indicates excellent planning ability in the use of money and making limited resources go a long way. He says he exhausted all resources before applying and gives a detailed account. The family lived on less than a full allowance while receiving unemployment compensation. They have exhausted their credit at the grocery store. The landlord is threatening eviction because of rent arrears of two months. He explains he went through all this because it is so painful for him to apply for welfare. The man is obviously honest and reliable. Under these circumstances, a conscientious Case Worker would find that

(A) it is unnecesary to verify the foregoing information in order to establish eligibility
(B) it is necessary to verify the facts given above in order to establish eligibility
(C) the interviewer should be free to decide whether any verifications are needed
(D) eligibility considerations should be waived and immediate grant made in order to help the man feel better.

15. Miss Lowe applies for public assistance and is able to account for her work history and her financial expenditures with the exception of three months in 1987. As acting intake interviewer it would be your responsibility to inform her that

(A) she will remain ineligible until she accounts for her complete work history
(B) her application can be accepted, but that certain verification will have to be made as to her statements regading lack of resources
(C) she is obviously hiding pertinent information and that her application cannot therefore be considered
(D) she obviously had some source of help in 1987 and that she should use this source again.

ANSWER KEY

1. C	4. B	7. D	10. A	13. D
2. C	5. C	8. B	11. B	14. B
2. A	6. C	9. C	12. A	15. B

IV. Judgment

1. When a family asks the help of the Eligibility Specialist because they are consistently exceeding their food and clothing allowance, he or she should

   (A) use the services of the home economist for consultation on the management problem which has developed
   (B) order the family to live within their budget allowance
   (C) ignore the situation as it is the family's responsibility to make ends meet
   (D) recommend small increases in the food and clothing allowance for this family.

2. When a client requests that the Department of Social Services take some action because her unemployed husband is indifferent to her and unconcerned about the welfare of their children, the Eligibility Specialist should

   (A) inform the husband that he will be cut out of the grant if he does not change his attitude
   (B) advise the woman to separate and try to build a life apart from her husband
   (C) tell the woman to appeal to the Family Court to have her husband ordered to spend his evenings at home
   (D) suggest that the woman discuss this matter with a private family agency

3. Knowing that a client needs a period of rest and that another agency can arrange this, it would be the responsibility of an Eligibility Specialist to

   (A) notify the client of this resource and suggest that he apply there if he wishes to
   (B) try to make all the arrangements for the client, telling the other agency her or she knows all about the client's situation and can supply information on him
   (C) tell the client that unless he applies to the other agency, he or she will do so for him
   (D) tell the client he seems insufficiently interested in getting well enough to work and the Department of Social Services may discontinue his assistance.

4. The homemaking center of the Department of Social Services furnishes the services of mother's aides to families to help in caring for their children because of the mother's temporary incapacity or absence. Mother's aides can assume responsibility for such household duties as feeding infants, preparing meals, cleaning the house, etc. They are mature, responsible women with previous homemaking experience who have passed a literacy test and have undergone a thorough physical examination. According to current thinking in the field, for the Eligibility Specialist assigned in any case where a mother's aide is furnised, to use the mother's aide as a source of obtaining confidential information for the Department would be

   (A) advisable; as a result of contact with the family, the mother's aide will have observed many details concerning their daily activities
   (B) inadvisable; while the mother's aide will have observed many details concerning the daily activities of the family, she has not been trained to interpret these observations
   (C) advisable; the mother's aide has been thoroughly examined as to her ability to perform her duties in the household
   (D) inadvisable; the mother's aide has a primary obligation to the family rather than to the Department.

5. One of your clients finds it necessary to be away from home for two weeks and arranges with her mother to care for her children, for whom she receives an aid to dependent children grant, without notifying your department about this plan. You discover her absence, however, when making a periodic revisit to the client's apartment. In view of these facts it would be most advisable to

   (A) stop the grant immediately inasmuch as you are unable to see the client at this time
   (B) let the grant continue as the temporary planned absence of the client does not affect her eligibility
   (C) tell the client's mother that a recipient of aid to dependent children may not leave her children even for a temporary period
   (D) order the client's mother to wire her return within two days or the grant will stop.

6. Assuming that careful interpretation has been given but an applicant for public assistance refuses to accede to the necessary procedures to establish his eligibility for aid, the most preferable of the following courses of action for the Eligibility Specialist would be to

(A) do nothing further
(B) grant temporary aid in the hope that the applicant will change his mind
(C) try to ascertain why the applicant feels as he does but to respect his decision if he refuses to change his mind
(D) proceed to check on all the facts possible even though the applicant has not given his permission.

7. The best of the following reasons for which a public assistance agency should not insist on certain standards of cleanliness as a factor in eligibility to receive public assistance is that it is generally acknowledged that

(A) people have a right to decide how they will live, provided their mode of living does not hurt others
(B) standards of cleanliness vary so much among people as to make one standard impracticable
(C) a little dirt has never hurt anyone
(D) it would take too much of the Eligibility Specialist's time to maintain a constant check on this factor.

8. Assume that a certain Mr. Sears applied for aid three weeks ago. As he had not yet received any assistance, he comes to see the Eligibility Specialist, claiming department neglect. A checkup of Mr. Sears' status reveals that his application has been active pending receipt of a reply from a former employer. When informed of this contingency, Mr. Sears offers to expedite matters by getting in touch with the employer himself. The best way to handle this case would be to tell Mr. Sears that

(A) the determination of his eligibility is the responsibility of the Eligibility Specialist alone
(B) it would help if he could hurry the reply
(C) if he discusses this with the employer, the information will be invalidated
(D) he should just go home and wait.

9. Before beginning to demolish a slum area, the families concerned should be assisted, when necessary, in moving. The families' social adjustment is more likely to be achieved, according to case work theory, if the family moves to

(A) a neighborhood chosen by the agency, because the agency is in a position of know what is best for the family
(B) a neighborhood chosen by professional social workers, because social workers will choose a better neighborhood
(C) a neighborhood chosen by the family itself, because people should be permitted to make their own plans
(D) a neighborhood chosen because relatives live nearby, since relatives are always helpful.

10. Social workers are generally agreed that except for the problems presented in individual cases, financial dependency should be treated as a

(A) symptom of general industrial unrest
(B) manifestation of individual inadequacy and personality maladjustment
(C) problem in individual and family relationships
(D) symptom of economic and personal problems

11. John Smith, an unemployed carpenter, age 40, lost a leg in an accident five years ago. This is his first application for public assistance. The least valid assumption for the Eligibility Specialist to make prior to investigation is

(A) he should be classified as permanently unemployable
(B) he is receiving Workers' Compensation
(C) although disabled, he may do well in suitable employment
(D) his physical handicap may limit his opportunities for re-employment.

12. When conducting a first interview with a foreign client who is applying for aid, the skill of the Eligibility Specialist is indicated by

(A) discussing the situation with the client without any particular consideration of his cultural background
(B) explaining to the client that he will probably find it difficult to get work because of the prejudices of English speaking persons against foreigners
(C) utilizing his or her familiarity with the cultural background of the client in order to promote the purpose of the interview
(D) explaining to the client how his cultural background affects his dependency.

13. It is important for the Eligibility Specialist to realize that the use of authority is

(A) natural only to the aggressive person and that any of its manifestations should be avoided

(B) indicative of an assumption of power which the Eligibility Specialist should not hesitate to apply in all instances.

(C) a necessary technique for the Eligibility Specialist to make the client conform to the agency policies

(D) inherent in the role of the Eligibility Specialist and he or she should be aware of its potential uses and abuses.

14. Suppose a client whom you are investigating has borrowed $25 in order to purchase an evening gown for one of her children who is being graduated from high school. She is planning to repay the loan at the rate of one dollar a week, and presents verification of this transaction as well as of the purchase. As an Eligibility Specialist you would be complying with the best case work principles by

(A) telling the client her grant will be reduced in view of her ability to manage on a dollar less each week

(B) telling the client that she must never do this again

(C) explaining to the client how her action will make it more difficult for the family to get along on their limited grant

(D) suggesting that she return the dress and repay the borrowed money in this way.

15. The best of the following principles to keep in mind in handling persons who comes to social agencies is

(A) destitution is not the only reason for opening a case

(B) families of the same size should be given the same amount of relief regardless of other factors

(C) one can usually accomplish more by the use of authority than by suggestion and cooperation

(D) persuasion by means of reasoning is always effective.

16. Mr. Durand, a widower with three children, had been receiving aid for about two months. The Case Worker noticed on a visit that the children had new clothing. Mr. Durand explained that the clothing came from an aunt in a distant city. He stated that the aunt could not help regularly and asked that no contact be established with the aunt. Since the aunt was not legally responsible, the Case Worker consented to this arrangement. About two weeks later, the worker was told by a neighbor that Mr. Durand was working regularly. The neighbor did not know where Mr. Durand was employed. The best of the following procedures for the Case Worker to follow is to

(A) go to Mr. Durand at once and accuse him of concealing assets

(B) investigate the matter further before taking action

(C) cut the family off assistance without further investigation

(D) tell Mr. Durand that the Case Worker would never again believe anything he said and that other Case Workers would be informed of Mr. Durand's unreliability.

17. The Grover family consisted of a mother and five children. The father had disappeared five years before. The oldest boy, 17, unable to find work, considered leaving home in order not to be a burden to the family. The family owned their own six-room home, renting out one room for $60 a month. Mrs. Grover did day work, but did not earn enough to cover expenses. Her health was poor. A partial aid to dependent children allowance was granted. The best practice for the Case Worker to follow in this case would be to

(A) encourage the oldest boy in his plan to leave home

(B) determine whether the allowance should be increased to permit Mrs. Grover to stay home

(C) get in touch with neighbors to determine if Mr. Grover has been seen recently

(D) urge the Department of Aid to Dependent Children to grant the full allowance immediately.

18. Mr. Semple was sent to prison in 1985 as a result of conviction for robbery. He will not be eligible for parole until 1996. His former employer is giving the family a small weekly allowance. The family owns a home, but has heavy taxes to pay and interest on the mortgage. The family consists of three children, none of whom is older than 16. No payments have been made since Mr. Semple left home and there is no income, other than the employer's allowance. Jack, the second oldest boy, is in the seventh grade in school and wants to go through high school. His IQ is 74. The family has lived in New York City for 25 years. The best of the following procedures is to

(A) refer Mrs. Semple to the Division of Aid to Dependent Children
(B) warn Mrs. Semple that the children may turn out to be like the father
(C) urge Jack to continue through high school
(D) use the agency's influence to get Mr. Semple paroled at once.

19. A Social Service division was helping the family of Jane Jones. Board money from her brother, James, helped to cut down the amount of aid the family received. A hospital dispensary worker informed the investigator that James was receiving regular treatments for syphilis at the dispensary. The disease was in the non-infectious stage, and the dispensary stated that the family was in no danger of contracting the disease. James had asked the medical social worker not to tell his sister of his condition because he feared that it would worry her. The best of the following procedures for the Case Worker to adopt is to

(A) initiate with the sister a discussion of the danger of syphilitic infection, permitting her to draw her own conclusions
(B) tell the sister about the brother's condition without telling her the source of the information
(C) leave the health matters of the man in the hands of the medical social worker
(D) question the sister about the morals of the brother.

20. The best of the following practices in handling cases in social agencies is to

(A) use indirect questioning sometimes in preference to direct questioning in order to obtain more complete information from the client
(B) use general terms in preference to specific terms in writing case records
(C) give advice and make promises freely in a first interview in order to gain the confidence of the client
(D) attempt to increae the client's nervous tension so that he or she will be more anxious to find work.

21. Assume that in making your first visit to the home of an applicant for aid to dependent children, you find the bed unmade, the dishes unwashed, and the furniture so dusty that you cannot find a clean place to sit down, although it is already three o'clock in the afternoon. The applicant has four small children. Under the circumstances described, you should inform the applicant that

(A) she is ineligible for the grant because she does not give her children the proper physical environment
(B) her application will be investigated and her eligibility determined
(C) her application will be investigated but if her home in not cleaned up when you visit next week, her application will be rejected
(D) if found eligible for aid to dependent children, she must take instruction in house-keeping from the welfare center home economist.

22. A 15-year-old girl calls on you, the Eligibility Specialist, to say that her mother is negligent and buys clothing for herself and treats her male friends to movie dates with her grant from aid to dependent children. According to the most generally accepted social case work principles, you should tell the girl that

(A) the grant will be stopped immediately
(B) she does not have to put up with that kind of environment and can arrange to leave her mother immediately
(C) you will take this matter up with her mother and see her again at some future time
(D) she should file a formal complaint against her mother.

23. From the case history on a client described as a delinquent individual, illiterate, shy, regarded by others with annoyance or condescension, who hardly ever engages in group activities and never goes to church, movies, or theater, the Case Worker would be justified in forming the conclusion that

(A) the social isolation is responsible for the delinquency
(B) the delinquency is responsible for the social isolation
(C) both the poverty and isolation are responsible for the delinquency
(D) a single case is insufficient for the inference that social isolation is regularly associated with poverty and delinquency.

ANSWER KEY

1. A	6. C	11. A	16. B	21. B
2. D	7. A	12. C	17. B	22. C
3. A	8. B	13. D	18. A	23. D
4. B	9. C	14. C	19. C	
5. B	10. D	15. A	20. A	

V. Public Health

1. Among persons handicapped by blindness, the ones who may be expected to display a range of experience most comparable with that of normal persons are those who

   (A) receive no special consideration from others
   (B) are closely protected by their relatives and friends against the severe limitations imposed by their handicap
   (C) are urged to greater attainments than would be expected of normal persons in order to compensate for their affliction
   (D) are urged to understand their potentialities and limitations and are encouraged to make the most of their opportunities.

2. Medical social work is distinguished from other forms of case work by the fact that

   (A) it is always performed by a trained nurse
   (B) it is always carried on directly under the supervision of a physician
   (C) it is directed primarily at bringing about conditions suitable for medical treatment and recovery of the patient
   (D) it relates only to chronic ailments that allow a sufficient length of time for service to make it effective.

3. The nutritive value of foods is determined principally by

   (A) specific gravity
   (B) caloric content
   (C) mineral content
   (D) enzyme components.

4. A knowledge of nutrition is of importance to a Case Worker chiefly because

   (A) it adds to his or her stock of cultural information
   (B) it helps him or her to understand the client's needs and may assist in formulating a plan for meeting these needs
   (C) the Case Worker should be familiar with modern sociological theories and practices
   (D) the Case Worker is thus enabled to act as a nutrition expert.

5. The term vital statistics is most commonly applied to such data as

   (A) births, deaths, and marriages
   (B) unemployment rates and cost of living indices
   (C) numbers of persons applying for public assistance and costs of public assistance administration
   (D) costs of health and safety education.

6. An occupational disease is one which arises from

   (A) continued employment in particular types of work
   (B) an accidental injury sustained by the employee
   (C) continued unemployment
   (D) dependence on public assistance.

7. That part of medicine which relates to foods is called

   (A) mastication
   (B) deglutition
   (C) pediatrics
   (D) dietetics.

8. The disease in connection with which the Schick test is best known is

   (A) diphtheria
   (B) tuberculosis
   (C) typhoid fever
   (D) syphilis.

9. A contributing factor to the decline in the death rate in the United States within recent years is generally considered by authorities to be the

   (A) decline in the incidence of heart disease
   (B) shorter hours of work in industry
   (C) decline in the incidence of infectious diseases in childhood
   (D) increase in the number of group medical treatment plans.

10. The population of the United States is said to be "aging," that is, there are more older people

proportionately now than in the past. The most probable reason for this is the
(A) increasing knowledge of diseases of older age groups
(B) constantly declining birth rate and immigration rate
(C) increase in public hospital and clinic facilities
(D) unemployment and increased leisure among older age groups which has decreased physical wear and tear.

11. The essential purpose of Health Education is to
(A) lower the cost of medical service to the public
(B) advertise public medical service
(C) instruct the public in the value of good medical services
(D) give the public information on self-treatment.

12. The most accurate of the following statements about visiting nurses is that they
(A) may visit families independently of a physician to give instruction in hygiene or minor services such as baths to patients
(B) always restrict their work to bedside service to the sick patient and take no responsibility for other members of the family
(C) never visit a family except on order of a physician
(D) always give service free of charge.

13. The surest test of whether the authorities of public health administration in a large city are doing effective work is seen in the
(A) decrease in death rates from yellow fever, smallpox, pneumonia, and mumps
(B) decrease in death rates from typhoid, diphtheria, and tuberculosis
(C) decrease in death rates from diabetes, heart disease, and cancer
(D) increase in the birth rate.

14. The best of the following methods of combating communicable diseases is
(A) fumigating homes in which persons with contagious diseases have been living
(B) inoculating against typhoid fever all persons known to have been in contact with a typhoid patient
(C) imposing a quarantine period upon all incoming vessels
(D) enforcing the law requiring reporting of communicable diseases.

15. Authorities on health education emphasize certain things that all persons should do as a preventive measure. The most important of these is
(A) routine X-ray examination of the teeth
(B) a cold shower every morning
(C) annual typhoid inoculation
(D) annual medical examination.

ANSWER KEY

1. D	4. B	7. D	10. B	13. B
2. C	5. A	8. A	11. C	14. D
3. B or C	6. A	9. C	12. A	15. D

VI. Procedures and Records

1. "In spite of the need which most of us have of finding rules and procedures to guide us, we must face the difficulty at the outset that there is no such thing as a model case "record." Of the following, the best justification for this statement is that

   (A) records should be written to suit the case
   (B) case recording should be patterned after the best models obtainable
   (C) rules cannot be applied to social case work because each case requires individual treatment
   (D) the establishment of routine and procedures in social work is an ideal which cannot be realized.

2. Of the following, the best statement in regard to the efficiency of the Eligibility Specialist in a public assistance agency is

   (A) clerical efficiency automatically speeds up the satisfaction of clients' needs
   (B) clerical efficiency automatically increases skill in client relationships
   (C) clients resent clerical efficiency in social work
   (D) clerical efficiency automatically meets the client's needs.

3. A woman applying for aid says that her husband is a drunkard, beats her, and mistreats her children. The Eligibility Specialist, when referring this case to a Case Worker, should make a notation that this man should be

   (A) committed to an institution for alcoholics
   (B) taken to court and ordered to keep the peace
   (C) referred to a psychiatric clinic
   (D) none of the above.

4. The essential purpose of the face sheet of a case record is to present

   (A) identifying data about the particular individuals in the social situation who present a problem to the agency
   (B) intimate personal facts about the persons concerned in the social situation
   (C) identifying data about the persons concerned in the social situation
   D) a social diagnosis of the family for reference purposes

5. One of the primary functions of an Eligibility Specialist is to

   (A) receive and record all complaints
   (B) interview all applicants for aid
   (C) take inventories of materials and supplies received
   (D) receive the commodities to be used by needy persons.

6. Writing a case record in a busy agency involves knowledge of acceptable practices in social case recording. Below are given four practices an interviewer might follow in writing up a long first investigation. The best practice is to

   (A) put down verbatim in the presence of the client everything he or she says
   (B) omit from the record any mention of agreements or promises made by the Case Worker
   (C) omit any mention of tension observed between members of the family, describing only what has to do with the economic condition of the family
   (D) give a picture of the problem as it appears to the family.

7. The one of the following which is not a good practice in writing up a case is

   (A) include everything of importance said by the Case Worker
   (B) give a clear account of the client's difficulties
   (C) record any line of action the Case Worker may have agreed to follow
   (D) make the case record as lengthy and as detailed as possible.

8. Of the following, the least valid reason for the maintenance of the case record in public assistance administration is to

   (A) furnish reference material for other Case Workers
   (B) improve the quality of service to the client
   (C) show how the public funds are being expended
   (D) reduce the complexities of the case to manageable proportions.

9. A public assistance agency will lean more on forms than a private agency in the same field of activity because

(A) forms simplify the recording responsibilities of newly appointed Eligibility Specialists

(B) public welfare records are of the family agency type

(C) the government framework requires a greater degree of standardization

(D) more interviews and visits are made in connection with public assistance cases.

ANSWER KEY

1. A	3. D	5. C	7. D	9. C
2. A	4. D	6. D	9. C	

VII. Interpretation of Social Work Problems

FICTITIOUS SCHEDULE OF MONTHLY ALLOWANCES FOR ASSISTANCE (To be utilized only for answering Questions 1 to 6.)			
Item of Expense	Allowance for Recipient		
	ADULT	CHILD 13-18	CHILD under 13
Food	$75.96	$70.00	$60.00
Clothing	$18.00	$16.80	$15.80
Rent Utilities Personal Incidentals		As paid by the Client $2.40 per person $1.40 per person	
Do not assume that the facts in the above schedule are either actual or current. They are not. They were simply devised to test your ability to apply facts in solving the kinds of problems that are part of your work.			

1. The Anderson family, consisting of father, mother, and four children, ages 4, 10, 15, and 17, is eligible for public assistance. The rent is $160 a month. Public assistance granted on the basis of the above items is given semi-monthly. According to the schedule shown, the proper semi-monthly grant for this family would be

   (A) $688
   (B) $516
   (C) $347.96
   (D) $172

2. Assuming that all the expenditures except rent were reimbursable under the State Welfare Law to the same extent that reimbursements for assistance are now being made to the city, the annual cost to the city for all the items included in the public assistance budget of the Anderson family would be approximately

   (A) $1920
   (B) $6431.04
   (C) $8260
   (D) $5058.

3. Mrs. Peet is 67 years old and applies for old age assistance. She lives with her widowed niece who has a family of three children. The rent of the apartment is $112.00 a month. The niece has agreed to pay for the utilities of the whole group and also to give Mrs. Peet some money for personal incidentals, provided that Mrs. Peet can pay one-fifth of the rent. On medical advice, a special diet allowance of $15.44 a month is authorized for Mrs. Peet in addition

   to the regular food allowance. The proper monthly grant for Mrs. Peet would be

   (A) $96.96
   (B) $112.40
   (C) $131.80
   (D) $161.44

4. Mrs. Scalise applies for aid for herself and her two children ages two and four. Her rent costs $130.00 a month. She is separated from her husband, who contributes $36 a week by court order. It has also been verified that Mrs. Scalise earns $22.40 a week doing piecework at home. Assuming that for budget computation purposes the Department considers 4.3 weeks as equivalent to one month, the monthly grant in this case would be

   (A) $96.32
   (B) $135.84
   (C) $154.80
   (D) $251.12

5. A 36-year-old sightless widower applies for aid to the blind. His rent and utilities are met by relatives with whom he lives. In aid to blind cases, $17.40 per month is allowed for expenses incidental to blindness as substitute for the personal incidentals item in the schedule. Under the circumstances, the proper monthly grant would be computed at

   (A) $89.40
   (B) $111.36
   (C) $78.00
   (D) $128.00

6. John Burke is 52 years old and needs supplementary assistance. He pays $74.00 a month for his room and he earns $84.00 a month doing odd jobs. Basing your computations on these facts and on the schedule, you can determine that the proper semi-monthly grant for Mr. Burke would be

(A) $167.80
(B) $83.80
(C) $43.88
(D) $25.28

7. "The knowledge and understanding of situations and of people attained through social case work may well serve as a basis for sound social action and for effective social welfare planning." The most logical assumption that the social Case Worker can draw from the statement made above is that

(A) since social welfare planning is related to broad social issues and needs, it is unnecessary to consider the individual
(B) the individual is the only unit to be considered in planning of effective social welfare programs
(C) all social planning should be directed primarily toward the individual and his or her needs
(D) knowledge of the individual attained through social case work can be effectively utilized in planning a broad social welfare program.

8. The inability of people to obtain employment during a time of economic depression is an example of the principle that

(A) anyone who really wants a job can get one if he or she tries hard enough
(B) the more capable people get jobs when jobs are scarce
(C) at certain times employment is not available for many people irrespective of ability, character, or need
(D) full employment is a thing of the past.

9. If the budget allowance, T dollars, granted each child under V years of age, is increased W percent of the base figure every X years, the percentage increase in the budget per child for a family of Y children all under V minus P years of age would, at the end of P years, be

(A) $\dfrac{W\,T}{P\,X}$

(B) $\dfrac{V \text{ minus } P}{Y\,X}$

(C) $\dfrac{P\,W}{X}$

(D) none of the foregoing.

10. "The real worth of the Family Court cannot be estimated in dollars and cents." This statement most nearly means

(A) the taxpayers should not begrudge the cost of administering this court, no matter how large
(B) the importance of this court to the community is the service that it renders in the preservation of family life
(C) the cost of administering the court must increase from year to year
(D) the value of the court's work in terms of dollars and cents should be ignored by the taxpayers.

11. During the year 1980, N families applied for aid, representing an increase of M families over the number applying in 1978. In 1979, however, the number applying was P less than in 1978. If there were R investigators in each of the 3 years, the average case load per investigator in 1979 was

(A) $\dfrac{N \text{ minus } M}{PR}$

(B) $\dfrac{N \text{ minus } M \text{ minus } P}{R}$

(C) $\dfrac{M \text{ plus } N \text{ minus } R}{P}$

(D) $\dfrac{N \text{ plus } M \text{ plus } P}{R}$

12. If it is assumed that the study of anthropology has no value for social work, then

(A) no anthropologist should be interested in social work
(B) no primitive cultures have any meaning for social workers
(C) persons who study anthropology should be interested in social work
(D) primitive cultures have meaning for the student of modern society.

13. It has been found by a research study in England that, during the time that Social Insurance has been in effect, there has been a decrease in the consumption of alcohol. The most valid assumption on the basis of this information is that

(A) people receiving Social Insurance tend to spend their money on alcohol
(B) Social Insurance income is so small that people cannot afford to buy alcohol
(C) the use of alcohol is a means of escape from an intolerable situation
(D) a decrease in the consumption of alcohol may be related to the receipt of Social Insurance.

Two excerpts of written material, which you are to read and study carefully, follow. Each excerpt is immediately followed by a number of statements which refer to it alone. You are required to judge whether each statement

(A) is entirely true
(B) is entirely false
(C) is partly true and partly false
(D) may or may not be true, but cannot be answered on the basis of the facts as given in the excerpt.

Choose the letter preceding the answer which is the best of those suggested and write it next to each question. Be sure to consider only the facts given in the excerpt to which the statement refers.

"The child labor provisions of the Minimum Wage Act prohibit any producer, manufacturer or dealer to ship or deliver in interstate commerce any goods produced in an establishment which has employed oppressive child labor in the previous thirty days. Oppressive child labor is defined as employment of children under 16 years of age. Exception is made for children of 14 or 15 in kinds of work other than manufacturing or mining in which it will have been determined by the Chief of the Children's Bureau, work will not interfere with school, health, or well-being. However, employment of children 16 or 17 years of age is prohibited in any occupation found and declared by the Chief of the Children's Bureau to be particularly hazardous or detrimental to health."

14. The Minimum Wage Act sets up minimum wages and hours for children who are legally permitted to work.

15. The Minimum Wage Act makes no provision for children over 16 years of age.

16. The employment of children of any age in a hazardous occupation is considered oppressive child labor.

17. According to the Act, a producer in New York State may not employ oppressive child labor for goods which he intends to ship to New Jersey, but is not affected if he sells the goods within New York State.

18. The Chief of the Children's Bureau may determine what exceptions may be made for children of 14 engaged in farming, and for children of 16 engaged in only manufacturing and mining.

In each of the following seven questions, a quotation is given in which one word or two consecutive words are incorrect and destroy the true meaning. Select the option which, if inserted in the place of the incorrect word or words, will make the most logical and correct statement.

19. "Efforts to deal constructively with the juvenile delinquent have been thwarted by the commonly held beliefs of a decade or two ago that most of them are social failures. The evidence against that is today overwhelming.

(A) retarded
(B) normal child
(C) psychotic adult
(D) adult mentality.

20. "Perhaps startling to some persons, although a commonplace to the public assistance workers themselves, is the recently ascertained fact that of those persons who became eligible for unemployment compensation, more than 90% had notified the assistance offices of the receipt of their agreement with the agency, before official notification was received from the unemployment compensation authorities."

(A) work assignments
(B) benefit checks
(C) insurance pensions
(D) endowment policies.

21. "The public aid program must focus upon ways and means of training and of maintaining the skills of its clients, must play an aggressive leadership role in the placement of its clients in labor camps, and must do this fully aware of the importance of preventing the flooding of

the labor market with persons forced to accept substandard sweatshop wages."

(A) relief categories
(B) government projects
(C) public institutions
(D) private industry.

22. "The psychoanalysts evolved theories as to the stages of intellectual development through which the personality matures and threw much light on the life situations and mental mechanisms by which this process is thwarted."

(A) psychological
(B) abnormal
(C) emotional
(D) retrogressive.

23. "Popular belief in the efficacy of punishment by imprisonment is apparently based on ignorance of the statistics on classification. While the figures supplied by prison officials are as low as 39% for some states, they are as high as 78% in others, and the general average for the whole country is approximately 64%. Some authorities frankly express their opinion that large numbers of prisoners emerge from existing institutions worse than when they entered."

(A) probation
(B) recidivism
(C) health
(D) perversion.

24. "When aid standards are discussed it is often difficult to work out the problem which centers about granting allowances to provide health and decency standards and also what the self-supporting family can afford for itself. The subsistence diet procedure in aid administration has been one method used to meet this problem."

(A) grocery order
(B) cash grant
(C) budgetary deficiency
(D) security wage.

25. "With the increasing interest in the contribution of group experience to individual growth, there has developed within the past few years, in several communities, considerable cooperation between case work agencies and those agencies in the public welfare field."

(A) child guidance
(B) mental hygiene
(C) community housing
(D) group work.

In each of the following questions 26–30, twelve possible answers are suggested. Next to each question, write the letter of the three answers which, of those suggested, are the most superior according to the instructions governing each question-item.

26. "The problem of the family rearing of children in a modern city is due, in part, to the survival of older attitudes which are in a practical way incompatible with modern urban conditions, and to the absence of definite patterns of guidance in a changing society for parents whose intelligence quotient may not be very high. No ethic has yet risen to take the place of the one followed in the Victorian era. The individual no longer has moral problems solved by the family group. The heterogeneity of society and the rapidity of social change make impossible specific formulae which tell one what to do in different situations. Right and wrong have to be figured out by the individual, which calls for a high I.Q. and some ability to think in an emotional situation."

Of the following, select three options which best illustrate the implications of this paragraph.

(A) Since modern society has fewer ethics than the Victorian era, attempts should be made to provide patterns of behavior for families

(B) Parents who do not have high I.Q.s cannot bring up their children properly in a changing society without assistance

(C) Parents with high I.Q.s can be counted upon to think more clearly than parents with average I.Q.s in emotional situations

(D) The family can be helped to solve the children's problems if specific formulae, now lacking, are provided

(E) In our present society parents are given patterns by which they may gauge their attitudes and behavior toward their children

(F) Since the family no longer has any influence over its individual members, one should deal directly with each member of the family group as individuals

(G) Since many parents do not have high I.Q.s, modern patterns of guidance should be provided for them

(H) Social change, which develops more rapidly than formulae for meeting it, creates problems for the individual as well as for the family

(I) Since people are not as emotional as they used to be, individuals with high I.Q.s are not apt to need assistance in meeting their problems

(J) The children in the modern family may not depend upon their families for definitions of right and wrong

(K) The family is no longer a unit of society because modern urban conditions have broken down parental authority

(L) Present society has not evolved generally accepted patterns of behavior com-parable to those of the Victorian era

27. "The handling of public assistance funds seems very simple to those who have never pondered on the power which is concentrated within giving assistance: unleashed, it can destroy morale and self-respect; harnessed, it can preserve courage and rebuild self-confidence. The keystone to sound assistance administration is fairness. In other words everyone who is eligible for assistance under the organization's policies should be able to secure financial help, whether or not he or she is civil or rude. Often township poormasters have a tendency to work off old grudges or present irritations by considering not a family's resources, but their reputation and courtesy. Case work brings a disciplined use of power."

Of the following options, select three which most clearly illustrate the meaning of the above paragraph.

(A) Civil behavior on the part of applicants is indicative of the extent of the client's need of assistance

(B) A family's experience with assistance to-day vitally influences the pattern of its life tomorrow

(C) The power inherent in the assistance giving situation has a deleterious effect on clients

(D) Clients' behavior is not important to the Eligibility Specialist in his or her function of administering assistance

(E) The power of the person administering assistance is not inherent in his or her situation

(F) Case work is a method of disciplining clients

(G) Fairness on the part of the Eligibility Specialist does not depend upon determining financial need on the basis of the client's behavior

(H) Case work is a method of determining assistance needs in accordance with the client's resources and his or her value to society

(I) A disciplined use of power means that the Eligibility Specialist only uses his or her power over the client when persuasion fails

(J) The Eligibility Specialist can eliminate the power inherent in the assistance giving situation if he or she is fair to the client

(K) The client's civility or rudeness may not be an indication of the extent of his or her financial need

(L) The power inherent in the aid giving situation builds up morale and self-respect when the Eligibility Specialist treats all clients in the same way.

28. "Why do you pry into my private life? You have my cancelled bank book. You've seen my dispossess notice. Do you think I'd let things like that happen if I had any way to stop them?" Such questions made the Eligibility Specialist, often convinced of the client's need, ask, "Why investigate?" Of the following, which three explanations best represent accepted social work concepts as to the reason for investigation?

(A) It is a policy of the agency not to grant assistance unless every clue has been investigated

(B) Need is relative and people with a lower standard of living may be able to get by with less income

(C) Investigation tends to clear up the client's fears of arbitrary action by defining his or her status and responsibilities in relation to the agency

(D) It is both administratively sounder and psychologically easier for clients that there should, in general, be basic requirements in any determination of eligibility

(E) The investigation places an additional responsibility on the client at a time when he or she wants to be dependent, temporarily at least, upon someone else

(F) The investigation is a method of finding out whether or not the client has a tendency to remain permanently on assistance

(G) The honest client does not need investigation, but other clients do and it would be difficult to explain why some clients should and other clients should not be investigated

(H) The client's potentialities for independence may be discovered or developed during the investigation process

(I) Investigation must be made in order to complete the case record which is necessary before assistance can be given

(J) Assistance without investigation is too easy and will tend to make the client too ready to accept assistance as a means of livelihood

(K) If the case is so urgent that immediate assistance without investigation is necessary, a private agency should be used

(L) Investigation leads to an intimate relationship between the investigator and the client

29. The three major purposes for which professional social work uses publicity today are to

(A) restrict the social audience to professional workers in its own and allied fields

(B) change mental attitudes and behavior patterns in order to assure mental and physical health

(C) enlist public assistance in securing or enforcing social legislation

(D) secure necessary financial support for social servies whether publicly or privately financed

(E) present services and problems which are distinctly isolated from normal community life

(F) place responsibility for interpretation exclusively in the province of the specialist

(G) enlist public opinion to prevent social, economic, and political changes

(H) limit areas of interpretation to those which provide tangible results

(I) develop social services as ends in themselves for the protection of the underprivileged groups

(J) increase understanding of social needs and social purposes

(K) guarantee the continuance of democratic processes by combatting subversive propaganda

(L) isolate services to avoid confusion with current public health programs

30. In working with the problems of American-born children of foreign-born parents, modern social workers are concerned with (Select three of the following options)

(A) helping the children to have a sense of pride in their backgrounds

(B) securing estimates of the number of illegal entries of aliens into the United States

(C) discovering the continuance of foreign customs and folk festivals

(D) mediating in conflicts of cultural differences between parents and children

(E) referring all such problems to group work agencies

(F) organizing community forces into compulsory Americanization enterprises

(G) assisting the parents to carry out punitive measures consistent with the standard of their background

(H) discouraging the formation of foreign interest groups in community centers

(I) knowing the culture and resources of ethnic communities

(J) reducing cultural conflicts by helping the children to forget their backgrounds

(K) encouraging the children to overcome feelings of inferiority by disregarding the influence of the ethnic community

(L) assisting the children in their adjustment by defending attitudes contrary to parental opinions

31. Merely looking at a client is enough to tell an intelligent Eligibility Specialist

(A) whether the client is lying

(B) whether the client is actually in need

(C) whether the client is likely to cooperate

(D) none of the foregoing.

32. A family consisting of five persons has one employed member earning K dollars a month. The family receives a total semi-monthly assistance grant of L dollars. If the rent allowance is M dollars, and the amount spent for food is twice that for rent, the amount spent monthly for all items other than food and rent is

(A) K plus 2L minus 3M

(B) $\dfrac{M \text{ plus } K \text{ plus } L}{5}$

(C) K plus L minus 2M

(D) $\dfrac{L \text{ minus } 2M}{5}$

33. In a survey of N families on assistance, it was found that P percent consists of 2 persons. Q

percent of the N families consist of one parent and one child. The percent of families on assistance which consists of 2 persons not of the parent-child category is

(A) larger that W percent but less than P percent

(B) $\dfrac{\text{P minus Q}}{\text{N}}$

(C) $\dfrac{\text{PQ}}{\text{N}}$

(D) P minus Q

34. In the following instances, cooperative behavior which results from loyalty to the same objective is best exemplified by

(A) the citizens of a community forming a committee for the purpose of building a school

(B) employer and employee agreeing to a conference for the purpose of arriving at an equitable wage settlement

(C) people attending a championship tennis match held for charitable purposes

(D) a conquered people accepting aid from their conquerors.

35. It is often held that cooperative activity is difficult to achieve because "individuals are basically selfish" and their alleged selfishness makes it difficult, if not impossible, to subordinate their individual wills to the collective enterprise. The chief factor overlooked in such a conception of the matter is that

(A) there is no necessary discrepancy or conflict between selfishness and cooperation

(B) people do not seek to further their self-interest by competitive activity

(C) competition and cooperation are essentially alike

(D) most successful people are not selfish.

ANSWER KEY

1. C	8. C	15. B	22. C	29. C,D,J
2. B	9. C	16. B	23. B	30. A,D,I
3. C	10. B	17. A	24. C	31. D
4. B	11. B	18. C	25. D	32. A
5. B	12. B	19. A	26. H,J,L	33. B
6. C	13. D	20. B	27. B,G,K	34. A
7. D	14. D	21. D	28. C,D,H	35. A

VIII. Case Work Techniques

1. The skill of the Eligibility Specialist in conducting the first interview with a client in a public assistance agency is stressed as important because
   (A) the attitude of the client toward assistance may be observed at this time and his or her future reactions determined
   (B) after the first interview the client may compare notes with other clients and change his or her story
   (C) it may establish a mutual understanding between the client who expresses needs and the worker who interprets the agency
   (D) if the worker is not skillful, the client may secure information about the agency policies which he or she may use later to his or her own advantage.

2. A most significant result of doing a good job is that
   (A) the clients will be grateful and tell others of the good service they have received
   (B) the functions of the agency will be interpreted to the community which is responsible for the program
   (C) the supervisor will give the worker a higher rating because the clients will never complain
   (D) the newspapers will give publicity to the program only if the work is well done.

3. From the social point of view, the most desirable requisite for a potential Eligibility Specialist to have at the outset is
   (A) a desire to return full value for the taxpayer's dollar
   (B) knowledge of eligibility requirements for assistance
   (C) understanding of the functions of the Department of Social Services
   (D) a desire to help people meet their problems.

4. Your client and his wife are quarreling continually. This is having a bad effect upon the children and causing friction in the home. The husband has been unemployed for some time. You would
   (A) arrest the client
   (B) commit the children to institutions
   (C) determine the underlying cause
   (D) cut off assistance.

5. An anonymous letter is received by your office stating that one of your clients has several unacknowledged children in good financial circumstances. You would
   (A) cut off assistance immediately
   (B) attempt to verify the information
   (C) bring charges for refund
   (D) trace the writer of the letter.

6. A son of your client secures work. You do not know any of the details. You would
   (A) continue assistance as before
   (B) cut off assistance immediately
   (C) ascertain length of employment and wages
   (D) summon the employer to court.

7. An applicant for assistance moved about a great deal in the city since becoming a resident of New York. His required time of residence is still questionable. You would
   (A) refuse assistance because of non-residence
   (B) return him to his birthplace
   (C) make efforts to verify his residence
   (D) turn him over to the Transient Bureau.

8. A member of a client's family develops a definite mental condition. His presence in the home jeopardizes the welfare of the family. You would
   (A) call a police officer
   (B) call an ambulance
   (C) obtain a mental examination
   (D) subdue him yourself if necessary.

9. A client obtains work which lasts for two months at wages which are twice as much as his assistance allowance. You would
   (A) continue assistance
   (B) cut off assistance temporarily
   (C) cut off assistance permanently
   (D) require a refund for benefits paid.

10. A husband on assistance meets with an accident and is taken to the hospital. You would
   (A) discontinue assistance because the hospital is taking care of him
   (B) increase assistance because of the situation
   (C) adjust the family budget during his absence in the hospital
   (D) require married children to support the family

11. A family applies for assistance. The man was born in Ireland but is a citizen. He is 66 years old, able to work but unemployed. You would

    (A) refer him to the State Department of Labor Employment Division for work
    (B) grant assistance because of need
    (C) refer him for old age assistance
    (D) deny assistance on grounds that he is able to work.

12. A client brings to his home the family of a married son from another state who is unemployed. He asks for increased assistance to cover additional needs of the son's family. You would

    (A) discontinue assistance because the client brought the family in without permission
    (B) increase assistance to take care of additional needs
    (C) communicate with the legal residence of son's family for reimbursement of additional assistance
    (D) bring charges against the son for trying indirectly to get assistance for a non-resident.

13. You find that a client has withheld the information that he and his son own jointly a piece of property. Sale of the property is pending in which the client feels that his interests are being endangered. You would

    (A) continue aid during the transaction
    (B) discontinue aid because of fraudulent statements as to assets on the part of the client
    (C) aid the client in protecting his interest in the property so that remibursement of the assistance grant is assured
    (D) make a claim on the property because of aid granted.

14. You find that a applicant has a war-connected disability for which he never thought he could receive a veteran's pension. He has the necessary papers to prove his war disability. He is in extreme need. You would

    (A) grant immmediate assistance because of need
    (B) transfer him to another center
    (C) arrange for him to stay at a lodging house until he finds work
    (D) refer him to the Veteran's Administration for assistance.

15. A child of one of your clients develops tuberculosis of the lung and is rapidly getting worse. The welfare of the entire family is thus endangered. You would

    (A) increase assistance because of sickness
    (B) discontinue assistance because of the health menace created
    (C) arrange hospital care for the child
    (D) send the child to a summer camp to get well.

16. An applicant has previously been denied assistance because a son in the home was working. The son marries and establishes an independent home. You would

    (A) deny assistance because of the son's marriage
    (B) grant assistance because of need
    (C) force the son to support his parents
    (D) make the parents live in their son's new home.

17. A client whom you inform that assistance will be decreased threatens to kill you the next time he receives his assistance check. You would

    (A) reason with him, pointing out the cause of your action
    (B) tell him you are not afraid of him and will be ready for him the next time you call, armed with a weapon of protection
    (C) bring a special officer with you the next time you visit his home
    (D) discontinue assistance because of his threats.

18. You find that a married brother of an applicant is reputed to be wealthy and able to support his brother. You would

    (A) deny assistance because the brother is able to support the applicant
    (B) interview the brother and attempt to obtain help for the applicant
    (C) bring action against the wealthy brother because his brother is liable to become a public charge
    (D) grant assistance immediately because of need.

19. When a client receives assistance, he or she

(A) gives up the right to manage money in his or her own way

(B) is justified in assuming that he or she has proved eligibility for assistance and is free to use the money according to his or her best judgment

(C) is limited in spending the money only for expenditures itemized in the agency budget

(D) is obligated to keep an itemized list of expenditures.

20. A widow with a girl 17 years old and a boy 18 years old applies for aid. There are rumors that she has been supported by a boarder living in her home and the moral relationship is questioned. You would

(A) ascertain the facts and grant aid if warranted

(B) deny assistance because boarder seems to be able to support the family

(C) refer the applicant to the Board of Child Welfare for a widow's pension

(D) bring charges immediately against the mother for jeopardizing the morals of her children.

ANSWER KEY

1. C	5. B	9. B	13. C	17. A
2. B	6. C	10. C	14. D	18. B
3. D	7. C	11. C	15. C	19. B
4. C	8. C	12. C	16. B	20. A

IX. Social Work With Children

1. Eight-year-old Johnny, on whose account his mother is receiving aid to dependent children, is becoming a truant from school. Disturbed by the course of events, his mother appears at the center and informs you, her Case Worker, that her efforts to stop Johnny's truancy have been unavailing. You should tell Johnny's mother that

   (A) the grant will be discontinued since Johnny's truancy is evidence of her failure as a parent
   (B) she can be referred to a specialized agency in the community
   (C) you will institute court action to remove Johnny from his home environment
   (D) you will give her two months to straighten out the problem before taking further action.

2. A woman appears at your center and asks for advice on what to do as she would like if possible, to be able to remain at home with her three children, ages four, seven, and ten. She declares that her husband has been killed and she is unable to manage on her old age and survivors insurance. Assuming the facts to be true as stated, the Eligibility Specialist should advise her

   (A) to apply for aid to dependent children
   (B) to try to find a job
   (C) to apply for more money under old age and survivors insurance
   (D) that there are no other public financial resources available in her case.

3. "From a mental hygiene point of view, those parental attitudes are good which offer to the child emotional security; that is, a feeling of stability, permanence, and safety; acceptance, that is, a feeling of belonging and being welcome for what he or she is, free to be a child, to be held only to a child's accountability for actions and not forced prematurely to act according to an adult code; freedom for experience, that is, an environment which offers opportunities for trying out his or her own abilities, interests, ideas, and games—a freedom that includes the right to feel and to express feelings both of affection and aggression."

   According to the ideas expressed in the paragraph

   (A) a family in which there is economic dependence cannot be good for children
   (B) emotionally secure children do not have feelings of aggression
   (C) children should not be held accountable for their actions
   (D) parental attitudes are inadequate which do not give the child feelings of belonging and freedom for experience.

4. One of the deleterious effects of child labor from the social work point of view is that it inevitably deprives the child of

   (A) valuable discipline
   (B) opportunities for play
   (C) a sense of responsibility
   (D) opportunities for companionship.

5. Aid to Dependent Children is premised upon the assumption that

   (A) children are better off with their mothers under any circumstances
   (B) children should not be removed from their homes because of poverty alone
   (C) children should not be removed from their homes because of behavior problems alone
   (D) children whose mothers work are generally neglected.

6. A child was born out of wedlock to a certain Ms. Smith and has been placed in a private foster home. Ms. Smith is unable to pay anything toward the child's care. She asks about visiting her little girl. The most desirable reply for the Case Worker to make in this situation would be that Ms. Smith

   (A) cannot visit the child because she would exert an adverse influence over her
   (B) should not visit since she is not paying for the child's care
   (C) should not visit because it will be difficult for the child to explain to her friends that her mother is unmarried
   (D) has the same right as any other mother to visit her child.

7. The best thing to do with a problem child is to

    (A) advise the parents to maintain strict discipline
    (B) ask the police to watch the child
    (C) put the child on probation
    (D) follow an individual plan after analysis of the case.

8. The modern practice in the child care field recognizes the boarding care of children is desirable

    (A) at all times
    (B) under no circumstances
    (C) provided there is adequate supervision of the boarding-home
    (D) in very few cases.

9. The most widely accepted of the following principles of child welfare work is

    (A) foster homes in which children are placed should be, so far as practicable, of the same religious persuasion as that of the child
    (B) no illegitimate child should ever be permitted to stay with its mother
    (C) it is important that prospective foster parents be far above the average in their social and economic status
    (D) no child should be placed with foster parents until arrangements have been completed for having the foster parents adopt the child.

10. Anthony, age 8, has had many difficult experiences in his life. His father's whereabouts are unknown, as he deserted when Anthony was two years old. His mother, whom he loved dearly, died three months ago. Since that time he has been living with his grandmother, who is old and ill, and cannot care for such an active little boy. Together the grandmother and you, the social Case Worker, have decided that placement in a foster home is essential for Anthony's well being. You know he will resist any change in his living arrangement. Accord-

ing to acceptable case work practice, the best of the following methods for you to apply in this situation is to

    (A) take the boy to his new home without telling him anything beforehand
    (B) explain that it is necessary to move him and that he is going to a very nice place where he will be happy and have many things he does not have now
    (C) tell him you are sorry if he feels bad about it, but grown-ups know best what is good for him and tell he will have to do what they say
    (D) give the child a chance to get to know you before he is moved and to express his feelings in relation to the plan which is being made for him.

11. Suppose you, as a Case Worker, are considering institutional care for several different types of children for whom removal from present homes is indicated. Of the following, the type least suited for such care would be

    (A) a child needing observation, study, and treatment for a severe crippling condition
    (B) a 5-year-old boy who resents adult authority
    (C) a family of six brothers and sisters who are devoted to each other
    (D) a normal 3-year-old girl whose mother is dead and whose father is employed at night.

12. It is generally agreed among psychologists that children need to have certain experiences in order to develop into healthy, well-integrated adults. Of the following, it is most important to the development of the pre-adolescent child that he or she

    (A) live in a good neighborhood
    (B) have a room of his or her own
    (C) have nice clothes
    (D) have the feeling that he or she is loved and wanted by the parents.

Answer Key

1. B	4. B	7. D	10. D
2. A	5. B	8. C	11. D
3. D	6. D	9. A	12. D

X. General Review

1. Of the types of mental breakdown listed below, the disorder that ordinarily occurs at the most advanced age is

   (A) cerebral arteriosclerosis
   (B) neurasthenia
   (C) dementia praecox
   (D) paresis.

2. The cost of old age assistance is borne

   (A) entirely by the local government
   (B) entirely by the federal and state governments
   (C) entirely by the federal government
   (D) by the federal, state, and local governments.

3. Most old age assistance programs have been limited in general to the financial and physical needs of the aged because

   (A) it is impossible to determine their other needs with any degree of practicality
   (B) social agencies are unwilling to enlarge their responsibilities for the care of the aged
   (C) old people are not interested in social participation
   (D) Social Service administrators have not been given the means to undertake more augmented programs.

4. During a period of economic adjustment when unemployment is on the rise, the invention of a labor-saving device would, in the long run, be economically and culturally

   (A) unsound, because it would stir up unrest among the organized labor groups
   (B) unsound, because it would result in accelerating unemployment
   (C) sound, because the rise of unemployment is a temporary phenomenon while the labor-saving device would add permanent values
   (D) sound, because it would enable the user to produce more with the small working population still employed.

5. The chief purpose of insurance adjustment is

   (A) maximum protection to the client at minimum cost
   (B) to reduce the number of persons receiving assistance
   (C) to make sure that insurance companies do not lose money
   (D) to investigate solvency of insurance companies with which clients are concerned.

6. The parole movement of releasing prisoners before the expiration of their sentences is based mostly on the assumption on the part of the taxpaying public that

   (A) prison officials and parole officers can watch the paroled prisoners closely and help them adjust themselves in the community at the same time
   (B) recidivism is greater for persons serving their full sentence
   (C) it sends the parolees out with an obligation rather than a score to settle
   (D) total costs for prison administration are materially reduced when a large percentage of the prison population has the terms of incarceration reduced.

7. A small town without a hospital is located near a large city which boasts of its excellent medical facilities. These facilities are extended liberally to non-residents who come from adjacent centers which do not have hospitals of their own. If it is shown statistically that the death rate of the small town is lower compared to that of the large city, the most logical inference for the alert Case Worker to make is that

   (A) small-town life is more healthful than living in a big city
   (B) the statistical data have been improperly manipulated
   (C) death rates should not be determined by political boundaries
   (D) the deaths of non-residents have boosted the death rate of the large city.

8. The greatest limitation on the general effectiveness of marriage courses in college curricula is

    (A) there is no evidence to prove that such courses result in better matches and happier homes
    (B) successful completion of such courses is no indication that the knowledge contained in the courses will be successfully applied by the students who have taken them
    (C) there is no complete agreement as to whether the family, the church, or the school should be responsible for guiding marriage education
    (D) most of the people who marry are ineligible to enroll in such courses.

9. The least accurate of the following statements regarding intelligence is that

    (A) a person's intelligence is not directly related to biological factors
    (B) persons differ radically in the degree of intelligence they have
    (C) persons cannot learn beyond the limits of their native intelligence regardless of the amount and kind of effort they expend
    (D) ill health, isolation, and certain kinds of temperament may seriously limit the proportion of one's intelligence which may actually be able to be put to use.

10. The only educative agency which can properly be thought of as really starting with a "clean slate" in developing a person's behavior is the

    (A) family
    (B) play group
    (C) church group
    (D) elementary school.

11. Councils of social agencies or welfare councils are

    (A) organizations of executives of private social work agencies whose function it is to clear the programs of their respective agencies so as to avoid duplicating one another's work
    (B) federations or associations of agencies with formal representation of joint planning of social work in a way so that every agency can contribute its most appropriate service to the whole, avoid duplication, and study gaps

    (C) federations of social agencies for the sole purpose of joint and more effective financing of their work
    (D) advisory committees or bodies composed of both board members and executives, who pass on and approve or veto the actual or proposed programs of social agencies.

12. Of the following types of cases, medical social work seems to be the least needed, according to various studies, in cases of
    (A) recurrent and chronic illness
    (B) physical handicap
    (C) invalidism
    (D) acute illness.

13. Adoption is best defined as a
    (A) friendly and informal agreement by which the second husband agrees to provide for the children of his wife by the first husband during their minority
    (B) legal instrument in the form of an affidavit made out before a notary public by which the father legitimizes the child born to his wife before their marriage
    (C) legal process as described above, but valid only if approved by a children's agency, which for that purpose, and in accordance with the needs of the case can override the will of the natural parent
    (C) method by which a person legally assumes full parental responsibility for a child that is not his or her own child, adoption being made by authority of a court having suitable jurisdiction.

14. A "pay as you go policy" is most nearly one in which
    (A) annual expenditure does not exceed annual income
    (B) money is expended to meet new needs
    (C) a bond issue is the instrument for raising money
    (D) the budget is never balanced.

15. Of the following, the most important of the present housing difficulties is
    (A) financing bodies refuse to give mortgage money for use in residential construction, reserving their funds for factory, office, and mercantile construction
    (B) people in the slums are so used to their kind of housing that they refuse to go to better places, and if they do, they soon reduce the best housing to slums, depress values, and so make investment in multiple dwellings unprofitable

(C) the cost of new construction on modern standards does not provide apartments cheap enough for low-income rent and still be profitable for investment

(D) it is impossible to build low rental houses profitably from private investment and it is illegal and unsound to use public subsidies.

16. Social Security legislation, as enacted by the federal government, is characterized by the fact that

(A) it makes widows' pensions compulsory throughout the United States

(B) it is the first comprehensive security law which provides health insurance as well as other forms of social insurance and pensions

(C) if offers unemployment and old age benefits only where the states do not already provide these

(D) it carries into effect a combination of state and federal operation, of employer and employee contribution, and a gradual development of the system over the years.

17. The Visiting Teacher may be of assistance to the Case Worker in understanding family problems because the Visiting Teacher is able to

(A) explain the child's social problems and assist in their cure by remedial teaching of reading or other subjects

(B) explain the needs of the family for clothing and provide for these needs

(C) explain the social and educational maladjustments of school children and assist in meeting their needs

(D) explain the effects of dependency upon school children and assist in obviating these effects by providing free lunches.

18. Accepted Social Work practice holds that assistance in kind is less useful to client and community than assistance in cash because

(A) assistance in kind is inflexible and tends to develop dependent attitudes in clients

(B) it is impossible for clients to maintain a balanced diet on grocery orders issued in kind

(C) assistance in kind is economically unsound and keeps less money in circulation

(D) friction between the agency and the tradespeople is the usual result of assistance issued in kind.

19. According to current thinking, the public welfare agencies should consider the private social agencies as

(A) separate and competing agencies with a different purpose and function

(B) cooperating agencies whose advice and support should be sought

(C) independent agencies concerned entirely with people who have emotional and behavioral problems

(D) part of the public agency with whom cases may be interchanged because they are serving the same purpose.

20. In public assistance administration, the basic determinant of eligibility for assistance is

(A) need

(B) citizenship

(C) need through no fault of the applicant

(D) settlement.

21. Analysis of migratory agricultural workers indicates that, in general, the most characteristic definition of them is that

(A) they are not an ill-defined, undifferentiated group who are not concerned with a stabilized occupation

(B) they are a constantly shifting, undifferentiated group who are not concerned with a stabilized occupation

(C) they are not a well-defined, differentiated group who are concerned with a stabilized occupation

(D) they are an ill-defined, constantly shifting group who are jacks-of-all-trades and not concerned with a stabilized occupation.

22. The work of the Case Worker may be considered a protection to the community because it includes

(A) recording anti-social attitudes and serious grievances expressed by clients which may be destructive to society

(B) recognizing potentially serious health and behavior problems and referring them to the appropriate services for care

(C) recording the incidence of disease and promoting community programs for prevention based on the data thus secured

(D) recognizing the potential criminal tendencies which are inherent in economic dependents.

23. The most modern point of view among those who offer social treatment to the blind is that

    (A) because of their handicap the blind should be given special privileges such as being allowed to live together so that they may associate on the basis of their common handicap, preference in placement of jobs suitable for them, etc.

    (B) as many of the difficulties in which blind persons find themselves come from causes other than their blindness, which serves to heighten their difficulties, treatment should be based upon their total situation rather than their handicaps

    (C) blind children should secure their complete education in special schools and colleges provided for them and should not have to go to the regular high schools and colleges where they will be unable to adjust themselves

    (D) sheltered workshops for the blind and the provision of vending stands in public buildings are an unfortunate means of support for blind persons since they emphasize their handicap.

24. The best definition of parole is:

    (A) "A continuation of the social policy, or social control, instituted by the state when it first places the law-breaker under apprehension."

    (B) "The shortening of the prison term of an offender against the law who is then no longer subjected to the disciplinary control of the state."

    (C) "A form of clemency or leniency granted to law-breakers under apprehension who have established records for good conduct and who cannot be returned to the institution."

    (D) "The withholding of punishment of an adult offender due to the clemency of the court in an individual instance warranted by the compliant behavior of the offender."

25. The provision of free hot lunches to needy schoolchildren may have some disadvantages because

    (A) dietitians cannot prepare food of sufficient variety to satisfy the children and at the same time conform to minimum budget requirements

    (B) fewer children are now in need of free hot lunches because their families are on public assistance and are receiving adequate budgets

    (C) school principals are not in favor of maintaining lunchrooms in the elementary schools because of the difficulties of providing this service

    (D) those who cannot afford to buy their lunches are apt to be identified as dependent children.

In questions 26–30 below, Column I consists of items referring to certain characteristics of areas usually found to exist in most American cities. Column II describes four sections into which the general sociological pattern of the modern city may be divided. Select the description in Column II to which the reference in Column I is most appropriate.

Column I

26. The area in which a predominantly male resident population would probably be found.

27. The area in which a "slum" would be located if it existed in this city.

28. The area in which the most prominent citizens of the community would probably be found living.

29. The area likely to contain the sparsest resident population.

30. The area likely to be inhabited by middle-class families.

Column II

(A) Retail stores, eating establishments, movie theaters, offices of professional people and business organizations.

(B) Made-over private dwellings, rooming houses, cheap hotels, pawnbrokers, wholesale business establishments.

(C) Less crowding than in above area, more modern houses, fewer children.

(D) fashionable suburbs, homes of professional and business leaders, relative cleanliness and modernity.

ANSWER KEY

1. A	7. D	13. D	19. B	25. D
2. D	8. D	14. A	20. A	26. B
3. D	9. A	15. C	21. A	27. B
4. C	10. A	16. D	22. B	28. D
5. B	11. B	17. C	23. B	29. A
6. A	12. D	18. A	24. A	30. C

HOUSING AND SOCIAL WELFARE QUIZZER

1. It is generally agreed by those who have closely studied the housing shortage in this country that, of the new housing needed in the next decade to meet the shortage and to raise standards, the greatest part will be required to

    (A) house families now seeking separate dwellings
    (B) house new families formed during the period
    (C) maintain a suitable percentage of vacancies
    (D) replace substandard dwelling units.

2. The best statement as to where slum dwellings and slum areas are found, in the United States, is

    (A) in New York and several other of the largest cities
    (B) in nearly all large cities
    (C) in nearly all towns and cities of every size
    (D) in nearly all towns and cities of every size and in nearly all rural areas.

3. The one of the following which is least characteristic of a slum area is

    (A) high disease rate
    (B) high incidence of fires
    (C) high rate of juvenile delinquency
    (D) high tax rate

4. The most important step in improving the housing conditions of low-income families living in slum dwellings is to

    (A) demolish slum dwellings in areas where conditions are worst
    (B) enforce existing building and tenement regulations more strictly
    (C) provide satisfactory housing at rents which they can afford
    (D) replan residential and commercial areas more carefully.

5. The statement has been made that "slum dwellers create the slums." This is generally

    (A) true because slum dwellers are both unsanitary and unhealthful in their habits
    (B) true because environment is as strong a force as heredity in molding character
    (C) untrue because slum dwellers do not care to keep their dwellings in clean and sanitary condition
    (D) untrue because slums are caused by conditions which are not under the control of the slum dweller.

6. The building of some scattered new housing in a slum area is generally

    (A) undesirable because the need to adhere to new zoning ordinances will make such construction economically unsound
    (B) undesirable because it may be unable to maintain itself against the surrounding slum
    (C) desirable because it may serve as the focus for an overall improvement of living conditions
    (D) desirable because it may provide an incentive for other new construction.

7. The high tax expenditures in slum areas tend to decrease upon the demolition of the slum buildings and rehousing of the population. The expenditures which decrease least rapidly are those for

    (A) delinquency prevention
    (B) fire alarms
    (C) garbage collection
    (D) street cleaning.

8. It has been said that home ownership is a magnificent ideal and that the greatest good would be attained when every family in the country

owned its own home. The chief limitation of this belief is that

(A) changing economic and labor conditions may cause the loss of much of the home owner's investment

(B) it applies only to ownership of one-family dwellings

(C) it would discourage large-scale speculative building activity

(D) public housing would then no longer offer serious competition to private construction.

9. Slum areas and bad housing are expensive to a city chiefly because

(A) crime and delinquency flourish there

(B) higher rents are usually charged there than the tenants can afford

(C) more city services of all kinds need to be provided

(D) such areas generally represent the larger portion of the city.

10. Tenancy in low rent government housing projects is usually limited to people of low income. Of the following, the principle upon which this limitation is most probably based is that

(A) government housing activities should be limited to providing housing for those low income groups for which private industry cannot provide decent housing at a profit

(B) the total amount of desirable housing that is available in a community is limited, the first choice of the better housing should be offered to people of low income

(C) low rent housing developments should not pay high taxes

(D) people of high income do not usually want to live in government housing projects.

11. "Studies of cities have shown that the rate of juvenile delinquency was highest in areas where housing was least adequate." On the basis of this quotation, it is most correct to say that

(A) no relationship can be established at all since bad housing is but one factor among many that may cause delinquent behavior

(B) provision of adequate housing is probably the most effective tool in combating juvenile delinquency

(C) areas of substandard housing are generally areas of high juvenile delinquency

(D) slum areas are less effectively policed than other areas in the cities in which the studies were conducted.

12. Studies on the relation of juvenile delinquency and housing have in general indicated that the

(A) effect of poor housing operates independently of family relationships, regardless of city size

(B) larger a city, the more significant is the factor of poor housing in causing juvenile delinquency

(C) relationship between poor housing and juvenile delinquency is almost non-existent, regardless of urban size

(D) size of a city has little significance in the relation between juvenile delinquency and poor housing.

13. The term "site coverage" as it is usually used in reference to housing projects means

(A) the area occupied by the buildings alone divided by the total area of the project

(B) the area occupied by the buildings and recreation areas divided by the total area of the project

(C) the area occupied by the buildings and recreation areas divided by the total area of the project excluding streets

(D) the area occupied by the present buildings previously on the site.

14. "Impairment of desirability and usefulness resulting from changes in the arts or in design, or from internal influences which make a property less desirable for continued use" is most nearly a definition of

(A) blight

(B) depreciation

(C) deterioration

(D) obsolescence.

15. "A collection of legal requirements, the purpose of which is to protect the safety, health, morals, and general welfare of those in and about buildings" is most nearly a definition of

(A) Administrative Code

(B) Building Code

(C) Welfare Code

(D) Sanitary Code.

16. An area where dwellings predominate which are detrimental to safety, health, or morals, because of dilapidation, overcrowding, lack of ventilation, and other similar faults is termed a

(A) blighted area

(B) condemned zone

(C) slum area

(D) tenement district.

17. The theory that the housing needs of the lower-income groups will be met when the higher-income groups move out of their present housing into newly constructed homes and buildings is known as
(A) concurrent use
(B) economic mobility
(C) filter down
(D) housing fluidity.

ANSWER KEY

1. D	5. D	9. C	12. D	15. B
2. D	6. B	10. A	13. A	16. C
3. D	7. A	11. B	14. D	17. C
4. C	8. A			

JUDGMENT IN SOCIAL WELFARE SITUATIONS

1. The one of the following laws of learning which would be most helpful in securing tenants' compliance with the rules and regulations of a housing project is

   (A) adults do not learn as rapidly as children
   (B) effective remembrance is based on periodic repetition
   (C) emotional acceptance generally precedes understanding and compliance
   (D) understanding is the basis of compliance.

2. As the population of cities increases, there is a decrease in the proportion of the developed urban area which is used for

   (A) commercial purposes
   (B) industrial purposes
   (C) parks and open areas
   (D) residential purposes.

3. The statement that building new homes for the upper-income groups will thereby create a supply of older buildings for the lower-income groups is not tenable unless

   (A) the concurrent elimination of slum dwellings take place
   (B) the erection of potential new slums is prevented
   (C) private enterprise has the facilities to build for all families in the upper-income groups
   (D) the low-income groups are able to afford the buildings thus vacated.

4. Of the following, the most effective way to reduce the monthly cost of home ownership is to secure reductions in

   (A) interest rates
   (B) maintenance expenses
   (C) property taxes
   (D) the capital cost of the house.

5. If valid criteria have been used in tenant selection for public housing projects, the result most likely to be attained is

   (A) homogeneity of tenant characteristics will be assured
   (B) larger federal subsidies will be required
   (C) neediest families will receive the greatest proportion of assistance
   (D) the underlying conditions of slums will be ameliorated.

6. It has been claimed that "subsidized housing for workers who cannot pay rent high enough to secure good housing on a profit basis is, in effect, subsidizing low wages for the benefit of parsimonious employers." The defect of this argument is that

   (A) it fails to distinguish between money wages and real wages
   (B) sanitary and decent housing costs more than slums
   (C) wage and hour legislation would then be unnecessary
   (D) wages have not been high enough in the past, prior to the time subsidized housing became available, to enable the average worker to secure good housing.

7. "The enforcement of existing or procurable legislation regarding public health, safety, and morals would eliminate slums without the use of public funds." An important defect in this statement is that

   (A) compulsory increases in standards mean higher rentals
   (B) existing acceptable housing is still insufficient to meet housing needs
   (C) it assumes the continuation of a high level of home building activity by private enterprise
   (D) legislation regarding public welfare is absolutely necessary for civilized urban life.

252

8. The degree of social intelligence which a person possesses can best be determined by the

    (A) extent of success the person has in getting along with people
    (B) score obtained on a test of social intelligence
    (C) judgment of a psychologist in an interview with the person
    (D) person's own judgment of his or her success in dealing with social situations.

9. A study made of residents in a public housing project one year after it was open for occupancy showed that there was less crime, less disease, and fewer divorces than in a group of the same size and average income living in a slum area. This shows that

    (A) slums tends to breed crime, disease, and marital discord
    (B) public housing projects have a beneficial effect upon the health and morals of the inhabitants
    (C) the inhabitants of the public housing project are healthier than those of the slum area
    (D) the data are insufficient to make any of the foregoing conclusions.

10. If a hereditary characteristic skips a number of generations in a family, the characteristic probably is

    (A) dominant
    (B) mutant
    (C) linked
    (D) recessive

11. Because of present housing conditions in New York City, there are families on the public assistance caseload who require some assistance because of payment of high rentals. This group could be helped best by

    (A) providing satisfactory housing at rents which they can afford
    (B) creating a "relief village" on the outskirts of town where they could live at reduced rents
    (C) providing homemaker services so that the mothers of these families can seek employment
    (D) urging them to move to less congested areas outside of New York.

12. The one of the following factors which is the greatest obstacle in the assimilation of immigrant groups is

    (A) the difference in the customs and patterns of the present and former environments
    (B) language difficulties
    (C) the difference in the standards of living enjoyed in the old and the new environments
    (D) the contact which the immigrants maintain with friends and relatives who have remained in the immigrants' former environment.

13. The one of the following statements which best describes the relationship which exists among environment, intelligence, and learning to read and write is that

    (A) proper environment is necessary to make the most of one's intelligence in learning to read and write
    (B) there is no relationship among environment, intelligence and ability to read and write
    (C) a person with low intelligence cannot learn to read and write, regardless of environment
    (D) intelligence develops with reading and writing, regardless of environment.

14. Sociologists feel that the individual today has certain basic social needs arising out of group life in our modern culture. One of the most important of these needs is the need to

    (A) gain personal recognition from the peer group
    (B) get away from the influence of the peer group
    (C) lead and control the peer group as often as possible
    (D) submerge individuality and desires to the pattern and desires of the peer group.

15. The study of facial contours and the structure of the skull as a means of determining intelligence or aptitude is considered to be

    (A) a valid means of determining intelligence
    (B) of little use in determining aptitude for a job
    (C) valid for inherited mental characteristics but invalid for learned behavior
    (D) significant in determining basic intelligence and mechanical aptitude.

16. Assume a young, healthy-looking male client who is jobless and on public assistance tells you he feels and thinks he may have AIDS. As his Case Worker, you should first
    (A) assure him that he is probably all right, not to worry, and to find a job
    (B) inform him he will be ineligible for public assistance if he has AIDS, but may be able to receive SSI
    (C) refer him to his doctor or to a health provider who is knowledgeable about AIDS to learn the truth
    (D) assure him that he will not be cut off public assistance if he has AIDS.

17. Assume the father of an ADC family living in a single room occupancy hotel expresses fear that his children will develop AIDS since there are drug users and homosexuals in the hotel. You, his Case Worker and the Worker for several other families living in the hotel, should
    (A) remind him that the hotel management is responsible for this kind of problem and tell him to speak to them about it
    (B) remove the family from the dangerous situation by arranging for space in a city shelter for them
    (C) remind him that parents, not the public assistance agency, are responsible for the health, safety, and welfare of their children
    (D) discuss the entire matter with your supervisor to determine what investigation should be made of the situation at the hotel and what authorities or individuals should handle such an investigation.

18. Assume that it is Friday and you are planning your schedule for the following week. The final session of a 10-session training class you are required to take is scheduled for 2 p.m. Thursday. It will last all afternoon and will be a review of all the material that has been covered as well as talks by specialists in certain matters not covered in past sessions. Assume also that your agency requires you to visit the homes of clients on a planned basis. In planning your activities for Thursday, of the following, your most efficient and correct use of time would be to plan to
    (A) skip the training session since it is largely a repeat of information that has already been covered
    (B) visit one AFDC family near the training center whose previously scheduled visit you had been forced to cancel because of illness

    (C) visit one family on public assistance who are known to have long-standing problems which should be discussed. The family resides a considerable distance from the training center and you must first check in at your office before going to the field.
    (D) refrain from going to the session and copy a co-worker's notes so that you will not miss anything.

19. Assume that a client calls with an emergency problem which appears to require an immediate home visit. You, his Case Worker, are handling the supervisor's phone messages since she is at an important meeting with the Agency's director. Of the following, your best action is to
    (A) tell the client you cannot leave the office but that he should come to the office to see you as soon as possible
    (B) send another Case Worker to visit the client and to handle the emergency
    (C) schedule a visit to the client for the following morning
    (D) request another Case Worker to handle the phone, leave a note for your supervisor explaining the situation, and visit the client immediately.

20. It is often good case management procedure for the Worker to set up a personal "tickler" file in order to have easy accessibility to the essential matters involving each case responsibility. Of the following, the information least needed to be included on most cases would be
    (A) client's name, address, and phone number, if any
    (B) case number for reference to the actual case record
    (C) medical history of each client
    (D) dates when required visits are made.

21. Assume you are the Case Worker for an elderly woman not working and living alone who is constantly visiting the social service office and holding long conversations unrelated to her case with you, your supervisor, your co-workers, and with anyone else who is around. You should understand that this client
    (A) may be trying to tell you something of vital importance related to her eligibility
    (B) is trying to ingratiate herself with staff so that she will be given special consideration

(C) is in need of psychiatric help and should be referred to a clinic for consultation and therapy

(D) may be lonely and seeking the companionship of other people but not knowledgeable about community programs and activities which might be of interest to her.

22. Assume that a new Case Worker sits next to you in the public assistance office and is constantly besieging you with questions, only some of which are connected with your agency's work. As a result, you are somewhat behind in your own responsibilities. Of the following, you should initially

(A) report to your supervisor that the new Worker needs further training

(B) request that your desk be moved without giving an explanation

(C) say nothing to the supervisor or to the new Worker but remain after working hours to complete your responsibilities in a timely manner

(D) explain to the new Worker that you will be glad to answer pertinent questions related to her duties but that you must complete your own work on time.

ANSWER KEY

1. D	6. D	11. A	15. B	19. D
2. D	7. B	12. A	16. C	20. C
3. D	8. A	13. A	17. D	21. D
4. D	9. D	14. A	18. B	22. D
5. C	10. D			

DETERMINING ELIGIBILITY FOR PUBLIC ASSISTANCE AND HOUSING QUIZZER

1. The one of the following which would be least acceptable as proof of residence at a specific address is a (an)

    (A) automobile driver's license
    (B) gas and electric bill
    (C) hospital clinic appointment card
    (D) life insurance premium receipt.

2. The head of a family applying for an apartment in a low-rent housing project is a widow who was born in a foreign country, married a citizen of the United States in 1971, and has lived here since then. At the time of her marriage, she was not a citizen of the United States. The one of the following which would be required as proof of her citizenship is

    (A) proof of naturalization in her own right
    (B) proof of her marriage, inasmuch as her husband was a citizen
    (C) proof of her marriage and proof of her husband's citizenship
    (D) proof of her marriage, together with proof of continuous residence in this country.

3. The development of a fixed pattern for all initial interviews of applicants for public housing is

    (A) desirable chiefly because it helps to provide a complete record in the least time
    (B) desirable chiefly because it permits the development of a uniform procedure and simplifies the training of interviewers
    (C) undesirable chiefly because it fails to provide for the varying circumstances of individual applicants
    (D) undesirable chiefly because it sacrifices rapport in order to secure uniformity.

4. Of the following methods of beginning an interview with an applicant for an apartment, the most desirable is to
    (A) allow the applicant to discuss his or her housing problem
    (B) assure the applicant of your interest in his or her need for housing
    (C) discuss the purpose of the interview
    (D) discuss some impersonal topic familar to everyone.

5. In order to attain accurate information when interviewing an applicant for public housing, a housing assistant should not
    (A) allow the applicant to qualify his or her answers
    (B) anticipate the applicant's answers
    (C) ask one question at a time
    (D) ask questions at first which are easy for the applicant to answer.

6. The time when it is generally considered desirable to add to the record subjective comments concerning an applicant and family is
    (A) during the interview
    (B) right after the interview has been concluded and the applicant has left
    (C) right after the interview has been concluded but before the applicant has left
    (D) at the end of the day, after all interviews have concluded.

7. "The interviewer's choice of words may determine the success or failure of the interview." To be successful in this respect, the interviewer should be careful to
    (A) adjust terminology to the language of the applicant
    (B) employ expressions similar to those of the applicant
    (C) speak in terms which are easily understood
    (D) use correct technical terms with such explanations as are necessary.

8. When conducting a first interview with an applicant for an apartment who speaks English poorly, the skill of the housing assistant is indicated by

(A) asking the applicant to return the following day when a staff member familiar with the applicant's language will be available

(B) creating a spirit of rapport in spite of the language difficulty

(C) explaining to the applicant how his or her language handicap affects eligibility

(D) explaining to the applicant that he or she would probably find it difficult to get along with the other tenants because of their prejudice against foreigners.

9. A porter employed at your project asks you if a friend of his whose application was processed by you has been approved as eligible for an apartment at your project. Of the following, the most appropriate action to take is to

(A) ascertain the relationship between the porter and the applicant before discussing his status

(B) discuss the facts of the situation confidentally with the porter to develop a cooperative relationship with him

(C) inform him of the tenant's status only if you actually know the final decision on this application.

(D) inform the porter that the applicant wiill be notified shortly of the results of his application.

10. Assume that an applicant for an apartment in a public housing project objects to answering a question concerning whether he has any income other than that which he recieves from his regular employment. The best course of action for the housing assistant to take is to

(A) advise the applicant that he is ineligible and terminate the interview

(B) advise the applicant to reconsider his refusal to answer and then ask the question again

(C) go on to the next question and return to this one later in the interview when better rapport has been established

(D) inform the applicant of the reason for asking the question and tell him he must answer.

11. At an interview to determine whether an applicant is eligible for public housing, the applicant gives information different from that which she submitted on her application. The most advisable action to take is to

(A) cross out the old information, enter the new information, and initial the entry

(B) enter the new information on the applicant form and initial the entry

(C) give the applicant another application form, have her fill it out correctly, and resume the interview

(D) give the applicant another application form to fill out, and set a later date for another interview.

12. In interviewing, the practice of anticipating an applicant's answer to questions is generally

(A) desirable because it is effective and economical when it is necessary to interview large numbers of applicants

(B) desirable because many applicants have language difficulties

(C) undesirable because it is the inalienable right of every person to answer as he or she sees fit

(D) undesirable because applicants may tend to agree with the answer proposed by the interviewer even when the answer is not entirely correct.

13. A follow-up interview was arranged for an applicant in order that he could furnish certain requested evidence. At this follow-up interview, the applicant still fails to furnish the necessary evidence. It would be most advisable for you to

(A) advise the applicant that he is now considered ineligible

(B) ask the applicant how soon he can get the necessary evidence and set a date for another interview

(C) question the applicant carefully and thoroughly to determine if he has misrepresented or falsified any information

(D) set a date for another interview and tell the applicant to get the necessary evidence by that time.

14. In reviewing applications of prospective tenants you notice that an application was approved by

a management assistant who is the daughter of the applicant. You should

(A) reject the application and reprimand the management assistant

(B) review the application and notify the group of management assistants to refer to you all applications of friends and relatives

(C) approve the application but warn the management assistant of punishment if a similar incident should occur

(D) reject the application and make no further reference to the matter.

15. An applicant complains to you that the management assistant who investigated her disqualified her on racial grounds only. You should

(A) explain to the applicant that racial discrimination is illegal

(B) call the management assistant and demand to know why the tenant was disqualified

(C) review the report of the management assistant and accept or reject it

(D) assign the case to another management assistant for investigation.

16. In checking applications of prospective tenants which have been passed upon by a management assistant you discover an error which has led to the acceptance for an application which should have been rejected. You should

(A) approve the application and reprimand the management assistant

(B) reject the application and advise the applicant of the error

(C) assign the application to another management assistant to be investigated further

(D) approve the application and advise the applicant to remove the disqualifying factor.

17. A management assistant under your supervision reports to you that the application of a prospective tenant, which has been assigned to her, is that of a friend. You should

(A) reprimand the management assistant for accepting an application from a friend

(B) tell the management assistant to supply you with intimate details of the family history of the applicant

(C) assign the application to another management assistant

(D) reject the application.

18. Of the following, the most important reason for registration of applicants for low-rent public housing with the Social Service Exchange is to

(A) avoid duplication of services to the family of the applicant

(B) determine the current economic status of the applicant

(C) inform other social agencies of the current need of the applicant for low-rent housing

(D) provide a more complete picture of current and possible future needs of the family.

19. When an initial interview is being conducted one way of starting is to explain the purpose of the interview to the applicant. The practice of starting the interview with such an explanation is generally

(A) desirable because the applicant can then understand why the interview is necessary and what will be accomplished by it

(B) desirable because it creates the rapport which is necessary to successful interviewing

(C) undesirable because time will be saved by starting off directly with the questions which must be asked

(D) undesirable because the interviewer should have the choice of starting an interview in any manner he or she prefers.

20. When a housing assistant visits the home of an applicant to obtain necessary eligibility verification she finds present in the room an 8-year-old son. In order to conduct the interview properly, the most reasonable action that the housing assistant should take with respect to the boy is to

(A) allow the boy to stay, but warn him not to make any comments during the interview

(B) ask the parent to send the child to another room to emphasize the confidential nature of the visit

(C) elicit from the child details of his interest, school record, and health to demonstrate to the parent the attitude of management

(D) greet the child, but direct the interview toward the parent or adult members of the family.

21. After you have secured all the necessary information from an applicant, he shows no intention of leaving, but starts to tell you a long

personal story. Of the following, the most advisable action for you to take is to

(A) explain to the applicant why personal stories are out of place in a business office
(B) listen carefully to the story for whatever relevant information it may contain
(C) interrupt him tactfully, thank him for the information he has already given, and terminate the interview
(D) inform your supervisor that the time required for this interview will prevent you from completing the interviews scheduled for the day.

22. The information which the interviewer plans to secure from an individual with whom he or she talks is determined mainly by the

(A) purpose of the interview and the functions of the agency
(B) state assistance laws and the desires of the individual
(C) privacy they have while talking and the willingness of the individual to give information
(D) emotional feelings of the individual seeking help and the interviewer's reactions to those feelings.

23. Generally, the most effective of the following ways of dealing with a person being interviewed who frequently digresses from the subject under discussion or starts to ramble is for the interviewer to

(A) tell the person that he or she, the interviewer, will have to terminate the interview unless the former sticks to the point
(B) increase the tempo of the interview
(C) demonstrate that he or she is a good listener and allow the person to continue
(C) inject questions which relate to the purpose of the interview.

24. "Being a good listener" is an interviewing technique which, if applied properly, is desirable mostly because it

(A) catches the client more easily in misrepresentations and lies
(B) conserves the energies of the investigator
(C) encourages the client to talk about personal affairs without restraint
(D) encourages the giving of information which is generally more reliable and complete.

25. When questioning applicants for public assistance or public housing, it would be best to ask questions that are

(A) direct, so that the applicant will realize that the interviewer knows what he or she is doing
(B) direct, so that the information received will be as pertinent as possible
(C) indirect, so that the applicant will not realize the purpose of the interview
(D) indirect, so that they can trap the applicant into making admissions that he or she would not otherwise make.

26. The chief reason for a social investigator or a housing assistant to conduct an interview with a new applicant in complete privacy is that the

(A) interviewer will be better able to record the facts without any other worker reading the case notes
(B) applicant will be impressed by the businesslike atmosphere of the agency
(C) interviewer will be able to devote more time to questioning the applicant without interruption
(D) applicant will be more likely to speak frankly.

ANSWER KEY

1. C	7. C	12. D	17. C	22. A
2. A	8. B	13. B	18. D	23. D
3. A	9. D	14. B	19. A	24. D
4. C	10. D	15. C	20. D	25. B
5. B	11. B	16. B	21. C	26. D
6. B				

READING INTERPRETATION
QUESTIONS

1. "Expansion, succession, and mobility have played a part in determining the social characteristics of the slum. The immigrant populations that have poured into the transitional zones of American cities have not sought the slum, have not created slums, but have been forced by their low economic status to live in the low rental dwellings created in these zones by the city's expansion. The variety of cultural backgrounds immigrant groups have brought with them have contributed to the cultured confusion of the slum." On the basis of this quotation, the least accurate of the following statements is
   (A) as the population of a city expands and moves out of certain areas, these areas tend to change in character
   (B) slums have been created by the variety of immigrant cultured backgrounds
   (C) the low earnings of immigrants have forced them into housing left behind in expansion process
   (D) the cultured confusion of the slum existed before the influx of immigration.

2. "A general area in which unsanitary or substandard housing conditions exist may include land, either improved or unimproved, and buildings or improvements not in themselves unsanitary or substandard. Demolition or rehabilitation of the latter may be necessary for effective replanning or reconstruction of the entire area." On the basis of this quotation, it would be most accurate to state that
   (A) an area may be considered substandard from the housing viewpoint even though it contains some acceptable housing
   (B) in replanning an entire area, little if any consideration need to be given to buildings or improvements not in themselves unsanitary or substandard
   (C) it is not easy to determine the exact boundaries of slum areas
   (D) under existing law, only substandard dwelling quarters may actually be demolished.

3. "The slum is not only a grimy mass of brick and mortar that can be torn down and demolished; it is also a way of living—a whole series of habits, attitudes and sentiments." On the basis of this quotation, it would be most correct to state that
   (A) demolition of substandard housing in slum areas will provide the basis for a new way of living
   (B) desirable urban community life is menaced by the existence of a social class forced into inferior housing and living standards
   (C) substandard housing and inferior living conditions constitute social problems of the first magnitude
   (D) the slum is imprinted in the lives of the people that occupy it, both adults and children.

4. "There is urgent need to proceed as rapidly as possible with the revision of existing zoning regulations, especially as to so-called 'unrestricted' districts. These districts, in which much current private building activity is going on, are to all intents and purposes unzoned." If the revision referred to in this quotation were to be placed in effect, an immediate result would probably be that

   (A) blighted areas would be saved and prevented from becoming slums
   (B) new industrial and business construction would have to conform to whatever regulations are set up
   (C) slums would be eliminated
   (D) the unsightly and uneconomic mixture of land uses found in many neighborhoods would disappear.

5. "The housing problem itself clearly is a consequence of the lack of proper distribution of income and wealth, unemployment, and other

economic factors." On the basis of this quotation, it would be most correct to state that

(A) eradication of unemployment is the key to the housing problem

(B) good housing could generally be available for all if every family had adequate income

(C) proper distribution of housing is a basic factor in solving the housing problem

(D) slums are a direct result of the unavailability of acceptable housing.

6. "Human society in a slum area is extremely mixed. A majority of the adults are self-respecting, law-abiding working men and women in low-paid or irregular occupations, who want to bring their children up right and have them get on in the world. A smaller group has been pushed down from a higher income level by illness, accident, or incompetence." On the basis of the above quotation, it would be most accurate to state that

(A) adults earning good salaries should not live in slum areas

(B) children who are raised in a slum area are more likely to present problems of juvenile delinquency

(C) residents of slum areas include adults who formerly had a higher income level

(D) self-respecting, law-abiding working men and women in low-paid occupations are as likely to be found in slum areas as anywhere else.

7. "A considerable body of substandard housing can be made acceptable by repairs and modernization. For this reason and others, the volume of substandard housing is much greater than the volume reasonably recommended for demolition. On the other hand, any slum clearance scheme will involve the demolition of some houses, which if located elsewhere, would not need to be demolished. No locality large enough for neighborhood development is made up completely of housing unfit for use." On the basis of the quotation, it would be most correct to say that

(A) a combination of unsanitary conditions exists only in slum areas which need to be redeveloped

(B) clearing slums always involves demolition of some acceptable housing

(C) localities which need to be redeveloped contain substandard housing only

(D) repairs and modernization are an acceptable substitute for redevelopment of a slum area.

8. "Zoning ordinances have generally served a highly useful purpose in preserving neighborhoods unspoiled for the greatest good of the greatest number. Zoning has been a boon to families of moderate means. The wealthy could always protect themselves by living in restricted districts or owning large estates. Working people well enough off to live in new sections have been helped too, those in older sections very little, those in slums not at all." On the basis of this quotation, it may properly be assumed that

(A) adequate zoning laws will, over a long period, rehabilitate slum areas

(B) business districts do not benefit from zoning laws

(C) home owners need the protection afforded by zoning laws

(D) new homes for families of moderate income can change the character of a decadent area.

9. "Complete absence of policy hampered the World War II housing program from the start. Operations were again centralized in federal government. As further appropriations were authorized, a dozen uncoordinated federal agencies began to scramble for a share of the purse. They competed for sites and personnel, sometimes out-bid one another. In one city, one agency actually blocked off another's street." On the basis of this quotation it would be most correct to assume that

(A) appropriations for war housing reflected wartime rush and confusion

(B) centralization of federal war-housing operations would have resulted in a more coordinated program

(C) centralized authority can bring order out of chaos

(D) overlapping functions and operations of different bureaus lead to inefficiency.

10. "Tearing down slums may be esthetically satisfying and emotionally soothing but it does not, of itself, improve the housing conditions of low-income families. Slum clearance tends to impose additional hardships on tenants and does nothing to remedy the underlying condi-

tion." On the basis of the above quotation it would be most correct to state that

(A) healthful decent housing for low-income families implies the demolition of slums

(B) healthful decent housing within the means of low-income families must be provided before slums can be torn down

(C) low-income families are forced to live in slum areas

(D) slum clearance is a necessary preliminary to improving housing conditions of low-income families.

11. "More damage has been done to the health of children of the United States by a sense of chronic inferiority due to consciousness of life in substandard dwellings than by all the defective plumbing those dwellings may contain." Of the following the most reasonable conclusion that may be drawn from this statement is that

(A) esthetic satisfaction in the home and its surroundings has some bearing on the physical well-being of children

(B) normal physical and mental development is not possible when children are conscious of the substandard nature of their homes

(C) psychiatric treatment is a necessary component of the adjustment of the children of slum families after transfer to public housing projects

(D) the physical aspects of good housing are far less important in the healthful development of children than the provision of adequate play facilities

(E) the replacement of defective plumbing can have little effect on the health of children in slum areas.

12. "Across the years, our social sense has decreed that every position of social leadership, every place of influence, every concentration of social power in the hands of an individual, every instrument or agency that has aggregated to itself the power to affect the common welfare, has become by that very fact a social trust that must be administered for the common good. In our moral world, the social obligations of power are real and unescapable." On the basis

of this quotation, it would be most correct to state that

(A) an individual engaged in private enterprise does not have the social responsibility of one who holds public office

(B) social leadership carries with it the obligation to administer for the public good

(C) in our moral world, the abuse of power is real and unescapable

(D) social leadership depends upon the aggregation of power in the hands of an individual or in an agency that wields concentrated influence.

13. "Personnel selection has been a critical problem for local housing authorities. The pool of qualified workers trained in housing procedures is small and the colleges and universities have failed to grasp the opportunity for enlarging it. While real estate experience makes a good background for management of a housing project, many real estate people are deplorably lacking in understanding of social and governmental problems. Social workers, on the other hand, are likely to be deficient in business judgment." On the basis of this quotation, it would be most accurate to state that

(A) colleges and universities have failed to train qualified workers for proficiency in housing procedures

(B) social workers are deficient in business judgment as related to the management of a housing project

(C) real estate experience makes a person a good manager of a housing project

(D) local housing authorities have been critical of present methods of personnel selection.

14. "The financing of housing represents two distinct forms of costs. One is the actual capital invested and the other is the interest rate which is charged for the use of capital. In fixing rents the interest rate which capital is expected to yield plays a very important part." On the basis of this quotation, it would be most correct to state that

(A) the financing of housing represents two distinct forms of capital investment

(B) reducing the interest rate charged for the use of capital is not as important as economies in construction in achieving lower rentals

(C) in fixing rents, the interest rate is expected to yield capital gains justifying the investment

(D) the actual capital invested and the interest rate charged for the use of this capital are factors in determining housing costs.

15. "The housing authority faces every problem of the private developer and it must also assume responsibilities of which private buildings are free. The authority must account to the community; it must conform to federal regulations; it must provide durable buildings of good standard at low cost; it must overcome the prejudices against public operations of contractors, bankers, and prospective tenants. These authorities are being watched by anti-housing enthusiasts for the first error of judgment or the first evidence of high costs, to be torn to bits before a congressional committee." On the basis of this quotation, it would be most correct to state that

(A) private builders do not have the opposition of contractors, bankers, and prospective tenants

(B) congressional committees impede the progress of public housing by petty investigations

(C) a housing authority must deal with all the difficulties encountered by the private builder

(D) housing authorities are no more immune from errors in judgment than private developers.

16. "Another factor that has considerably added to the city's housing crisis has been the great influx of low-income workers and their familes seeking better employment opportunities during wartime and defense boom periods. There was one such influx during World War II, and another coincided with the Korean War and defense build-up. The circumstances of these families forced them to crowd into the worst kind of housing and produced on a renewed scale the conditions from which slums flourish and grow." On the basis of this quotation, one would be justified in stating that

(A) the great influx of low-income workers has aggravated the the slum problem

(B) New York City has better employment opportunites than other sections of the country

(C) The high wages paid by our defense industries have made many families ineligible for tenancy in public housing

(D) the families who settled in the city during World War II, the Korean War, and the defense build-up brought with them language and social customs conducive to the growth of slums.

17. "Much of the city felt the effects of the general postwar increase of vandalism and street crime, and the greatly expanded public housing program was no exception. Projects built in congested slum areas with a high incidence of delinquency and crime were particularly subjected to the depredations of neighborhood gangs. The civil service watchmen who patrolled the projects, unarmed and neither trained nor expected to perform police duties, were unable to cope with the situation." On the basis of this quotation, the most accurate of the following statements is

(A) neighborhood gangs were particularly responsible for the high incidence of delinquency and crime in congested slum areas having public housing programs

(B) civil service watchmen who patrolled housing projects failed to carry out their assigned police duties

(C) housing projects were not spared the effects of the general postwar increase of vandalism and street crime

(D) delinquency and crime affected housing projects in slum areas to a greater extent than other dwellings in the same area.

18. "Another peculiar characteristic of real estate is the absence of liquidity. Each parcel is a discrete unit as to size, location, rental, physical condition, and financing arrangements. Each property requires investigation, comparison of rents with other properties, and individualized haggling on price and terms." On the basis of this quotation, the least accurate of the following statements is

(A) although the size, location, and rent of parcels vary, comparison with rents of other properties affords an indication of the value of a particular parcel

(B) bargaining skill is the essential factor in determining the value of a parcel of real estate

(C) each parcel of real estate has individual peculiarities distinguishing it from any other parcel

(D) investigation of each property is necessary in relation to rent and price.

19. "In part, at least, the charges of sameness, monotony, and institutionalism directed at public housing projects result from the degree in which they differ from the city's normal housing pattern. They seem alike because their very difference from the usual makes them stand apart. In many respects, there is considerably more variety between public housing projects than there is between different streets of apartment houses or tenements throughout the city." On the basis of this quotation, it would be least accurate to state that

   (A) there is considerably more variety between different streets of tenements throughout the city

   (B) public housing projects differ from the city's normal housing pattern to the degree that sameness, monotony, and institutionalism are characteristic of public buildings

   (C) public housing projects seem alike because their deviation from the usual dwellings draws attention to them

   (D) the variety in structure between public housing projects and other public buildings is related to the period in which they were built

20. "The amount of debt that can be charged against New York City for public housing is limited by law. Part of the City's restricted housing means goes for cash subsidies it may be required to contribute to State-aided projects. Under the provisions of the State law, the City must match the State's contributions in subsidies, and while the value of the partial tax exemption granted by the City is counted for this purpose, it is not always sufficient." On the basis of this quotation, it would be most accurate to state that

   (A) the amount of money New York City may spend for public housing is limited by annual tax revenues

   (B) the value of tax exemptions granted by the City to educational, religious, and charitable institutions may be added to its subsidy contributions to public housing projects

   (C) the subsidy contributions for State-aided public housing projects are shared equally by the State and the City under the provisions of the State law

   (D) the tax revenues of the City, unless implemented by State aid, are insufficient to finance public housing projects

21. "Maintenance costs can be minimized and the useful life of houses can be extended by building with the best and most permanent materials available. The best and most permanent materials in many cases are, however, much more expensive than materials which require more maintenance. The most economical procedure in home building has been to compromise between the capital costs of high quality and enduring materials and the maintenance costs of less desirable materials." On the basis of this quotation, one would be justified in stating that

   (A) savings in maintenance costs make the use of less durable and less expensive building materials preferable to high quality materials that would prolong the useful life of houses constructed from them

   (B) financial advantage can be secured by the home builder if he or she judiciously combines costly but enduring building materials with less desirable materials which, however, require more maintenance

   (C) a compromise between the capital costs of high quality materials and the maintenance costs of less desirable materials makes it easier for a home builder to estimate construction expenditures

   (D) the most economical procedure in home building is to balance the capital costs of the most permanent materials against the costs of less expensive materials that are cheaper to maintain

ANSWER KEY

1. B	6. C	10. B	14. D	18. B
2. A	7. B	11. A	15. C	19. B
3. D	8. C	12. B	16. A	20. C
4. B	9. D	13. A	17. C	21. B
5. B				